James Godkin

The Religious History of Ireland, Primitive, Papal, and Protestant

Including the evangelical missions, Catholic agitations, and Church progress of the

last half-century

James Godkin

The Religious History of Ireland, Primitive, Papal, and Protestant
Including the evangelical missions, Catholic agitations, and Church progress of the last half-century

ISBN/EAN: 9783337325466

Printed in Europe, USA, Canada, Australia, Japan

Cover: Foto ©ninafisch / pixelio.de

More available books at **www.hansebooks.com**

RELIGIOUS HISTORY OF IRELAND

PRIMITIVE, PAPAL, AND PROTESTANT

INCLUDING THE

EVANGELICAL MISSIONS, CATHOLIC AGITATIONS, AND CHURCH PROGRESS OF THE LAST HALF-CENTURY

BY

JAMES GODKIN

AUTHOR OF 'IRELAND AND HER CHURCHES' ETC.

HENRY S. KING & CO.
65 CORNHILL & 12 PATERNOSTER ROW, LONDON
1873

CONTENTS.

CHAPTER I.
ANCIENT IRELAND AND ITS HISTORY.

                       PAGE

Irish Historians—Celtic Divines Abroad—Ancient Irish Schools—Iona and St. Columba—Legends of St. Columba 1–25

CHAPTER II.
MYTHOLOGY AND HAGIOLOGY.

Gods and Saints—Miracles of the Irish Saints—Religious Foundations   26–37

CHAPTER III.
THE CHURCH OF ST. PATRICK.

The Church of St. Patrick—Apostolic Succession .   38–48

CHAPTER IV.
ANCIENT MONUMENTS.

Ancient Monuments—Royal Irish Academy—Round Towers—Norman Architecture—Temples and Crosses—Celts no Builders—Cormac's Temple, Cashel—Kilmelchedor—Sculptured Crosses 49–72

CHAPTER V.
PATRONS AND PILGRIMAGES.

Heathen Customs — Clonmacnoise — Kildare — Ardmore — Innisfallen Loughderg—Glendalough 73–90

CHAPTER VI.
THE CHURCH OF THE PALE AND THE REFORMATION.

Invasion and Progress—Race and Creed—The Pope and Ireland—The Reformation 91–110

CHAPTER VII.

A CRUSADE AGAINST THE REFORMATION.

An Irish Crusade—Religious Persecution—James I. and the Catholics—The Viceroy and the Jesuit—Sir Arthur Chichester—Flight of the Ulster Chiefs 111–122

CHAPTER VIII.

THE PLANTATION OF ULSTER BY JAMES I.

Plantation of Ulster—Preparing the Way—Six Counties Confiscated—The London Companies—The Irish Society—Exclusive Policy . . . 123–133

CHAPTER IX.

FOUNDATION OF THE PRESBYTERIAN CHURCH.

The Presbyterian Church—Graces of Charles I. . 134–140

CHAPTER X.

THE ESTABLISHED CHURCH UNDER CHARLES I., LAUD, AND STRAFFORD.

The Established Church United—The Presbyterians Persecuted—Strafford and the Black Oath—State of the Church 141–149

CHAPTER XI.

THE MASSACRE OF 1641.

Catholic Insurrection—Proofs of the Massacre . . 150–162

CHAPTER XII.

THE CATHOLIC CONFEDERATION.

Catholic Confederation—Owen Roe O'Neill—The Pope's Nuncio—Battle of Benburb 163–170

CHAPTER XIII.

RELIGION UNDER CROMWELL—THE SOLEMN LEAGUE AND COVENANT.

Cromwell's Policy—What is Ireland—Confiscation—Rooting out the People—Wolves, Priests, and Tories—Solemn League and Covenant—The Independents—Milton and the Presbyterians—Henry Cromwell's Government 171–195

CHAPTER XIV.

THE RESTORATION OF PRELACY.

Jeremy Taylor and the Presbyterians—Macaulay on English Rule—Home Rule under James II.—The Act of Attainder 196–207

CHAPTER XV.

THE REVOLUTION AND THE PENAL CODE.

Penal Code—Odious National Comparisons—Cromwell and William III. —The Protestant Interest—The Charter Schools—Pictures of the Rival Churches—Bishop Doyle—George IV. and the Roman Catholic Bishops 208–227

CHAPTER XVI.

EVANGELICAL MISSIONS.

Noble Evangelists—English Missionaries—Evangelism in Dublin—Religious Societies—Public Discussions—Established Church Home Missions—The Parochial System 228–243

CHAPTER XVII.

CATHOLIC AGITATION.

The Catholic Association—George IV. and the Emancipation Act—The Monster Grievance—The Church Question—Church Temporalities Act—The Archbishop of Dublin 244–257

CHAPTER XVIII.

THE TWO CHURCHES MILITANT IN CONNAUGHT.

A Popular Archbishop—Proselytism—O'Connell and Archbishop Trench —The New Reformation—Irish Church Missions—Romanist Reaction . 258–269

CHAPTER XIX.

PROGRESS OF ROMANISM.

Archbishop McHale—Primate Crolly—Cardinal Cullen—'Dens' Theology' Papal Infallibility—Catholic Liberalism 270–282

CHAPTER XX.

PROGRESS OF PRESBYTERIANISM.

Progress of Presbyterianism—Dr. Cooke—Cooke and O'Connell—Triumph of Dr. Cooke—Political Non-entity of Presbyterians—Liberals in the Assembly—Career of Dr. Cooke 283-299

CHAPTER XXI.

THE DISESTABLISHED CHURCH—RELIGIOUS EQUALITY.

Irish Church Act—New Church Constitution—Revenues of the Freed Church—Revision of the Prayer Book—The Education Question—Conclusion 300-313

CHAPTER I.

ANCIENT IRELAND AND ITS HISTORY.

WHEN the history of a vanquished nation, which has resisted for centuries, is written by the conquerors, it is not likely to be very impartial. It is still less to be relied on if the writers be ignorant of the language of the people, whom they hate or despise. For those who wish to judge fairly in such a case, it is desirable to hear the accredited organs of the subject race, that they may know what they have to say for themselves. One story is good till the other is told. This maxim should be remembered even where the temptations to misrepresentation are not so very great. If we believe the bundle of affidavits which one party to a suit, some claimant to an estate, lays on the table of the Court, he is the most injured of men. If we believe the bundle, sworn to by equally credible witnesses on the other side, he is the principal agent in a wicked conspiracy, aiming at robbery and sustained by perjury. It is only by comparing the evidence on both sides, and carefully sifting it, that we can hope to arrive at the truth. A difficult task at all times, even to minds the most judicial; but never more difficult than in a case where two such nations as England and Ireland are at issue about the facts of history in the troubled and distant past, touching interests on one side far dearer than those of property. It is amazing with what facility men of superior, and even critical, minds receive worthless testimony when it falls in with their wishes or their prejudices. Not less wonderful is the tenacity with which national animosities grow and flourish from generation to generation, despite the efforts of good men to extirpate them, despite the silent influence of education in changing the nature of the soil in which they are rooted.

'I have observed that every modern historian who has undertaken to write of Ireland commends the country, but disparages the people. It grieved me to see a nation hunted down by ignorance and malice, and recorded as the scum and refuse of mankind, when, upon strict enquiry they are found to have made as good a figure, and to have signalized themselves in as commendable a manner to posterity, as any people in Europe. The valour of the old Irish, and particularly their fixed constancy in the Christian religion and the Catholic faith, ought to be honourably mentioned as a standard and example for ages that follow.' This has not been written in reply to any living historian, advocating the case of England v. Ireland. It was written 270 years ago by a priest, hiding from persecution in the wood of Aharlow, in the county Tipperary. This was the Rev. Jeoffry Keating, D.D., who devoted himself to the Irish Mission, after spending twenty-three years at the College of Salamanca. During his retreat in the forest he compiled a History of Ireland, from the time of *Noah* down to the English Conquest by Henry II. His book was composed in *Irish*, although, as his translator, Mr. Dermod O'Connor, informs us, he was perfectly skilled in the English language. It is an advantage to have such a history, because those of us who have the misfortune to be ignorant of the native tongue are constantly told by Irish antiquaries, even of the present day, that we are thereby disqualified for understanding the ancient history of the country. Dr. Keating himself continually taunts English authors with their manifest unfitness on this very ground.

It is true that we may not be able to read the Irish MSS. in which the old chronicles of Erin are written. But we ought certainly to be capable of comprehending the contents of those chronicles when they are translated for us faithfully by those learned Irishmen who were taught Gaelic by their mothers, and who have been studying and teaching it all their lives. Some of the ablest of these men, encouraged and supported by the public, have translated all the most valued of those ancient treasures, accompanied with an immense mass of illustrations; hoping to meet the wish expressed so warmly by Dr. Johnson, the great lexicographer, by giving us a true history of the times when Ireland was the *quiet* abode of sanctity and learning. If we find these to a large extent worthless as materials of real history, it is not because we are without the means of appreciating them. Translators must have the philosopher's stone if they can transmute fables into facts and legends into truth—legends propagated in an age of boundless credulity.

Dr. Keating had as little patience with sceptics in his time as the monks of the dark ages had in their day. In the preface to his History he gave hard knocks to some of their number:—
'Never,' he exclaims, 'was any nation under heaven so traduced by malice and ignorance as the ancient Irish.' For example, *Strabo*, without any knowledge of their annals, charged them with living on human flesh; whereas, no instance of the kind was on record, except the single case of a lady named Eithne, daughter of a King of Leinster, 'whose fosterers fed her with the flesh of children in order to make her the sooner ripe for matrimonial embraces.' But this was done to accomplish a prediction. I wonder how many babies did she consume. *Pomponius Mela*, again, with equal falsehood, described the ancient Irish as a people 'ignorant of all virtue.' But perhaps the most stinging remark of all those ancient criticisms was that of a waspish author named *Solinus*, who asserted that there were no bees in Ireland, that Irish children received their first food on the point of a sword, and that the fathers washed their faces in the blood of the enemies they had slain. As to the bees, they were so numerous, both in hives and trunks of trees, that the land might be said to flow with honey as well as with milk. *Ex uno disce omnes.*

From the classical calumniators, Father Keating turns to the English, 'who have never failed to exert their malice against the Irish, and to represent them as a base and servile people.' Foremost among those offenders was *Cambrensis*—'an inexhaustible fund of falsehood.' He had the hardihood to assert, among other fables, that there was a fountain in Munster which made the hair of the head grey when dipped in it, and another fountain in Ulster which at once restored it to its original colour. Worse still, he said that Irish enemies were reconciled by kissing the relics of the saints, and drinking each other's blood. This, Cambrensis boldly asserted, 'with his usual effrontery, without proof or foundation.' Of a piece with this, was his story about the inauguration of the O'Donel. In that fiction, 'compounded of ignorance and malice,' he reported that the ceremony was performed in this manner:—All the inhabitants of the country were assembled on a high hill; here they killed a white mare, whose flesh was boiled in a great cauldron in the middle of a field; when it was sufficiently boiled the King was 'to sup the broth with his mouth (without a spoon) and eat the flesh out of his hands without the assistance of a knife or other instrument, but with his teeth only. Then he divided the rest of the flesh among the assembly, and afterwards bathed himself in the broth!' The real ceremony was the presentation of a white rod by one of the chiefs, who advancing, said, ' O King! receive the command of thy own country, and distribute justice impartially among thy subjects.' No wonder the historian denounces Cambrensis for introducing ' in the room of a laudable custom, a savage and abominable practice, with no foundation in truth or history; the effect of inveterate malice, which urged him on into absurd and monstrous relations.' The kings of the O'Donel race, we are assured, were princes of strict piety and exemplary virtue, who abhorred a ceremony so odious. This, therefore, he adds, was 'another falsehood of Cambrensis, which ought to destroy his credit for ever among lovers of truth, and brand on him an indelible mark of infamy to all posterity.'

Dr. Keating, coming down to his own times, says: 'There is *one Spencer*, a writer of a Chronicle,' who dared to assert that an English King, Edgar, had jurisdiction in Ireland. ' But what is most surprising in this audacious writer is, that he should undertake to fix the genealogies of many of the gentry of Ireland, and to pretend to derive them originally from an English extraction.' ' It is surprising to me,' says the Doctor, 'how Spencer could advance such falsehoods; he was a writer that was unable to make himself acquainted with Irish affairs, as being a stranger to the language; and, besides, being of a poetical genius, he allowed himself an unbounded license in his compositions. It may be the business of his profession to advance poetical fictions, and clothe them with fine insinuating language in order to amuse his readers,' &c.

Stanihurst, another of Mr. Froude's predecessors, was no better qualified than Spencer to write a history of Ireland. What right had he to 'pronounce sentence upon the arts and sciences, the laws and customs of the Irish, when he understood not a word in the language, could not read their books, nor converse with the learned professors?' Besides, he was 'overrun with prejudice, set to work by men who naturally abhorred an Irishman.' Though he had neither abilities, nor proper materials, to write a history of Ireland, he was 'big' with this production for some years, and by the help of spleen and ill nature, he was at last delivered of it, to the great joy of his English patrons, who had bribed him for breeding his litter of calumnies against the Irish. Stanihurst had spoken strongly against the Irish language, and expressed a wish that it had been extirpated—a sentiment which Father Keating justly denounced as pagan and barbarous. In the same spirit he reprobates *Hanmer, Campion, Moryson,* and other English writers on his native country. Even the learned Camden does not escape censure. He asserted that it was the custom of the country that ' the priests, *with their wives and children,* had their dwelling in the churches consecrated to divine use, where they feasted, rioted, and played music, by which means those holy places were desecrated.' In answer to this foul charge, Dr. Keating says, it must be observed ' that this irreligious custom had not been practised for many ages, except in the most uncivilised part of the kingdom, and by a sort of clergy who pretended to be exempt from ecclesiastical discipline; and he cites Gerald Cambrensis as bearing testimony to the piety of the clergy, who were pre-eminently distinguished by their chastity. Another slander against the clerical order put forth by Campion, our Irish-speaking historian repels with an indignation and simplicity which are rather comic. It was a device said to have been resorted to by a very covetous bishop, to excite the liberality of the faithful. He told his congregation that, some years before, St. Peter and St. Patrick had a very violent contest about an Irish Galloglach whom St. Patrick wanted to get into heaven; but St. Peter objected to the Hibernian soldier, and in his anger he struck the Irish saint with his key, and broke his head. They were therefore asked to contribute as a sort of testimonial or compensation to their outraged national patron. In reply to this story, Father Keating seriously asks, ' Can it be supposed that a Christian of the meanest capacity would believe that St. Patrick, who died above a thousand years ago, and St. Peter should quarrel and come to blows; and that St. Patrick should have his head broken by St. Peter's key, as if the key had been made of iron, which everybody knows is nothing material, but implies the power of binding and loosing.'

Seeing, however, that his country was so grievously wronged by such misrepresentations, Dr. Keating, being a man of advanced age, with valuable experience, acquainted with the ancient authors in their original language, undertook to write a true history of Ireland, and thus vindicate the character of a noble nation. If it be objected that the chronicles of Ireland are liable to suspicion, he replies, that no people in the world took more care to preserve the authority of their public records, and to deliver them incorrupt to posterity. 'They were solemnly examined and purged every three years in the royal house of Tara, in the presence of the nobility and clergy, and in a full assembly of the most learned and eminent antiquaries in the country. The authority of these public records cannot be questioned, when it is considered that there were above 200 chroniclers and antiquaries whose business it was to preserve and record all actions and affairs of consequence relating to the public. They had revenues settled upon them for their maintenance and to support the dignity of their character. Their annals and histories were submitted to the examination and censure of the nobility, clergy, and gentry, who were most eminent for learning, which is evidence sufficient to evince their authority, and to procure them a superior esteem to the antiquities of any other nation, except the Jews, throughout the world.'

So much faith has the Irish author in the Celtic records that he sees no difficulty in their having kept such exact pedigrees that the genealogy of every genuine Irish chief could be traced back to Adam.—Both in heathen and Christian times the chronicles were composed in verse,—'that their records might be the less subject to corruption and change, that the obscurity of the style might be a defence to them, and that the youths who were instructed in that profession might be the better able to commit them to memory.' Hence the term 'Psalter,' as applied to the collections of these historical Psalms or poems. This, indeed, was the custom of all barbarous nations, as Mr. Tylor has shown in his

'Primitive Culture'; and Mr. Buckle has stated truly that those records which were preserved by the professional Bards, and taught to their children from age to age (the office being hereditary), were far nearer to the truth than the written chronicles which the clergy of the dark ages founded upon them. 'In this way,' says Mr. Buckle, ' the Christian priests have obscured the annals of every European people they converted; and have destroyed or corrupted the traditions of the Gauls, the Welsh, the Irish, the Anglo-Saxons, the Sclavonic nations, and even of the Icelanders. Nothing came amiss to their greedy and credulous ears. Histories of omens, prodigies, apparitions, strange portents, monstrous appearances in the heavens, the wildest and most incoherent absurdities passed from mouth to mouth, and were preserved with as much care as if they were the choicest treasures of human wisdom. For 500 years human credulity reached a height unparalleled in the annals of ignorance. In the whole period from the sixth to the tenth century there were in all Europe not more than three or four men who dared to think for themselves.'[1]

It is gratifying to know that the most illustrious of these independent thinkers were Irishmen. The German historian Mosheim pays no small tribute to their merit in this respect. Writing of the eighth century he says:—' The Irish, or Hibernians, who in this century were known by the name of Scots, were *the only divines* who refused to dishonour their reason by submitting it implicitly to the dictates of *authority*. Naturally subtle and sagacious, they applied their philosophy, such as it was, to the illustration of the truth and doctrines of religion; a method which was almost generally abhorred and exploded in all other nations.' In a note, he adds:—' That the Hibernians were lovers of learning and distinguished themselves in those times of ignorance by the culture of the sciences, *beyond all other European nations,* travelling through the most distant lands, both with a view to improve and to communicate their knowledge, is a fact with which I have long been acquainted, as we see them in the most authentic records of antiquity, discharging with the highest reputation and applause the functions of Doctors in France, Germany

[1] 'History of Civilisation,' vol. i. pp. 247, 258, 269.

and Italy, during this and the following century. But that these Hibernians were *the first teachers* of the scholastic theology in Europe, and so early as the eighth century illustrated the doctrines of religion by the principles of philosophy, I learned but lately from the testimony of Benedict Abbot of Ariane, in the province of Languedoc, who lived in this period, and some of whose productions are published by Baliesius in the 5th volume of his Miscellanies.'

Of the chief of these brilliant Irish lights Mosheim speaks farther on in his History :—' Johannes Scotus Erigena, the friend and companion of Charles the Bald, an eminent philosopher and a learned divine, whose erudition was accompanied with uncommon marks of sagacity and genius, and whose various performances, as well as his translations from the Greek, gained him a shining and lasting reputation.' The same historian, again referring to the state of the Church early in the ninth century, remarks :—' The Irish doctors *alone*, and particularly Johannes Scotus, had the courage to spurn the ignominious fetters of authority, and to explain the sublime doctrines of Christianity in a manner conformable to the dictates of reason and the principles of truth. But this noble attempt drew upon them the malignant fury of a superstitious age; and exposed them to the hatred of the Latin theologians, who would not permit either reason or philosophy to meddle in religious matters.[1]

Such prophets, however, had little honour in their own country; they left it then, as they leave it now for the same reason, because they refused to have their reason bound in the fetters of authority; and it is to prevent the existence of such thinkers among the Roman Catholics that the study of philosophy was to be, if possible, interdicted in the new national University. There never was so little freedom of thought among Catholics as at the present time. If the ecclesiastical authority had not extinguished the native spirit of freedom which shone so brightly in Johannes Scotus and Duns Scotus, could the nation have remained

---

[1] For an account of the persecution and hatred that Johannes Scotus suffered in the cause of reason and liberty, Mosheim refers to Du Boulay, 'Hist. Academ.' Paris, tom. i. p. 182. Also Mabillon, ' Acta Sanctor. Ord. Bened. Sacr.' vol. v. p. 392, and 'Hist. Littér. de la France,' tom. v. p. 416.

slavishly silent on the dogma of Papal Infallibility? The foreign testimonies in favour of the learning of the early Irish Christians are very numerous, and very strong. In addition to those already quoted, I give the following, which I collected many years ago.

Sir James Mackintosh, yielding to the force of ancient authorities on this subject, says:—' The Irish nation possesses genuine history several centuries more ancient than any other European nation possesses, in its present spoken language.' Thierry, a historian of greater research, if not of more philosophic genius, thus refers to the ancient Celts:—' The major part of the Irish were men with dark hair, with strong passions, loving and hating with vehemence, irascible, yet of a social temper. In many things, especially in religion, they were enthusiasts, and willingly intermingled the Christian worship with their poetry and literature, which was perhaps the most cultivated in all western Europe. Their island possessed a multitude of saints and learned men, venerated alike in England and in Gaul; for no country had furnished a greater number of Christian missionaries, animated by no other motive than pure zeal, and an ardent desire of communicating to foreign nations the opinions and the faith of their native country. The Irish were great travellers, and always gained the hearts of those whom they visited, by the extreme ease with which they conformed to their customs and ways of life.'

Camden says:—' No men came up to the Irish monks in Ireland and in Britain for sanctity and learning; and they sent forth swarms of holy men all over Europe: to whom the monasteries of Luxueil in Burgundy, Pavia in Italy, Wurtzburgh in Franconia, St. Gall in Switzerland, &c. &c., owe their origin. . . . Why should I mention almost all Ireland, with its crowd of philosophers, despising the dangers of the sea, flocking to our shores? . . . The Saxons also at that time flocked to Ireland from all quarters, as to a mart of literature. Whence we frequently meet, in our writers of the lives of the saints, " such an one was sent over to Ireland for education;" and in the Life of Fulgenis—

> Exemplo patrum commotus, amore legendi,
> Ivit ad Hibernos, sophiâ mirabile claros.'

Yet the French historian remarks: ' The old Celtic races,

seated on their native rocks, and in the solitude of their isles, will remain faithful to the poetic independence of barbarous life, until surprised in their fastnesses by the tyranny of the stranger. Centuries have elapsed since England surprised and struck them down; and her blows incessantly rain upon them, as the wave dashes on the promontory of Brittany or of Cornwall. The sad and patient Judea, who counted her years by her captivities, was not more rudely stricken by Asia. But there is such a virtue in the Celtic genius, such a tenacity of life in this people, that they subsist under outrage, and preserve their manners and their language.

'Whatever has been the result (of the law of gavelkind) it is honourable to our Celts to have established in the west the law of equality. The feeling of personal right, the vigorous assumption of the I, which we have already remarked in Pelagius and in religious philosophy, is still more apparent here; and, in great part, lets us into the secret of the destiny of the Celtic races. While the German families converted movable into immovable property, handed it down in perpetuity, and successively added to it by inheritance, the Celtic families went on dividing and subdividing, and weakening themselves—a weakness chiefly owing to the law of equality and equitable division. As this law of precocious equality has been the ruin of these races, let it be their glory also, and secure to them at least the pity and respect of the nations to whom they so early showed so fine an ideal.'[1]

'It was in reference to this period,' says O'Driscoll, 'that Ireland, by the unanimous consent of the European nations, was placed in the rank of a third empire; the Roman, the Constantinopolitan, and the Irish. Is this any evidence of her worth and her renown? It was not surely her extent, or her conquests in the world, that gave her this high place. Hers was not an empire purchased by the tears and sufferings of other nations, but by benefits conferred upon them. Her triumphs were peaceful triumphs, and such as in comparison with which Cressy, Agincourt, and Waterloo, fade into nothing. It is a vulgar thing to subdue a nation. Have not the Goths, and the Huns, and the Turks, and the Tartars, done this? But to give refuge

[1] 'Hist. France,' b. i. c. iv.

to many people, to instruct many nations—these are triumphs worthy of empire. The claim of Ireland to a third empire was established at the Council of Constance; and it was more glorious than the other two, for it was the empire of intellect and benevolence.'

Camden informs us, that 'the whole nation of the Irish were strong in their persons, peculiarly active, possessing a brave and elevated mind, sharp in their intellects, and warlike.' 'They were besides,' says Stanihurst, 'extremely hospitable, good-natured, and beneficent—of *all men the most patient in suffering, and rarely overcome with difficulties.*' Champion, and other Englishmen, describe them as religious, sincere, compassionate, full of energy in misfortune, good horsemen, passionately fond of war, charitable and hospitable beyond expression. And Hanmer tells us, that 'when Robert Fitzstephen and the brave knights of Britain invaded Ireland, they did not find cowards but valiant men, brave both as horse and foot.'

The learning of the ancient Irish schools was unquestionably superior for those ages; but how miserably dark they must have been! The whole circle of the sciences was composed of what the scholastic philosophers called 'The Seven Liberal Arts,' viz., grammar, rhetoric, logic, arithmetic, geometry, music, and astronomy. The three former were designated by the title of '*Trivium*' and the four latter by '*Quadrivium.*' In the greater part of the schools the public teachers ventured no farther than the first division. 'Nothing,' says Mosheim, 'could be conceived more wretchedly barbarous than the manner in which these sciences were taught, as may be easily seen from Alcuin's treatise concerning them, and the dissertations of St. Augustin on the same subject, which were in the highest repute at this time.'

I am indebted to the late Mr. Darcy Magee for the following notes on this subject sent me when I was writing the History of Irish education:—

'In the sixth century were founded the three great schools of Bangor in Down, Clonard in Meath, and Cluanmacnoise on the Shannon: St. Comgall founded the first, the monarch Dermidh the second, and St. Kiaran, called ' the Artificer,' the last. Their respective dates are fixed at A.D. 516, 549, and 548. They were governed each by its own set of rules. In 603 St. Carthagh founded the great school of Lismore on the Blackwater. See Usher's Antiq., Lannigan's Ecc. Hist., Colgan's Acta Sanctorum, Bede's Annals, Mabillon, the Bolandists, &c. Guizot, Hallam, Muratori, Brucker, and Mosheim, have all spoken of these institutions as most important agencies in advancing civilisation and revelation.

'There is no complete account of their system or systems extant in print, as far as I can learn. Harris, in his History of Dublin, refers to a manuscript by Florence McCarthy in the College library, containing some information respecting them. This much I have gathered from various expressions in the lives of their most distinguished scholars:—

The Scriptures were much studied in them all. St. Jerome, next after the Scriptures. That the students transcribed with their own hands some particular portions of the two Testaments. Most frequent mention is made of David's Psalms, St. Paul's Epistles, and St. Matthew's and St. John's Gospels. That singing of Psalms was a part of each day's exercise. Hence the name of Banchor or White-choir is derived by Harris: Muratori thinks that the Antiphonarium Banchorense, which he published from a copy in the Imperial Library at Milan, is a composition of the sixth century. That presidents of the schools were in most cases called Regents. That they were much frequented by natives of all the countries and islands of western Europe. That Latin versification was in high estimation with the students from the first, and that they had some knowledge of the Latin profane classics. That they studied much in the open air, in the fields and woods, where their teachers usually accompanied them.

'The Danish wars, which commenced in 807, and did not terminate until Brian's victory in 1014, ruined the four schools I have named, each being near the sea coast, and greatly injured the Irish literature which they had fostered.

'The most considerable students of Clonard were Columbcille, Eleran the Wise, Erigena (perhaps), and Marianus Scotus the Chronicler.

'Of Bangor, Columbianus, the founder of the continental seminaries of Luxeuil, Fontanes, and Bobio, Elfred of North-Humberland, and (it is said) Pelagius; Dungall, the astronomer of Bologna, mentioned by Muratori, &c.

'When the Danish wars had ceased, several great persons interested themselves for the restitution of the schools. St. Malachy rebuilt Bangor, and O'Brien, King of Thomond, repaired Cluanmacnoise; but before the work was finished, the English invasion arose and dashed it down. John de Courcy sacked Bangor, and Hugh de Lacy was killed while casting down the ancient school of Durrow.

'The Irish and the Anglo-Irish, who dared, went to Oxford, and Anthony A'Wood preserves many curious reminiscences of their battles with the Scottish and English students there, in which they were usually backed by the Welsh. Amongst the most eminent of them were O'Fihely, afterwards Archbishop of Tuam, Dunensis or Downensis Scotus, and "A Sacco Boses," the schoolmen.

'The Anglican Archbishops of Dublin tried hard about the beginning of the fourteenth century to found an university in this city. In 1320, Archbishop Bicknor succeeded. The building was annexed to St. Patrick's Cathedral, and sustained a struggling vitality till the time of the Reformation, when it died out. See Harris's Dublin, Cooke Taylor's Trinity College, Dublin Review, Wyse's Pamphlet, &c.

'For the Irish Catholic Colleges founded abroad during the penal times, *see* Ware, Antiquit. last section, *or* the "Irish Writers of the Seventeenth Century," and the *Hibernia Dominicana.*'

It is a glorious fact that the Northern nations owe the deepest debt of gratitude to Celtic genius, learning, and zeal. The early history of these nations records that many Irish ecclesiastics travelled among Batavian, Belgian, and German nations, propagating the knowledge of the truth, erecting churches, and forming religious establishments everywhere. 'This,' says Mosheim, 'was the true reason which induced the Germans, in after times, to found so many convents for the Scots and Irish, of which some are yet in being.' Of these Irish apostles, Columba was the leader and the chief.' What a wonderful record is the following, collected by Mosheim from the ecclesiastical historians of the sixth century! 'Columba, an Irish monk, had happily extirpated the ancient superstitions in Gaul and the parts adjacent, where idolatry had taken the deepest root. He also carried the lamp of celestial truth among the Suevi, the Boii, the Franks, and other German nations, and persevered in these pious and useful labours till his death happened A.D. 615. St. Gal, who was one of his companions, preached the Gospel to the Helvetii and the Suevi. St. Kilian exercised the ministerial function with such success among the Eastern Franks, that vast numbers of them embraced Christianity.'

Incomparably the best account of Colomba to be found in our language is the admirable little book on *Iona*, by the Duke of Argyll. I know no work better calculated to throw light on the primitive Irish monasteries, and dissipate the haze that surrounds them in the minds of those who have not been accustomed to study history in a critical spirit, combining sympathy with the love of truth. The most enthusiastic Irish Catholic of the present day could not celebrate more highly the fame of the Abbot of Iona than his Grace does, though no one has more reason than he to be jealous for the honour of his own country; but, while giving to the ancient Irish all the credit that their countrymen can claim for them, the Duke brings the spirit of a philosophic historian to bear on the times, and shows how naturally were produced the marvellous results which in after ages were ascribed to the exertion of miraculous powers.

'In the time and in the country of St. Columba,' says the Duke, 'the Celtic monasteries were not only the great missionary colleges of the Church, but they seem to have embraced and absorbed almost all that existed then of ecclesiastical organisation.' This is quite true, and of these organisations Iona was one of the first, and undoubtedly the most successful. 'We must remember,' continues his Grace, 'the fact that St. Columba was an agent, and a principal agent, in one of the greatest events the world has ever seen, namely, the conversion of the Northern nations. Nothing of the kind has ever happened for more than a thousand years. The world is still in a large proportion heathen. Christianity is indeed spreading, but mainly by the spread and migration of those races whose conversion was completed then. Converts are made in our own time; but nowhere—nowhere during a long course of centuries, have we seen whole nations accepting the Christian faith, and casting their idols to the moles and to the bats.'

The Picts in North Britain were the first converted. With what advantages of a temporal kind did the Irish missionaries approach those warlike tribes? 'Christianity was not presented to them in alliance with the imposing aspect of Roman civilisation. The tramp of the Roman legions had never been heard in the Highland glens, nor had their clans ever seen with awe the majesty and power of the Roman Government. In the days of Columba, whatever tidings may have reached the Picts of Argyll or of Inverness must have been tidings of Christian disaster and defeat. All the more must we be ready to believe that the man who at such a time planted the Cross successfully among them must have been of powerful character and splendid gifts. There is no arguing against the great monument to Columba, which consists in the place he has received in the memory of mankind.' (P. 52.)

It is difficult to realise in our minds the *remoteness* of the age in which this great place was won by an Irish soldier of the Cross, whose weapons, though purely intellectual and spiritual, were so mighty in demolishing the strongholds of heathenism. The Duke of Argyll helps us to do this by pointing out the stages through which the British nation has passed since that time. Fordun, and the fathers of Scottish history, lived 700 years later than the great Apostle of the Picts! In the days of Adamnan, Scotland was not Scotland, but *Albyn*; England was not England, the Heptarchy was not yet formed. The history of Scotland begins with Malcolm Conmore, when Columba had been dead more than 400 years. The oldest building now in Iona, supposed to be a restoration, by Queen Margaret of Scotland, was erected nearly 500 years after the death of the apostle. She died in 1092. The ruins that now exist are calculated to impress the mind with feelings of the deepest solemnity. But St. Columba had nothing to do with them, except that he made the ground whereon they stand holy. During more than 1,000 years its sanctity attracted pilgrims from all Christian lands, and made it the burial-place of kings, princes, bishops, and heroes.

The building which St. Columba erected as a church was a low quadrangular structure, made of wooden stakes and wattles. Around it separate cells or huts were constructed, of the same materials, for the monks and the visitors who went there as scholars to be instructed, as they now go to a university. A portion of their time was spent in manual labour, cultivating the ground, taking care of the stock, and fishing in the waters around the coast. The Duke of Argyll, the owner of the island, states that it now supports 200 cows and heifers, 140 younger cattle, 600 sheep, and 25 horses, and 'three score of the pachyderms so dear to the children of Erin.' Other lands were added from time to time, and gifts in abundance were brought by wealthy pilgrims and grateful disciples. Thus, though huts were multiplied and the population increased, supplies were not wanting. As missionaries went out into all lands, they were not unmindful of the rock whence they were hewn. The sacred Isle was their Jerusalem, and each of them might exclaim, 'If I forget thee, may my right hand forget its cunning!' The resources of the monastery were therefore increased by contributions from a thousand streams. Above all, the princes and the prelates who came to bury their dead within the sacred precincts did not come empty-handed. Iona, during 200 years—the golden age of the Irish Church— continued to be the fruitful mother of monasteries; and it is an interesting fact, that during 700 years every abbot but one was an Irishman. At length the Danes found out this sanctuary, and plundered it many times. Here is an ominous heading in the annals for 794: '*Vastatio omnium Insularum a Gentilibus.*' But 200 years are a long time for a monastery to flourish. Think of all that the British islands have witnessed and suffered since the revolution of 1689!

St. Columba was by nature a ruler of men. Remarkably tall, handsome, well built, with a powerful physique, great musical gifts, a magnificent voice for both singing and speaking, gentle in spirit and simple in his habits, full of benevolence and noble aspirations, his very presence inspired homage. He was idolised by the monks and students; and it was quite natural in those ages of credulity that legends should have clustered round his history. This was the more to be expected, as he, like most of the famous Irish saints, bore the name of a Pagan divinity. His case will furnish a good example of the transformations effected by the legend-mongers of the eighth, ninth, and tenth centuries.

When he resolved to establish in Scotland—then *Albyn*—a missionary college for the conversion of the heathen, he seems to have devoted himself to perpetual exile. But he felt that if he was anywhere in sight of his native land, if he could only behold the green woods of Inishowen, or the heather-clad mountains of Donegal or Down, he could not resist the temptation to relinquish his work and return to the home of his fathers. So when he and his companions cruised in their boats of hides along the Scottish coast, he landed at several points that seemed desirable for a settlement. But when, on ascending the highest hill, he saw his dear country, he gave orders to sail on, until at length he found in Iona all the seclusion that he required. Very touching and generous is the manner in which the Duke of Argyll records this incident in the life of the Irish Saint. Observing that Columba sailed on till he had got out of sight of Ireland, he says, 'He could not bear to see it, and live out of it. The passionate love of an Irish Celt for his native land seems to have burned in him with all the strength which is part of a powerful character.' (P. 78.)

Exceedingly beautiful, intensely noble, is the character of Columba thus presented in the simple garb of truth. Let us now see how it appears in the Psalters, Chronicles, and Annals, which were examined, tested, and expurgated every three years at Tara in presence of Kings, Princes, Bishops, and Bards; and for not believing which, all non-Irish speaking writers are denounced as ignorant and incompetent, if not grossly prejudiced and stupidly malignant.

According to the 'Chronicle of the Saints of Ireland,' Columba was descended from the Royal race of Ulster in a direct line from Niall, the great hero of the Nine Hostages. As farther evidence of this, Dr. Keating subjoins the following verses from an old poet, 'whose testimony cannot be disputed':—

> The most religious Columkill
> Descended from the royal race of Felix,
> Son of Feargus, most renowned in war,
> Son of the invincible Conall Gulban.

The child was baptized by the name of Criomthan, and he was always attended by a guardian angel, named Axall, and an evil genius, or demon, called Demal. He was sent to school at a monastery, and his master allowed him a weekly holiday, to play with the children in a neighbouring town. His amiable disposition made him so great a favourite with his youthful companions that when they saw him coming from the gate of the convent they used to lift up their hands in a transport of joy, exclaiming, 'Here comes Collum na Cille,' which in Irish means 'The Pigeon of the Church.' The Abbot Florence, therefore, directed that his gifted pupil should be always called by this name.

Notwithstanding this pleasing promise of his youth, it seems that Columba manifested when he grew up a very quarrelsome and revengeful disposition, which, no doubt, was the work of his indwelling demon. He was the promoter of three or four bloody battles between his countrymen. The first battle happened on this wise. During the sitting of the Royal Parliament, one member killed another 'against the established laws and privileges of that convention.' The murderer took refuge in a monastery, and was committed to the protection of Columba. But justice or vengeance pursued him, and put him to death, disregarding the sanctuary. 'This sacrilegious violence so enraged the saint that his passion urged him on to revenge, and roused by him the northern clan O'Neill took up arms in his defence.' 'In an outrageous manner they demanded satisfaction of King Dermod for violating the holy asylum, and putting the offender to death. The King thought to chastise their sedition with the sword, and marched against them with his forces; a terrible engagement followed, and after a bloody conflict, the royal army, supported by the provincial troops of Connaught, was defeated; and that martial clan, the O'Neills, obtained a complete victory, "not a little owing to the fervent prayers of Columkill."'

There is another account, called 'the Black Book of Molaga,' which represents the cause of this war differently. It was a dispute about a copy of the New Testament, transcribed by an unknown hand. Columkill took possession of it, alleging that as the copyist was unknown, he had as good a right to it as any one else. The matter was referred to the King of Ireland, who decided against the claimant, quoting the proverb, that 'the cow and the calf should always go together,' and, therefore, that the proprietor of the original had an undoubted right to the copy until the true owner appeared. This decision was resented by the dove-like saint, and he found means to engage the king in the war which ended in the memorable battle of Cuill Dreimme. He excited the other wars to avenge affronts which he received from different persons, so that his vindictive temper caused the shedding of an immense quantity of Irish blood.

Taking these facts into consideration, St. Molaise imposed upon Columkill a very severe penance: namely, that he should quit his native land and never more behold Ireland with his eyes, hoping that exile would be an effectual cure for his vindictive nature. He humbly submitted to the cruel penance. This is the reason ' why he never rested till he had got out of sight of the island.' But he returned many years after as Abbot of Iona, to assist in the decision of the great question about the threatened banishment of the Bards. How was he to do this without looking at his beloved country and breaking his vow? Quite easily; by wearing a close bandage over his eyes all the time he was in it. And thus, as the old chronicles record, Columkill religiously observed the commands of St. Molaise, 'and never was refreshed with a glimpse of light till the assembly broke up, and he returned into Scotland.' St. Molaise wrote a poem upon this occasion, wherein are these lines :—

> The pious Columkill with his retinue
> Sailed from the isle of Aoii and arrived
> In Ireland; but by the discipline of the Church
> Enjoined, he never with his eyes beheld
> The country.

The retinue mentioned consisted of twenty bishops, forty presbyters, fifty deacons, and thirty students of divinity. The fact that twenty bishops came in the train of an abbot sorely perplexed the chroniclers, a proof that they lived five or six centuries after the events they undertook to describe. Having imbibed their ecclesiastical ideas under the Roman hierarchy, which first brought diocesan episcopacy into Ireland, they could not understand that the 'bishops' of the monastic times were nothing more than doctors or professors—the title implying simply, that they had been authorised or designated by some abbot to go forth as teachers or missionaries. Father Keating endeavours to get out of the difficulty by quoting a passage from the history of the Venerable Bede, who says that 'the island of Iona had an abbot for its governor, to whom not only the whole province, but also the *bishops,* by an unusual order, owed submission.' But the case of Iona was not at all exceptional. Every abbot in Ireland had supreme jurisdiction over the clergy in his district, and these were generally called 'bishops,' of whom there were several in the same convent, engaged either as tutors and professors, or as preachers.

But when the illustrious Abbot of Hy (as the island was anciently called) made his appearance at the assembly, convened at Drumkeat, he met a very strange reception, which is instructive as showing, at least, what the chroniclers and the writers of the *Ancient Manuscripts* thought likely and credible, as happening in Ireland in 'the golden age of Christianity.' We are told that when Columkill came near Drumkeat—where the kings, princes, prelates, and nobles were assembled—the wife of Hugh, King of Ireland was incensed at his arrival, and commanded her son Conall to treat those religious 'foreigners' with contempt, to disregard their office, and not give them the least countenance or protection. The news of the evil design having reached the saint, he refused to enter the assembly till he had obtained satisfaction. 'Therefore he addressed himself to Heaven and importunately petitioned for an exemplary stroke of vengeance.' His prayer, which was granted, was this: that the queen and her waiting lady might be punished with 'a disease, which, though not incurable, should afflict them with long and lingering pains, and confine them to their apartments.' During the time the distemper continued, the superstitious people of the country about imagined that they had been turned into cranes.

But this ungallant retaliation for a singular example of Irish hospitality did not deter the wicked son of the queen from carrying out his mother's instructions in a most outrageous manner. The abbot was received with profound respect by the royal and noble assembly, and seated beside Conall, son to the King of Ireland. But this graceless prince gave the signal to his accomplices, a gang of roughs, whereupon they immediately began to insult the 'bishops from Iona,' pelting them with tufts and dirt till they were covered with filth, and some of them very much bruised by this violent and barbarous treatment.' St. Columba was amazed at the outrage, and demanded at whose instigation it was perpetrated. Finding that the king's son was the director and principal cause of this barbarity, 'he warmly represented to the prince the heinousness of the act; and, as the *Chronicle* goes on, he caused *twenty-seven bells to be rung*, and by these bells he laid the most heavy curses and dreadful imprecations upon him, which had the effect of depriving Conall of his sense and understanding, and in the end caused the loss of his estate, and of the succession to the crown of Ireland. This cruel prince, from the curse laid upon him by the ringing of the bells, was afterwards distinguished by the name of *Conall Clogach*.'

Another son, however, was respectful to St. Columba, and so he prayed for *him* as effectually as he had prayed against the other. He then paid an unwelcome visit to the Monarch of Ireland, who sat in a room apart from the rest of the assembly. His Majesty had great awe upon him when the saint came into his presence, 'for by the constant *success* of his prayers, he became a terror to the Irish court.' Columba's next visit was to the King of Ossory, whom the King of Ireland had cast into prison, where, loaded with chains, he was kept under a strong guard. Here the old *Chronicle* records a most miraculous event. A large pillar, as it were of fire, appeared in the air at night, exceedingly bright and terrible, lighting up the castle as at noonday; it hung directly over the apartment where King Scanlan was confined. Groaning under the weight of his irons, he heard a distinct voice, which called aloud, 'Scanlan, stand up! fear nothing! give me your hand, and leave your chains and fetters behind you.' The King obeyed, and the chains fell 'of their own accord.' The soldiers, who had fallen flat on their faces when they saw the bright pillar, now summoned courage to demand who had dared to force open the prison. The angel replied, that Scanlan, King of Ossory, was free, which answer confounded them, for they thought it impossible that any human power could make such a desperate attempt.

The King of Ireland had churlishly refused the earnest request of the saint to set his Royal prisoner at liberty, when St. Columba said he should be liberated, and that he would that very night 'untie the strings of his brogues,' while engaged 'in his midnight devotions.' This prediction was accomplished; for King Scanlan, staying with his deliverer at his lodgings, the latter 'being disposed to sleep, intended to take off his brogues, but was prevented by the king, who untied them. The saint, in surprise, demanded who had loosened his strings. The king replied that he had done it; which gave the saint great satisfaction, because he had frustrated the design of Hugh, the King of Ireland, upon that prince, and procured his delivery from a cruel imprisonment.'

Let us have one more exploit of the Dove of the Church before he returns in peace to his paradise, Iona, which his austerities made for him a purgatory. An old chronicle relates, that when St. Columba was in Ireland there lived a pagan priest in the '*county*' of Tyrconnel, who erected a temple of great beauty and magnificence, and among other curiosities of art and workmanship he made an altar of fine glass, which he adorned with the representation of the *sun* and *moon*. It happened that this priest was seized with a sudden distemper, which took away his senses, and he was without motion, as if in a swoon. 'The Devil, who it seems had a particular resentment against the man, took advantage of the opportunity, seized him with his talons, and was hurrying him away through the air. St. Columba looking up, perceived the fiend upon the wing bearing his prey, and when he was flying over him, the saint made the sign of the cross in the air above his head, which so astounded the Devil that he let go his hold and dropped the priest, who providentially fell at St. Columba's feet.' This deliverance was so gratefully received by the priest, that after a short discourse he became a convert to Christianity; when he had dedicated his temple to the Christian faith, he bestowed it upon St. Columba, and entered himself into a 'religious order, where he led a monastic life and became an eminent confessor for the faith of Christ.'

Such were the stories that passed for ecclesiastical history in the times when the Irish *Annals* were written. In the mass, those mediæval chronicles are distinguished by the most childish ignorance and credulity; they are plainly but clumsy travesties of the heathen mythology, adapted to monkish purposes, and are little more *historical*, in the true sense of the word, than fairy tales. In the story of the Pagan Priest there is a traditional glimpse of the beautiful temples and imposing Sun-worship of the Tuath da Danaans, who preceded the Celts as the rulers of the island. Dr. Keating informs his readers that *the Chronicle of the Irish Saints* and other ancient authorities take notice that there were twenty-two saints in Ireland named Columbkill, and says 'The first of which name was the saint whose piety and virtuous acts have been described, and in honour of whose name every one was desirous of that title, as a sort of check and restraint upon immorality and vice, and a signal example of temperance, charity, and every Christian virtue.' We learn from the same source that *the* Columba was naturally of a hale and robust constitution; 'for the author of his *Life* relates that when he used to celebrate mass or sing the Psalms his voice might be heard distinctly a mile and a half from the place where he was performing his devotions;' and as we find it expressly related in his *Vision*:

> St. Columba by his sweet melodious voice
> Expelled the evil spirits, who from the sound
> Precipitately fled; for by Heaven inspired,
> He charmed the good, but was a scourge and terror
> To the profane.

The power of his voice and its sweetness were the more wonderful when we consider his mode of life. The description of his austerities shows how the poetical legends of the Bards were worked up in the prose Chronicles. The 'ancient poet' sung:

> This pious saint as a religious penance
> Lay on the cold ground, and through his garments
> His bones looked sharp and meagre; his poor cell
> Was open to the inclemency of the winds
> Which blew through the unplastered walls.

Here is the version of the prose Chronicler: 'The Irish saint mortified his body by a continued course of abstinence and austerity, which, by this severe usage, became so macerated that his bones had almost pierced through his skin; and when the wind blew hard through the wall of his cell, which was unplastered, and forced aside his upper garment, his ribs became visible through his habit; for by fasting and other acts of devotion he was no more than the image of a man, and was worn to a very ghastly spectacle.' Though he spent 34 years in Iona out of the 77 of his life, by the Irish accounts he did not wish that his bones should rest out of Erin. Thus dying he remembered his favourite haunts:

> My soul delights to meditate and pray
> At Hy, the happy Paradise of Scotland;
> Derry, the glory of my native isle,
> I celebrate thy praise by nature blessed;
> To Dunn de Leathglass I bequeath my bones,
> In life a sweet retreat.

This must have been written by some one who did not know that in Columba's time and for centuries after, Scotland, or Scotia, was the name of Ireland, and that the Irish were called Scots.

Mr. John Stuart, in his work on the 'Sculptured Stones of Scotland,'[1] says that the Rev. Dr. Reeves, our greatest Irish antiquary, 'has amply illustrated the fact, so long of being recognised by our early historical writers, that Ireland was the *ancient Scotland*, and home of the Scotch.'[2] 'From the mother country,' writes Dr. Reeves, 'issued St. Columba and almost all the early saints of the Scottish calendar. Coming from Ireland, yet frequently visiting it, they maintained their old relation, so that their memory was equally cherished in either country, and a common day appointed to the festival of each.'

In the days of Columba the Picts had no less than seven Kings, the proud name assumed by the heads of clans, as in Ireland; and among them, says Mr. Stuart, 'there was wanting any principle of coherence or national unity, or any germ of diffusive vitality for civilising the masses.' The monasteries of the Picts were all subject to Iona.

In Ireland more than 300 religious houses are ascribed to the name Columba and Colman. Mr. Marcus Keane remarks that

[1] Published by the Spalding Club.   [2] Vol. ii. p. 47.

the numerous legends told of them in the most extreme counties of Ireland attest their Pagan origin; but the foundation of the names is to be sought for in Babylonian Mythology. The name 'Colmban' literally means the 'White dove,' from *Colm*, dove, and *ban*, white. The name Colman may also be rendered 'swift dove.' Mr. Keane thinks it probable that Colman is the name Colmban, only spelled as usually pronounced in the south of Ireland, the B not being sounded; and consequently we find Colmban as a distinguished saint in connexion with numerous establishments throughout the Northern and Midland Counties; while the name of Colman, given to 200 saints, is generally found in the Southern and Western Counties. St. Colman's religious foundations are said by Colgan to be no fewer than 300 ('Ulster Journal,' vol. i. p. 27). I am confirmed in the opinion that Colman and Colomb represent the same heathen divinity (Juno the dove) by the fact that Columban, Colman, and Mocholmog are in the *Martyrology of Donegal* identified as the same individual. And again the same authority informs us that Columnan was called Colman.[1]

[1] 'Towers and Temples of Ancient Ireland,' p. 79.

CHAPTER II.

MYTHOLOGY AND HAGIOLOGY.

OF the origin of the name Columba a curious account is given by Mr. Hislop in his learned work 'The Two Babylons.'[1] He states 'that in ancient Babylon the title of the Goddess-mother as the dwelling place of God was *Sacca*, or in the emphatic form *Sactha*, that is, the " Tabernacle." . . . Every quality of gentleness and mercy was regarded as centred in her; and when death had closed her career she was fabled to have been deified and changed into a pigeon, to express the celestial benignity of her nature. She was called *D'Juné*, or ' the Dove,' without the article *Juno*, a name of the Roman Queen of Heaven, which has the very same meaning; and, under the form of a dove as well as her own, she was worshipped by the Babylonians. The dove, 'the chosen symbol of this deified Queen, is represented with an olive branch in her mouth, as she herself in her human form also is seen bearing the olive branch in her hand.' He adds that in the sculptures at Nineveh, the wings and tail of the dove represented the *third* member of the Idolatrous Assyrian Trinity. In confirmation of this view it must be stated that the Assyrian Juno, or the *Virgin Venus* as she was called, was identified with the *air*. Thus Julius Fermicus says 'the Assyrians and part of the Africans believe the air to have the supremacy of the elements; for they have consecrated this same element under the name of Juno or the Virgin Venus. Why this air, thus identi-

---

[1] The author of 'The Two Babylons' was a learned Scottish clergyman. It was the work of many years, in which he was aided by several friends, who took an interest in antiquities, among them Lord John Scott. But his most valuable condjutor was an Irish gentleman, Edward J. Cooper, Esq., Markree Castle, for many years M.P. for the county Sligo. He died in 1863. An eminent amateur astronomer, he was author of a 'Catalogue of Ecliptic Stars.' The Royal Society speaks of him as ' a sincere Christian, no mean poet, an accomplished linguist and exquisite musician, who possessed a wide and varied range of general information.' He spent much money in the pursuit of knowledge.

fied with Juno, whose symbol was that of the third person of the Assyrian Trinity? why, but because in Chaldea the same word which signifies the "air" signifies also the *Holy Ghost*. The knowledge of this accounts entirely for the statement of Proclus that Juno imports the generation of *soul*. Whence could the soul, the spirit of man, be supposed to have its origin but from the spirit of God?'

Now as Colman or Columban literally means 'the white dove,' Mr. Keane infers from this quotation the fact that, as so many other unmistakeably Babylonish divinities are found among the names of Irish saints, this connection is sufficient to account for the 200 Irish saints bearing that name. There seems no doubt of Juno's having been worshipped in Ireland as *Da Mater*, 'the mother of the Gods;' her Irish name was *Una* or *Unan* or *Iun*, the dove, like the Hebrew; and this name is still preserved in Iona, the island in West Scotland sacred to St. Colman, the dove. Ion or Iun is also to be found as part of compound names in many localities throughout Ireland—the divine Incarnation, as her son was styled, *Mac Ion* or *Mac Owen*; we have therefore Kil Mac Owen, or Temple Mac Owen; and Kiledeus tells us that there were fifty-eight saints of the name of Mochuan. The name Una is frequently introduced into ancient Irish poetry. It is translated into the English name Winifred, a saint celebrated for holy wells. The name Una or Iun, with which many of the Holy Wells of Ireland were associated, has fallen into oblivion, and that of *St. John* has been substituted for it, both names being nearly identical in the Irish:—therefore it is that so many of *St. John's Wells* are found throughout Ireland.

Mr. Keane associates another name with *Da Mater* for the female nature—Daire, the 'oak.' Thus St. Dairebille or Belle Mullet, the Oak-tree; St. Dairearca, the 'oak of the Ark;' St. Dairmilla, 'or the four paps,' the mother of several Irish saints. Dairmaid, the oak twig, answers to the branch of Juno of Cuthite mythology, and there are fifty-eight St. Mochuans, the sons of the Dove.

It is an unquestionable fact, of which Mr. Keane has produced an irresistible array of historic proofs and illustrations, that the early Celtic saints became the actual inheritors of the glory and *prestige* of the heathen gods, while several Christian festivals observed at the present day were in reality, so far as the popular feeling is concerned, a continuation of Pagan worship. 'The May-pole ceremony, with its dancing and rejoicing, was in fact a common mode of keeping the feast of Baal at a distance from the Round Tower, or real May Pole, and it was continued among the peasantry as a harmless custom long after the Round Tower worship was interdicted, and after the knowledge of its real origin was lost by lapse of time. The Irish name of May Day at present is *La Baal Thinna*, "the day of Baal's Fire." The name of Baltinglass, the fire of the Green Baal, may be also traced to the same source, and it is probable that the name of the green god snake (Gad il glass) may have given rise to Ireland being first called "The Green Island," the Green God having been a name of the primeval Budh in Hindoo mythology.' I may add here that the *Shamrock* was the Persian emblem of the Trinity. The Magi divided the victim in three parts, and laid them on a species of *trefoil*. The rod of Mercury was called the 'Three-leaved Rod.' Shamrock composed the 'Melilot garland,' which in Egypt was the crown of universal dominion.[1] In later times the miracles of saints who were the patrons of certain places and churches were referred invariably to the fifth and sixth centuries, for the obvious reason that no celebrated saint could have been supposed to exist before the time of St. Patrick, the Apostle of Ireland. Hence the two or three centuries after him came to be celebrated as 'the golden age' of the Church in the Irish *Hagiology*, which began to be composed about the *tenth century*. The literature of the heathens seems to have been as far as possible destroyed by the Celts when they became Christians, as we read that St. Patrick caused more than 180 volumes to be burned. But heathen monuments and customs were not destroyed in Ireland at all to the same extent as in other countries which formed part of the Roman Empire. For example, in the early part of the seventh century the Christians made a raid on the banks of the Seine, and overthrew the statues, images, sacred oaks, filled the fountains and holy wells, extinguished the sacred fires, and shut up the caves, &c.

---

[1] 'The Two Babylons,' p. 303. Fifth edition.

While the Irish language and the ancient landmarks remain, it will be impossible to obliterate from the minds of the peasantry the traditions of Paganism; and even at the present day they preserve in their own tongue the primitive pronunciation of the names of the divinities, which, by varying the spelling and the pronunciation, have been converted into the names of celebrated ancient saints. Colgan, the Catholic antiquarian, observes that there were some names among the Irish saints in which sanctity seemed to be inherent, they were borne by so many. Thus he gives eleven names, each of which was borne by a number of famous saints: one by ten, one by fifteen, one by twenty, and so on up to thirty saints. The most popular saint was Cronan, called after Cronos, the Titan. St. Kiledeus, an Irish bishop, said to have lived in the seventh century, and quoted as one of the best authorities, states 'that there had been in the island sixty-two *classes* of saints who bore the same name, among whom were remarkable: 34 Mochiminus, 37 Moluans, 43 Molaises, or Lascrenes, 58 Mochuans, and 200 Colmans. In heathen times the Shannon, like the Ganges, was worshipped as a sacred river, and accordingly along its banks were twenty-five heathen temples, to which the Christian writers attached the same number of St. Shanuans.'

A very curious and comic result of the derivation of saintly names from pagan deities is the fact that there is in the Irish Hagiology a St. Devil, something like the French 'le Bon Diable.' The Irish of Devil is Dia Baal, literally the god Baal, but sounded Diul, which in the name of the saint was spelled Dichul, the sound of the 'ch' being omitted in pronunciation. 'This is one of the names,' says Mr. Keane, 'in which sanctity seemed to be inherent, as twelve saints are said to have borne it—St. Devil in Irish—and he was the patron of ten religious foundations!' The same author gives a list of no less than 200 of the most celebrated religious foundations on which stood pagan temples in all parts of Ireland, the names of the gods once worshipped there having been appropriated by *saints*, and as the same god was worshipped in many places, so we meet the same saint turning up in the most remote localities, north, south, east, and west. Thus we find the name of St. Budhe variously spelled associated with *forty* ecclesiastical establishments, nearly all ascribed to the fifth and sixth centuries. Mr. Keane gives the particulars of all these 200 places, and a most interesting record it is. St. Luan, the Moon, was connected with foundations extending over eight counties in Ulster, Leinster, and Munster. *Luan* is still the Irish name for moon, which was worshipped as the symbol of female nature.[1] There were ten famous places in which her worship flourished. The Gubban Saer, celebrated as the great builder, became a saint under the names of St. Gobban and St. Abban, and to him seventeen great ecclesiastical establishments were consecrated. Molach, one of the greatest of the Cuthite divinities, became St. Molach, whose temple would be pronounced in Irish, Teampul Molaice. He was the renowned patron of ten churches, in Sligo, Limerick, Fermanagh, Kerry, Cork, and Kilkenny. The well-known heathen divinity Dagan also became a saint, and reigned in Monaghan and Wicklow.

The galaxy of saints celebrated by the Irish annalists in their most authentic records as brightening and glorifying the ages succeeding St. Patrick were distinguished by many striking peculiarities. The names of several of them, as we have seen, signify the relationship to the heavenly bodies. They were, besides, a very aristocratic class, and not a few had royal blood running in their veins. This is not so much to be wondered at, because at that time royal blood was plentiful. The country with a population that could not have exceeded one million had five kings, and in each kingdom there were perhaps a score chiefs or princes, each wielding all but sovereign power within his principality. The relationship, however, was so close that they may be said to have constituted a sort of family party, and Mr. Keane affirms that this party comprised *nine-tenths of the founders* of the most ancient ecclesiastical establishments of Ireland, always excepting St. Patrick, who was a genuine Irish saint, although his biographers have ascribed to him much of the legendary history which originated in heathen mythology. Of course they did not appear in this light to such historians as St. Bernard, who collected the stories of their lives, or to Colgan,

---

[1] Ard-boe, County Londonderry, once the site of a Round Tower, means literally the Hill of Budh.

who compiled them in his great work, the *Acta Sanctorum*. If we admit the theory that the saints were really heathen gods and demigods, we can easily account for the fact that there was no important ancient ecclesiastical establishment in Ireland which had not several of the most celebrated saints connected with its foundation. It would be very natural to have half-a-dozen gods or demigods worshipped in the same place at the same time, but very strange to have a cluster of Apostolic missionaries thus located. But as in ancient Greece and Rome one divinity was specially honoured at a certain place, as Diana at Ephesus, so each Irish temple is ascribed to one pre-eminent saint as its founder. Yet although the saintly hierarchy boasted of royal and aristocratic blood, it is a curious fact that the names which the Annals assign to them are not the names borne by the *kings* or *chieftains* of the Celtic Irish. On the contrary more than one hundred of the brightest of those luminaries bore the heathenish names of Dagan, Molach, Diul, Satan, Budh, Mochue, Endee, and Mochtee. Archbishop Ussher mentions an *authentic* manuscript wherein the first Irish saints were divided into three regular orders, viz., Most Holy, Holier, and Holy,—the first resembling the sun, the second the moon, and the third the stars. St. Patrick did not come within the celestial orders. He worked alone, and Colgan gives us proofs, if we can accept them, that he did not work in vain, for with his own hand he consecrated 150 bishops with 5,000 priests, besides which he founded 700 churches. Those old saints were wonderfully active in the founding of churches and other religious establishments. St. Luan (the Moon) is said to have founded 100 monasteries, and St. Columban (the Dove), Juno, established no less than 300. If these things were done in a country like modern France, or England, or even Ireland at the present day, with an industrious population counted by millions, and large stores of national wealth, we might be well astonished. But the marvellous achievements ascribed by Canon Pope of Dublin to Cardinal Cullen are nothing in comparison to what was done by the least of those Irish saints in the sixth century, when a scattered pastoral people with their numerous petty chiefs were so liable to be plundered by marauding hosts, that they could never count on reaping or grinding what they had sown, their only mill being the quern worked by the hand of a woman. Then civil war was almost incessant, and as may be seen in the 'Annals of the Four Masters,' the end of the vast majority of the rulers was a violent and untimely death. In fact those Annals so far as they relate to worldly affairs are little more than an account of robberies and butcheries perpetrated by the Irish upon one another before the Danish invasions. We know from what we read within the period of authentic history that the 'hosting' parties did not always spare sacred treasures; but according to early annalists, the Church flourished amazingly in the midst of chronic anarchy and chaotic violence. If we believe our best ecclesiastical authorities, such as Colgan, St. Comgal was the father of 4,000 monks, all of whom were in the abbey of Bangor at one and the same time. St. Binden was the father of 3,000 monks. St. Finian educated 3,000 saints at Clonard, 'including the Twelve Apostles of Ireland.' St. Fechian presided over 3,000 monks at the abbey of Fore; St. Molaice ruled 1,500 monks, and St. Gobban 1,000; in all 12,500 monks governed by five saints, and all about the same time—not to mention St. Patrick's 5,000 priests, and all the monks of the numerous monasteries founded or governed by the multitude of other saints.

Some of the saints were women, and not the least successful. They were fruitful mothers in Israel, whether we understand the word in the natural or the spiritual sense. Derinila, ' of the Four Paps,' was the mother of a considerable number; but, notwithstanding the extra supply of ' paps,' she was thrown into the shade completely by the mother of St. Camin of Iniscaltra. In the ' Annals of the Four Masters ' (anno 669) we read, ' That beside the saint she had seventy children!' and although there were forty-three saints named Molaice, fifty-eight named Mochuan, and two hundred Colmans, and so on, in addition to the holy progeny produced by miraculously prolific mothers, yet the Irish historians pretended to decide the difference between all those saints of the same name—' by their several genealogies, and the diversity of the time and place of their birth. No wonder that Ireland was then called the Island of Saints.' Not only did they increase and multiply by natural generation as well as by spiritual propagandism, but they lived to a patriarchal age in the midst of unremitting and barbarous warfare. According to the 'Annals of the Four Masters,' St. Sincheall lived to the age of 330 years, St. Moeda to the age of 300, St. Darerca to 180 years, while St. Liban reached the age of 470, and 404 was the length of St. Ibhar's life. All this is given as *authentic history!*—the history of the 'golden age' of the Irish Church. Other authorities relate that St. Molaice lived 160 years, and St. Fechian 180, in the seventh century, while St. Cieran spent no less than *three centuries* labouring in the vineyard! The same age is assigned to St. Brendan, who at the end of 300 years was seen ascending to heaven in a chariot. It was in honour of this saint that the priests of Kerry organised a great pilgrimage some years ago to his shrine on the top of a mountain called by his name.

It would be quite in keeping with the ignorance and boundless credulity of the times in which the Irish Annals were compiled to find that those long-lived saints performed an immense number of miracles, and that there should be fantastic violations of the laws of Nature without any purpose of utility. We are prepared for anything in the Thaumaturgic line after reading of ten saints, the total of whose ages amounted to 3,090 years, giving an average of 309 for each. Among the books which the modern antiquaries of the Petrie and Wilde school consider authentic records and historic literature, which no one would discredit except sceptics who are ignorant of the treasures contained in the Irish language, is the 'Martyrology of Donegal.' In that we read that countless were the signs and miracles that God performed on earth by St. Cieran. 'It was he that used to order the stones to kindle at the puff of his breath.' It was he also that made fish honey, and oil out of a little bit of meat in the time of the fast, when Bremverina, Bar, and Cieran of Cluane came on a visit to him, as appears in his 'Life,' together with many other miracles. He used to be often immersed in a vat of cold water, for the love of the Lord. It was he who used to go to a rock, which was far distant in the sea, without a ship or a boat, and used to return again, as appears from his own 'Life.' 'Sixty years and three hundred (360) was his age when he yielded his spirit.' Of St. Senan the same book states that he expelled a monster from Iniscathaigh, which monster kept the island to itself until then. The same Senan loved to have sickness upon him, and his desire was so far gratified that he enjoyed thirty diseases on his body at the same time. St. Enda subjected his disciples (thrice fifty in number) to a severe trial of faith. They were to go out in turn upon the sea in a *currach*, or canoe, made of wattles, without any hide upon it at all. If there was no sin in the man, the salt water did not penetrate the currach; if there was sin, it came in pretty freely between the wattles. But the only one subjected to this mishap was Gigniat, the saint's cook. 'What hast thou done, O Gigniat?' said Enda. He answered, 'that he did nothing but put a little to his own share from that of Cieran.' Enda ordered him to leave the island. St. Mocuda had a congregation of 1,100 persons when he was abbot at Rathin—' and an angel used to address every third man of them.' St. Brendan of Kerry saw a wonderful bird coming in at the window, so that it perched on the altar, and he was not able to look at it in consequence of the sun-like radiance around it. 'Salute us, O cleric!' said the bird. 'May God salute thee!' said Brendan: 'who art thou?' 'I am Michael the Archangel, whom God hath sent to thee, to address thee, and to make harmony for thee.' 'Thanks be to Him!' said Brendan; 'thou art welcome to me.' The bird placed its bill behind the feathers of its wing, and sweeter than the music of the world was the music it made. Brendan was listening to it for twenty-four hours, and the angel took his leave of him afterwards.

Although this saint went up to the sky in a chariot in the year 553, the musical entertainment vouchsafed to him by the archangel was nothing in comparison to that afforded to St. Mochaoi. The historian says 'He went with seven score young men *to cut wattles to make a church*. He himself was engaged at the work and cutting timber like the rest. He had his load ready before the others, and he kept it by his side. As he was so, he heard a bright bird singing on the blackthorn near him. He was more beautiful than the birds of the world. And the bird said, "This is diligent work, O cleric!" "This is required of us in building a church of God," answered Mochaoi. "Who is addressing me?" "A man of the people of my Lord is here," he answered, i.e. an Angel of God from Heaven. "Hail to thee!" said Mochaoi, "and wherefore hast thou come hither?" "To address thee from thy Lord, and to amuse thee for awhile." "I like this!" exclaimed the saint. The bird then fixed his beak in the feathers of his wing. Three hundred years did Mochaoi remain this doing, having a bundle of sticks by his side in the middle of the wood, and the wood was not withered, and the time did not seem to be longer than one hour of the day.'

It is on the same authority we learn that St. Declan on one occasion, when he was coming from Rome, forgot a bell (which had been sent him from heaven) upon a rock which was in the port, and the rock swam after him, so that it arrived before the ship in Erin, and Declan was told that where the rock should touch ground, there God should permit him to erect a church, and this was afterwards fulfilled.

It is noteworthy that the places associated with the names of heathen deities with the prefix of Saint, and which are the sites of round towers and stone crosses, as Ardmore is—where this stone rests and is worshipped—are the places of pilgrimage to which the peasantry retain the most inveterate attachment, a devotion which has resisted most stubbornly the innovating authority of the priesthood. No power of the Church can destroy the faith of the Waterford people in St. Declan's Stone. Of a similar character is the first miracle ascribed in the 'Martyrology of Donegal' to St. Madchog. It is there related that he was brought to be baptized upon a flagstone, and upon this stone 'people used to be ferried out and in, just as in every other boat, to the island in the lake on which he was born.' Eithne, his mother, when she was bringing him forth, held a spinster's distaff, which was a withered stick of hazel, in her hand. This withered stick 'grew up with leaves and blossoms, and afterwards with goodly fruit; and this hazel is still in existence as a green tree without decay or withering, producing nuts every year.'

These are but samples of the mass of fabulous rubbish contained in the 'Annals of the Four Masters,' the 'Martyrology of Donegal,' and other literary treasures, which the most competent scholars have translated from the Irish language. The child-like simplicity, unconscious ignorance, and boundless credulity with which they were compiled by the Brothers O'Clery, three Donegal friars, and another comrade, as well as the ridiculous nature of their contents, prove them to be utterly unhistorical and worthless as guides to a knowledge of the early ages of the Irish Church. The 'Acta Sanctorum' are for the most part fables almost too absurd for the entertainment of children in a nursery, and nearly as destitute of any basis in fact as the Irish fairy tales. We can gather, however, from them and from other sources, from the monuments and traditions of the country, and in other lands, in England, Scotland, France, and Germany, that there were numerous schools in Ireland in the early ages of Christianity which were celebrated throughout Europe; that they were frequented by many foreigners, who became afterwards men of eminence; that many of the Irish ecclesiastics, and of the Irish people, had a passion for learning, and extraordinary zeal in propagating their opinions, with an unquenchable love for disputation on questions of theology and science. But when we behold the ruins of abbeys and colleges which Irishmen founded in Scotland, in Germany, and France, we are liable to come away with a false impression of their achievements, forgetting that those great institutions *grew* from very small beginnings, and that generally the Irish teacher, or professor, or apostle, only planted the acorn from which sprung the gigantic oak. An unwilling exile, or an ardent missionary from his native land, he took up his abode in some quiet retreat, generally a secluded romantic spot, and there he began to teach such pupils as came to him. As his fame spread abroad his disciples increased, some of them the sons of wealthy men, or powerful chiefs, or even of princes, disgusted with the strifes, violence, and bloodshed that prevailed in those turbulent times. They brought with them presents, liberal contributions for the support of the little fraternity. The young men of practical turn of mind set to work by way of exercise to reclaim and cultivate the soil around them, to sow and to plant, for the support and shelter of the community. The results were gardens well stocked with vegetables, smiling fields of corn, flourishing plantations. In due time came grants of land in various parts of the country, with a numerous tenantry. Gradually to the primitive hut, or 'oratory,' was added building after building, chapels, schoolrooms, and ultimately a large church and abbey, with dormitories, refectories, and all the rest of the monastic accommodation which we see in the ruins that attest the former grandeur of those establishments. But ages before there was a stone building—centuries before the president became a mitred abbot and a lord of Parliament, the Irish founder had passed away, perhaps to repeat the immortal work in some other locality, leaving to men of greater talent for organisation, and steadier perseverance and capacity for government, to carry on, extend, and perfect the work on the foundation which he had laid. The pioneer of civilisation does not deserve less honour because results which he never contemplated have arisen from his labours. When George Stephenson constructed a steam engine which travelled at the rate of six miles an hour, he had no idea that locomotives would be made to run twelve times that rate, or of the enormous extent and power of the present railway system. Yet there are few books so full of interest as the Lives of the early Engineers: would that we could have accounts as authentic of the labours, and struggles, and successes of the founders of the Irish monasteries!

CHAPTER III.

THE CHURCH OF ST. PATRICK.

THE numerous ancient *Lives* of St. Patrick are admitted to be full of fables. After a great deal of revising and sifting, the most probable accounts are given by Archbishop Ussher and Sir James Ware. But even by them a considerable quantity of the marvellous has been preserved. We are told that Patrick was *probably* born in 373, at Kirkpatrick, near the Scottish border, his father being a deacon, and his grandfather a priest: that when sixteen years old he was taken prisoner, and carried into Ireland, where he remained a slave for six years, herding cattle, and performing other menial service. Having escaped from bondage, he returned to his parents; then travelled over the Continent, spending several years at Rome, after which he was ordained deacon by his uncle St. Martin, Bishop of Tours, and priest by St. German, Bishop of Auxerre; he next went to Rome, where he was consecrated Bishop, and got a commission from the Pope to convert the Irish. In pursuance of this commission he arrived in that country in the year 432. There he is said to have travelled about for years, founding churches in many places. He came to Armagh in 445, and then we are told 'he laid out the city, built a church, and assembled around him a multitude of religious persons.' All these marvels he seems to have accomplished in two years; for in 447 we find him in the Isle of Man, building a church there. Nothing is said about the well-established fact that Armagh was one of the greatest of the 'high places' of the ancient heathen. The primitive meaning of the name is the 'high place of Macha,' a divinity worshipped by the Tuath-da-Danaans. In the immediate neighbourhood of the city was the famous palace of *Emania*, said to have been built by 'Macha of the Golden Hair,' 300 years before the Christian era. However, St. Patrick, on his return to Ireland, visited Dublin, where he forthwith converted the King, and laid the foundation of Patrick's Cathedral. He then hurried off to Munster, visited Cashel, baptized its King, and 'settled *the ecclesiastical authority* in the southern parts.' Having employed the next six years in fixing the Church of Ireland on a solid foundation, and having ordained bishops and priests through the whole island, according to the patterns he had seen in other countries, he went to Rome again, where he was received joyfully by the Pope, and sent back to Ireland with increased honours and powers. He at length died in his Abbey of Saul.

Of his successors at Armagh little or nothing is known for centuries. Some of them bore the double title of abbot and bishop, the cause of which is fully explained in 'The Life of St. Patrick,' by Dr. Todd. It has been in recent times contended by the established clergy that the Church of St. Patrick was truly and essentially an Episcopal church of the Anglican type. The identity is assumed as a fact clearly demonstrated, and on the strength of this assumption the Roman Catholic Church is regarded as an alien institution imposed upon the country, and possessing no right, human or divine, for persisting in its offensive intrusion. This theory was first fully expounded by the Rev. Robert King, in his 'Primer of the Church History of Ireland,' which has been made a class-book for divinity students in Trinity College, Dublin. This delusion should be at once dissipated by reading the most trustworthy Life of St. Patrick ever published.[1] 'The church of the native Irish,' writes Dr. Todd, 'was discountenanced and ignored by Rome as well as by England. It consisted of the old Irish clergy and inmates of the monasteries beyond the limits of the English Pale, who had not adopted the English manners or language, and were therefore dealt with as rebels. Many of these took refuge in foreign countries, or connected themselves with foreign emissaries, hostile to England at home; but at a subsequent period, when the Anglo-Irish Church had accepted the Reformation, the "*mere* Irish" clergy were found to have become practically extinct.'

---

[1] 'S. Patrick, Apostle of Ireland: A Memoir of the Life and Mission,' &c. By James Henthorn Todd, D.D., S.F.T.C.D., Regius Professor of Hebrew in University, &c.

In the twelfth century, when St. Bernard wrote the 'Life of St. Malachi, Archbishop of Armagh,' he complained in that work that up to his own times there had been in Ireland a 'dissolution of ecclesiastical discipline, a relaxation of censure, a making void of religion, and that a cruel barbarism—nay, a sort of Paganism —was substituted under the Christian name.' In proof of this, he said that 'bishops were changed and multiplied at the pleasure of the "Metropolitan" (Abbot) without order, without reason, so that one bishopric was not content with a single bishop, but almost every congregation had its own separate bishop.' From this it is quite evident that St. Bernard was ignorant of the constitution of the Irish churches, and equally ignorant of the ecclesiastical polity which prevailed throughout the Continental nations in the earliest and purest ages of Christianity. If every congregation in Erin had its bishop, instead of proving that the Irish Christians were corrupt, disorderly, and heathenish, it would prove only that they had adhered with fidelity to the primitive system of church polity, modified by the peculiar circumstances of the country, and by the genius of the Celtic institutions. The word *bishop*, in the sense in which it is used by Churchmen, and generally understood, means a prelate who rules over a number of parochial clergy, be the same more or less. There was nothing of the kind known in Ireland till it was imported by the Normans, and imposed by the Pope. During six or seven centuries after the mission of St. Patrick the word 'parish,' or its equivalent, does not once occur in the history of the Irish Church. But the parish, we know, is the basis of the ecclesiastical system in England and Ireland. The old Irish church was built without this foundation-stone of Episcopacy; and the first thing that Dr. Todd can find which at all resembles a diocese is indicated in the following words:—' The district which owed allegiance to the chieftain, and was inhabited by his followers, became the proper field of labour to *his* bishops and clergy, and this was the first approach to a *diocese*, or territorial jurisdiction, in the Church of Ireland.'

It is quite true, as St. Bernard remarked, that almost every religious community worshipping in one place had a bishop of its own. Not only so—it had sometimes several bishops, the favourite number being 'seven.' These bishops were ordained *per saltum*, that is, without passing through any intervening 'orders;' and the consecration was effected often by a single bishop or abbot with a simple formality of prayer and the imposition of hands. Nothing more therefore was implied by the title of bishop than that the bearer was in 'Holy Orders,' and enjoyed the status of a clergyman, being in fact equivalent to our professional distinction of 'Reverend.' The title conferred no jurisdiction whatever. After passing in review the chief Catholic authorities on the subject, and quoting from Lanigan, Colgan, and others, Dr. Todd gives the result of his inquiries in the following words:—'From the foregoing facts and anecdotes no doubt can remain in the mind of any unprejudiced reader that the normal state of Episcopacy in Ireland was, as we have described, *non-diocesan*, each bishop acting independently without any archiepiscopal jurisdiction, and either entirely independent or subject to the abbot of his monastery; or in the spiritual clanship, to his chieftain. The consequence of this was a great multiplication of bishops; there was no restraint upon their being consecrated. Every man of eminence for piety or learning was advanced to the order of a bishop as a sort of *degree* or mark of distinction. Many of these lived as solitaries or in monasteries. Many of them established schools for religious life and the cultivation of sacred learning, having no diocese or fixed episcopal duties; and many of them, influenced by missionary zeal, went forth to the Continent, to Great Britain, or to other heathen lands, to preach the Gospel of Christ to the Gentiles.' Again, he says:—'On the continent of Europe the Christian empire both in the East and the West was divided into Episcopal provinces and dioceses, based upon the ancient civil divisions, and the canonical regulations were closely connected with the institution of metropolitan and diocesan jurisdiction. In Ireland, where there were no metropolitans, no dioceses, and no fixed or legally recognised civil divisions of the country, these canonical rules were inapplicable, and therefore were disregarded.' The word 'archbishop' occurs in Irish Church history, but it was used in a sense totally different from its present meaning. The Irish word *ard-episcop* is not equivalent to archbishop: the word 'Ard' meaning 'high,' the compound denotes simply an eminent or celebrated bishop; and there might be several of such *archbishops* in the same town or district.

The number seven being one to which the ancient Irish evidently attached a sacred import, we frequently read also of seven bishops dwelling in one place. Thus the 'Martyrology of Donegal' mentions no less than six groups of bishops, seven in each group, and in three of them the seven bishops were brothers, sons of one father! But this list, says Dr. Todd, is 'completely eclipsed by the 140 groups of "seven bishops," of various churches and places in Ireland, who were invoked in the Irish Litany attributed to Aengus Cele De, or the Culdee, and probably composed in the ninth century.' We can easily imagine that owing to the virtue ascribed to the mystic number seven, there would be a desire to have that number of churches in every religious centre, each dedicated to some favourite saint, or erected for some popular missionary. We cannot otherwise account for such a plurality in a place like Glendalough, where the stationary population could hardly fill more than one, although the 'Cathedral' here was but a small building. It is said that there was once a 'city' in this place, but that term is applied to nearly all places that were monastic seats. It does not seem possible that there ever could have been anything like a populous town in this valley, surrounded by barren mountains, and glens covered with timber and jungle. It was undoubtedly the residence of the chief of the O'Tooles, who were a pastoral people, having boundless space for their flocks and herds, but caring little for tillage, and knowing nothing of the industrial arts. On Sundays and holydays, however, and on grand festivals, which were numerous, we can understand that if the seven churches were all open, they would not hold a tenth of the people assembled, and that they would be obliged to have some of their religious services in the open air, or in tents pitched for the occasion.

The early Christian missionaries always applied in the first instance to the local chieftain, whose conversion was usually followed by the submission of the sept. At or near his head-quarters in the straggling village, or township, they obtained permission to erect a wooden church, a school, and a dwelling-house, in which their principal converts lived in community, cultivating the piece of land they obtained, making disciples, and teaching the youth of the place. These communities were in some cases so numerous and prosperous that they became the *nuclei* of considerable towns or villages.

Referring to the Catalogue of Saints published by Archbishop Ussher, and supposed to have been compiled about the middle of the *eighth century*, Dr. Todd remarks that there is not the smallest allusion to diocesan or archiepiscopal jurisdiction; not a word is said of a Primacy in Armagh, or any peculiar authority vested in the successors of St. Patrick, except this:—that the first order, having one head, CHRIST, followed Patrick as their leader or guide; retained in the celebration of their mass the liturgy introduced by him, adopted the same tonsure and the same Easter which he had taught, and were so far united in discipline that what one of their churches excommunicated, all excommunicated or agreed to do so.

The second order of saints had received their liturgy from David, the celebrated bishop of St. David's in Wales. This order was also connected with the *Columban* churches in North Britain, Cumberland, and Durham. It was from this order proceeded 'that great stream of Irish missionaries who went forth to evangelise Europe at the end of the sixth and during some following centuries.' From them, says Dr. Todd, the Venerable Bede must have derived his information respecting the Scotic or Irish Churches. From them must have been obtained all the information respecting Ireland which is to be found in all the writings of Continental authors. And it is remarkable that in the writings of Bede we find no mention of *St. Patrick or of Armagh*. He speaks only of Columba and the presbyters or bishops of the second order of saints. And Adamnan, his biographer, although he once incidentally mentions St. Patrick, is silent as to *Armagh*. The Continental missionaries of the sixth and following centuries seem to have carried with them to Europe no traditions of Armagh or St. Patrick. This remarkable silence has appeared to some unaccountable, and even inconsistent with the existence of St. Patrick. Dr. Todd accounts for it by supposing the Irish saints of the second order were connected with the British or Columban churches, and not with the churches of St. Patrick. They were disposed to emigration, and their zeal carried them to the Picts of North Britain, and to the barbarous nations of the Continent of Europe, to win souls to Christ. He thinks there was no reason why they should say anything to their converts about Armagh or the successors of St. Patrick. They were in all probability more anxious to connect the churches and monasteries which they had founded on the Continent with Rome and the successors of St. Peter, from whom more effectual support might be obtained. But that they did not altogether ignore St. Patrick is evident from the great collection of canons which has been preserved in Continental libraries only, and was evidently compiled in one of the Continental monasteries connected with Ireland.

For my part I see no reason to think that those Irish apostles had the least wish to connect themselves and their churches with either Peter or Patrick, or that they cared anything about succession. Perhaps one reason why the missionaries were silent about the so-called successors of St. Patrick at Armagh was that they had little good to say of them. The most striking peculiarity connected with the ancient Irish Church was its clanship, and the fact that many of the abbots or chief rulers were not in holy orders at all; and when they were in orders, the rights of chieftaincy were enjoyed by the ecclesiastical princes in hereditary succession, according to Oriental custom. Thus the land granted in fee to St. Patrick, or any other ecclesiastic, conveyed to the Religious Society of which it became the endowment all the rights of a chieftain or head of a clan. Hence the Co-arb—that is to say, the heir or successor of the original saint, the founder—became the inheritor of his spiritual jurisdiction and official power in religious matters; while the descendants in blood, or 'founder's kin,' were inheritors of the temporal rights of property, although bound to exercise those rights in subordination to the ecclesiastical Co-arb. Hence there was sometimes a double succession or progenies, ecclesiastical and lay. In consequence of this system the property of the Church or abbacy at Armagh fell into the hands of a lay chieftain, and continued so for 200 years! Thus the pretended successors of St. Patrick, forming the chain of apostolic succession, were in reality mere secular men, who were obliged to employ clerical deputies to perform the functions of their office. The rank of feudal lord or chieftain absorbed the co-existing Episcopal or Sacerdotal character in the Co-arb. The '*Family*' of a monastery comprehended not only the bishops, friars or monks, and other religious inmates, but included also in many cases the clansmen who lived on the lands round the Abbey and its dependencies. Sometimes the abbot was a pluralist, and had under his rule several monasteries. For example, the abbot of Iona was the common head of the monasteries of Durrow, Kells, Swords, Drumcliff, and other houses in Ireland, founded by Columba. Hence the 'Family' of Columba was composed of the congregations and inmates and dependents of all those monasteries, together with the mother abbey of Iona. The feudal abbot was often able to call out a large body of fighting men to defend his establishment and estates, in which they had a joint property. In general, however, the family of the monastery consisted of the monk-bishops and their assistants. This mixture of the temporal and spiritual has been a source of the utmost confusion to ecclesiastical historians, who looked at the old Irish Church through the modern ecclesiastical system, and laboured to trace the line of apostolical succession from St. Patrick down to their own time. 'Even Ussher, Ware, and Lanigan,' says Dr. Todd, 'led away by the preconceived opinions as to the existence of diocesan succession from the age of St. Patrick, were unable to realise to themselves the strange state of society indicated by our ancient records, and the still more strange state of the Church, when bishops were without dioceses or territorial jurisdiction. Hence it is that these eminent writers took the modern state of the Church since the establishment of dioceses as the model of what they conceived was, or ought to have been, the state of the Church in the days of Patrick and Columkill, and thus they have confounded the ancient *Co-arbes* with *chorepiscopi*, and *erenachs* with *archdeacons*. Even Colgan, influenced by the same prejudices, fell into the same mistakes.' The hierarchical system, with its diocesan jurisdiction, was introduced at the close of the eleventh or beginning of the twelfth century, when lists were fabricated in order to escape the reproach of irregularity, which the Roman party among the Norsemen and English of that period had brought against the Irish Church. But, as Dr. Todd emphatically affirms, with reference to a regular succession in Armagh or elsewhere, '*the truth is, there was no such thing.*'

The monastic institutions, or clan-churches, were mutually independent and perfectly free from external authority, although they made repeated attempts to establish common rules of discipline, and to be so far united as that what one church excommunicated all should excommunicate. But the church followed the fortunes of the sept to which it belonged, and its establishments were plundered and burned without scruple in the course of the almost internecine war which the chiefs and tribes waged against each other. The Celtic abbeys had been plundered by the Danes for centuries before the Conquest; they were devastated by Anglo-Norman invaders for centuries after the Conquest; and they often became the prey of those native chiefs who should have united to a man in their defence. Nothing seems to have escaped the violence of the times but the Round Towers, which, sphinx-like, looked down upon the ruins of rudely constructed ecclesiastical buildings, their exemption being due to superstitious awe, regarding them as the work of supernatural powers. It should, however, be borne in mind that violence and war prevailed throughout all the Western nations as well as in Ireland, and that under the feudal system ecclesiastics were bound to military duty. We read in the Annals that in 799 the clergy were exempted from going on ' Hostings,' &c., that is, on the plundering expeditions of their tribes. But only seven years later, in 806, there was war (*bellum*) between the monasteries of Cork and Clonfert; and an immense number of the Cork ecclesiastics and clansmen were slaughtered.

With respect to the native independence of the Celtic Church, Dr. Todd remarks that it was not looked upon as coming from foreigners, or as representing the manners and civilisation of a foreign nation. 'Its priests and bishops, the successors of St. Patrick in their missionary labours, were many of them descendants of the ancient Kings and Chieftains, so venerated by the clannish people. . . . By his judicious management the institutions which he founded became self-supporting. They were endowed by the chieftains without any foreign aid. They were supplied with priests and prelates by the people themselves, and the fruits were soon seen in 'that wonderful stream of zealous missionaries, the glory of the Irish Church, who went forth in the sixth and seventh centuries to evangelise the barbarians of Central Europe.'

Next to the late lamented Dr. Todd, the most learned ecclesiastical antiquary in Ireland is the Rev. Dr. Reeves, of Armagh; yet he and Archdeacon Cotton, a divine of almost equal authority in this department, have been reading the old Church Records without the light thrown upon them by the great work the *Life of St. Patrick,* from which I have quoted so much. Thus Dr. Reeves observes 'that the diocese of Down in its present state is a collection of smaller *sees*, which have been reduced to the condition of parishes, and of districts, which in primitive times were not assigned to any bishopric. The same remark applies to Connor and most of the larger dioceses of Ireland.' He also observes that in primitive times there were bishops in two churches in the immediate neighbourhood of Downpatrick. It is surprising that Episcopal writers do not draw from facts like these the obvious and necessary conclusion that in those early ages the churches, by whomsoever founded, were nothing more than what we should now call parish churches, each in the midst of a certain district, the inhabitants of which composed the congregation, and that each of those congregations was independent. The modern diocese, with its prelate ruling over other pastors, was in fact the result of a series of usurpations, by which the weaker churches were brought into subjection for the aggrandisement of one influential and ambitious minister, who became a lord over God's heritage. There is no fact in ecclesiastical history better established than this. Archdeacon Cotton remarks that but few particulars can now be ascertained concerning the early prelates of Down, 'who appear to have been abbots of the convent of St. Patrick.'

So much for the Episcopal succession in a place which is supposed to have been specially honoured by the presence of the National Saint![1]

---

[1] It appears, however, in the course of time that the two Sees of Downpatrick and Connor were united. In 1609 James I. made the church of Downpatrick the cathedral of the diocese; but in 1662, Charles II. learning that it had fallen into ruin, and that

Archdeacon Cotton, speaking of the Diocesan Records in Ireland, says that 'the Registry of *Armagh* presents a splendid contrast to the others. This repository (alone of all Ireland) contains a venerable and valuable series of registers of some of the earlier prelates, which happily have escaped destruction.' 'In consequence of the disturbed state of the province of Ulster during a great part of the reign of Queen Elizabeth, most of the diocesan registers suffered the loss of their ancient records. Armagh was so fortunate as to escape this calamity.' The same high authority asserts that 'there seems to be no reasonable ground for doubting that this church was founded and endowed with its primatial dignity and pre-eminence by St. Patrick.' From these remarks of the venerable chronicler of the Irish Sees, we might expect a complete catalogue of the Primates of Ireland from the days of St. Patrick down; but when we turn to his 'complete repository,' we find that the ancient registers which he enumerates do not commence till beyond the middle of the fourteenth century—the first series being from the year 1361 to 1416. The Armagh line ought to be the backbone of the Irish Episcopal succession, but for 800 or 900 years there are no links to connect it with the apostolic founders. The most ancient seal of the See extant is that of Primate Dowdall, 1543-58. It bears the arms of the See, and in the middle under a canopy sits a bishop mitred; on one side is St. George, and on the other some other saint, probably St. Patrick.

it was inconveniently situated, constituted the parish church of Lisnagarvie, now Lisburn, the cathedral church. The same reason that influenced the King in removing the See from Downpatrick to Lisburn, should now influence the Queen in transferring it from Lisburn to Belfast. The superstitious veneration for antiquity with regard to ecclesiastical sites in the present day leads to the greatest absurdities, inconvenience, and waste of resources. Roman Catholics might be excused for having much more of that feeling than Protestants; but they have the good sense to imitate their ancestors, and transfer the head quarters of their church to the great centres of population and social influence. One of the absurdities of the old parochial system, too, may be seen in the capital of Ulster, where the parish of Shankill has a population of 120,000, the late vicar, its pastor, having an income of only £288, while numbers of district churches have been erected on every side.

CHAPTER IV.

ANCIENT MONUMENTS.

THE uniformity which pervaded the ancient Religion of Ireland is something wonderful. Notwithstanding the 'gods many and lords many' that received the worship and homage of the people—notwithstanding the diversity of races inhabiting the island; the succession of invasions and colonies; the revolutions and civil wars; the rivalry of clans, and the number of petty sovereignties, as well as the absence of any controlling central power or supreme general government, either actually within the historic ages, or visible even through the dim vistas of fabulous antiquity, we find all over the country—from the great central plain to the highest mountain ranges that girdle the island and the surrounding isles that stud the Atlantic—the same style of religious monuments indicating the same kind of worship, everywhere manifest. The Round Towers, the Sculptured Crosses, the Sacred Rocking Stones, the Holy Wells, the Patrons, the Pilgrimages, the Festivals, all the same. And what is most extraordinary, these traces of ancient worship were found to be so numerous, so completely omnipresent, if I may use the term, as to indicate the existence at some time or other of a population that occupied the whole area of the country. Remnants of their primitive worship survived through all changes to the beginning of the present century. Since that time they have been fast disappearing. Precious monuments of stone, with undeciphered records, have been worked into new buildings or broken up to pave the roads; holy wells have been closed by the hundred; patrons and pilgrimages have been abolished, chiefly through the influence of the Roman Catholic clergy, in consequence of their demoralising effects; cairns, cromlechs, stone circles, temple-like barrows, rude pillar stones, and even the grand old sculptured crosses have been demolished; the ploughshare has passed through spots haunted by fairies and other supernatural things, by which the peasant dared not pass alone at night, and one stone or tree of which he dared not remove by day.

It may be safely said that no island in the world, not even Cyprus, was more rich in materials for the antiquary and the historian engaged in the study of the early civilization of mankind. Some of these are buildings which have been a puzzle for many centuries as monuments of skill and art, for the existence of which in such a place and among such a people it is extremely difficult to account; but which are so full of interest and so creditable to the country, that we should expect men of all classes to preserve them with religious care. Yet I find a very eminent man, Dr. Stokes, Physician to the Queen in Ireland, and Regius Professor of Physics in the Dublin University, complaining with just indignation of 'the *wilful destruction*' of these ancient monuments. He states that the landed proprietors, the clergy, the farmers, the new settlers, and the native peasantry, all lend their hands 'to the work of obliterating these old witnesses of the country's history.' And, Dr. Stokes adds, of the different classes engaged in this barbarism, the landed proprietors have been most to blame, because they are for the most part without 'national associations.'[1]

The vast stone circles in one district alone—Canrrwmore, County Sligo—traced by Dr. Petrie and his associates on the Ordnance Survey, were originally 200 in number. They are now reduced to 100, quarried away for building, drains and road making. Dr. Petrie states that there is no such collection of Pagan monuments in the British Isles; 'in fact these exceed in number all that are in England and Scotland together.' The Ordnance Survey was intended to give a complete account of the country from the earliest times, and this task was accomplished to a certain extent with ability and care. But the Report was published for one county only, Londonderry, after which the staff was discharged, leaving in their office, Mountjoy Barracks, Phœnix Park, 400 quarto volumes of letters and documents relating to the topography, language, history, antiquities, productions, and social state of every county. Various pretexts were

[1] Notes on the ' Life of Dr. Petrie,' Preface.

made for suddenly stopping the work, chiefly the cost; the standing objection when Ireland is concerned. Strange to say, this was done when an Irishman, Mr. Spring Rice, was Chancellor of the Exchequer, and when the Liberal Lord Melbourne was Prime Minister. Dr. Stokes has a singularly suggestive remark upon this subject. He says: 'It seems as if some strong, though concealed influence had been brought to bear on the Government in reference to the danger of reopening questions of Irish local history.'

However that may be, in the year 1860 more than 100 vols. of MSS. with 11 vols. of drawings, indexed and bound, were presented to the Royal Irish Academy. What history or science may gain from the consignment of the materials to that learned body it is difficult to say. It has a house, a library and museum, and a small endowment from Government. Dr. Stokes quotes (p. 106) from the Rev. Dr. Romney Robinson, Astronomer Royal, the highest scientific authority in Ireland, an opinion which is not so very favourable as to lead us to expect much from its patriotic labours. Dr. Romney Robinson stated that the Academy had been then in existence for sixty years, that it had published nineteen volumes of Transactions, had given considerable sums for Prize Essays, and had formed a Museum of Irish Antiquities. 'Yet, in all those nineteen volumes, the only part that could satisfy a reasonable mind was the "Memoir on the Antiquities of Tara," which was published as a specimen of the kind of information collected in the course of the Survey. I think,' he continued, 'with the exception of that, the result of their sixty years' labour in the study of Irish Antiquities has been *almost worse than useless*.'

This condemnation, by such an authority, ought to set people thinking. How are we to account for the signal sterility of the Royal Irish Academy? If the love of truth inspired its directors, if they had not pledged themselves to conclusions which facts failed to support, they might long since have settled the question about the origin and use of the Round Towers, and might have spared themselves the cost of attempting to prove that the Irish Celts were great builders. This very memoir on 'Tara' might have convinced them of the contrary. Thomas Moore, in his 'History

of Ireland,' full of the spirit of his ' Irish Melodies '—and betrayed
by his subject into the magniloquent style of Ossian—referring
to the residences of the Irish kings, says:—' However scepticism
may now question their architectural merits, they could boast the
admiration of many a century in evidence of their grandeur.'
Dr. Stokes says that ' this sentence is not unworthy of the philosophic historian!' But he admits, at the same time, that 'the Royal
Palace at Tara must have been composed of wood and clay—for
no stone houses or fortresses ever existed there. There is a Tuath-
da-Danaan *Cathair*, but the Celts never added a stone.' Now, if
the most celebrated palace in Ireland, the grand residence of
the monarch at whose court the kings and princes of the whole
island were accustomed to assemble, taking rank according to
their pedigrees, the other kings having palaces of their own
attached to this magnificent temple of national justice,—if this
building was made of wattles and mud, if, during twelve centuries,
the Celtic sovereigns of the country never added a stone to the
one which they found there, is it not absurd to make them the
builders of the Round Towers, and the old temples of perfect
masonry found in connexion with them? Surely if they could
or would build with *stone anywhere*, they would have built a stone
palace at ' Tara of the Kings.' I do not ask the reader to compare their wooden palace with the early architecture of Babylon,
or Nineveh, or Egypt. Let him only compare it with what the
Spaniards found in Mexico. It seems a bold thing to dissent
from the Academy on such a question, after reading Dr. Petrie's
essay, and the learned and brilliant works of one of the most
eminent of its presidents, Sir William Wilde, whose splendid
works ' Lough Corrib,' the ' Black Water,' and the ' Illustrated
Catalogue' of the Royal Irish Academy, have won for him so
much credit. But Truth is greater than authority.

There is a famous stone palace, or fortress, in the north of
Ireland—*Grianan of Aliach*—' a Rath of beauteous circles,'
or *enceintes*, as Dr. Stokes describes it. But the ' Dinnseanchus,'
a topographical poem of the ninth century, records the names
of the builders as having lived centuries before the Christian era.
The Royal Irish Academy gave Dr. Petrie a special prize of large
amount for an Essay (which they published in a costly form) to

prove that the Round Towers and ancient temples constructed of regular ashlar masonry, of exquisite workmanship, were of no earlier date than the ninth or tenth centuries. The style of architecture he called 'Norman,' though it had existed in the country long before the Norman Conquest, and there was nothing like it in that age, either in Normandy or England; and Mr. Freeman, adopting Dr. Petrie's theory, says, 'Whatever richness of detail was allowed by the nature of the fabric, is found in a degree surpassed by the Romanesque of no other country.'

Mr. John Stuart, in his great work on the 'Sculptured Stones of Scotland,' by way of illustrating the fact that a high degree of refinement may be concurrent with barbarism, says that 'the Monarchs who lived within the earthen Raths of Tara and Emania were probably wearers of the massive torques and graceful tiaras of which so many have been found in Ireland.' No doubt they were; but would they have dwelt in earthen Raths if they could have built towers, castles, and fortresses like the Normans? The same author remarks that neither from Cæsar nor other classical writers do we get any intimation that the Druids used stone circles as temples. And he says, 'There are many references to the heathen priesthood of the Celtic people of Ireland in early annals of that country; but I have not been able to discover anything which would serve to connect them with the use of stone circles as temples.' In fact the Celts were always wonderfully shy of stones. They would not profane them with the stroke of a hammer, nor break one lest they should dislodge a god or spirit, who would punish them for the outrage. Dr. Petrie considers, rightly I believe, that the stone circles were all designed to be monuments or tombs; not altars or temples of the Druids, but the sepulchral beds of warriors. He was astonished at the multitude of these monuments all over the country, even in the parts now deemed wildest. He says, 'One can hardly look over a ditch without seeing some of these remains, such as a Rath, or a Cromlech, a Cairne, or a Stone Circle.' No doubt the circles were, in each case, the enforced work of years, performed by the enslaved people at the bidding of the conquerors, in honour of their king or chief, and his followers, slain in battle. It was so in Babylon and Egypt.

Mr. Fergusson remarks that the men of the Turanian race,— the Chinese, Egyptians, and Mexicans, were the great builders of temples, tombs, and monuments of stone. 'No Semite and no Aryan ever built a tomb that could last a century, or deserved to last so long.' The Jews and Arabs had no great care for temples,—one sufficed at the fountain head of their worship. Jerusalem and Mecca were enough for the faithful in each case, and to them the tribes went up from all lands to attend the festivals. Solomon's Temple, setting aside the ornaments of gold, silver, and brass, was no grander than a good parish church; and even for this Solomon was obliged to borrow an architect from the Semites.[1] The Semites were a separatist race, intolerant, and antagonist to all others; and they felt that loyalty to Jehovah obliged them to exterminate aliens, without respect to age or sex. It was a sin to spare even the children, while ridding the land of the accursed seed by which it was polluted. The Calvinists, holding the literal inspiration of the narratives of the Old Testament, imbibed their spirit and imitated their example. The Celt, on the other hand, more genial and light-hearted, mingled freely with other races. He was excessively fond of fighting; but he killed men from no higher motive than the love of plunder and the love of glory. He was inclined to be religious; but Mr. Fergusson asserts that no Celtic race ever rose to the perfect conception of the unity of the Godhead. They must have a hierarchy of demigods, angels, and saints; and they were always strongly addicted to the Budhist love of Relics, holy localities, and objects. According to this authority, the modern Celt is as much the slave of a casteless priesthood as ever the Budhist was; this priesthood representing on earth the hierarchy of heaven. With all the devotion and loyalty of the race, however, there is in the Celtic nature an irrepressible element of impulsiveness, impatience, and personal ambition, which renders a republic impossible among this people. No kingdom of theirs ever existed any length of time *by itself*, nor could exist. The same may be said of municipal institutions. All such institutions lapse into despotism. The king or the chief was always a despot; doubly so if he united the priestly

---

[1] Fergusson's 'History of Architecture,' vol. i. p. 51.

office with his temporal rule. The people loved to put themselves under his *patronage* as king and priest. Hence the most celebrated Irish saints were of royal blood. Hence the boundless influence of the Irish priest to-day, regarded as the protector of an oppressed people, a power with which English policy unfortunately invested him in past times, and cannot easily divest him of now.

' The brilliant thoughtlessness ' of the Celt made no provision for the future in this world—*built* nothing for posterity. However rude its surroundings, his home would do well enough; his forefathers lived in the same manner, and he did not want to be better than they. But he loved learning, and music, and poetry. None of his Bards built a great epic, but his lyric genius was unrivalled; and when he could get the proper culture he excelled in the fine arts. Mr. Fergusson says: ' Nine-tenths of the lyric literature of Europe is of Celtic origin.' . . . ' Where no Celtic blood existed, no real art is found. Not only architecture, but painting and sculpture have been patronized, and flourished in the exact ratio in which Celtic blood is found prevailing in any people of Europe.' [1]

Architecture being Mr. Fergusson's proper subject, I had hoped to find some light in his pages on the subject of the Irish Round Towers. But here he is not only unsatisfactory, but strangely inconsistent. He states truly that ' the Cathedrals of the Normans in Ireland were neither so large nor so richly ornamented as many English parish churches.' . . . ' There is scarcely a single parish church of any importance built in Ireland, beyond the limits of the Pale, in the middle ages—no church in Ireland before the Norman Conquest which can be properly called a *Basilica*—none divided into aisles, &c.' This also is quite true. But he goes on to say: ' Ireland possesses what may be properly called a Celtic style of architecture *peculiar* to Ireland. As in Greece, the smallness of the churches is remarkable. We must not look for the origin of the styles either in England or France, but in *a more remote locality,* whose antiquities have not yet been so investigated as to enable us to point out the source whence they were derived. All the old churches (meant to have

[1] Vol. i. p. 62.

stone roofs) exhibit that peculiar character of Cyclopean masonry which has led to such strange, though often plausible, speculations.' After stating that neither their details nor their masonry would excite remark if they were found in an Eastern country, he adds: 'Yet here they stand alone, and exceptional to every thing around them.' He speaks of 'their unfamiliar aspect; their *strange and foreign* appearance. They are among the most interesting of the antiquities of Europe.' Again referring to the style, he adds: 'It shows the strange Cyclopean masonry, sloping doorway, the stone roof, &c.; and at the same time so like some things in Lycia and in India, that it is not to be wondered at that antiquaries should indulge in somewhat speculative fancies in endeavouring to account for such remarkable phenomena.'

Now if those curious stone-roofed temples are all that is here said about them—so strange, foreign, and Oriental, one might expect that the writer of a History of Architecture would endeavour to trace the style to its source, 'in some remote locality,' and solve a problem so deeply interesting in a professional point of view. But Mr. Fergusson comes to a most lame and impotent conclusion. He says that the Irish, at a very early period, 'invented a style for themselves, and were perfectly competent to carry it out to a successful issue, had an opportunity been afforded them.' What! had they no opportunity during the 2,000 years in which they possessed and ruled that rich and beautiful island, unmolested by the revolutions that swept over the Continent? Nothing, down to the present time, has exceeded the beauty and exquisite finish of the temples, round towers, and sculptured crosses, which are all admitted to have been executed by the same people. If the artists were Celts, what was to hinder their building a magnificent palace at Tara in a similar style of masonry? Why did they not erect in Armagh a Cathedral worthy of St. Patrick and the Island of Saints? Will it be believed that after all that Mr. Fergusson had said of the antiquity, remoteness, Orientalism of this Irish style, which could not have come from England or France, because they had nothing of the kind, he comes to the conclusion that the temples in question belong to the 12*th century?* Could he be ignorant of the state of Ireland at that time? But why should we question *him*? Giving up the inquiry in despair, he followed Dr. Petrie and the Royal Irish Academy.

It is a curious fact that the records of the 12th century are silent respecting the erection of those beautiful churches and crosses which modern antiquarians assign to that period, while those records give very particular accounts of the erection of Gothic buildings of the same date—buildings much inferior as specimens of artistic skill, while the so-called *Norman* builders invariably chose ancient foundations ascribed to the 5th and 6th centuries for their sites. The conclusion drawn from these facts is that we must assign this style of architecture to a date as early at least as the 6th century. But if the Celtic Irish who preceded the Danes and the English had no architecture or sculpture in stone, the conclusion is irresistible that the towers and crosses, and ancient temples, were the work of the people whom the Celts conquered and superseded in the dominion of the country. By a singular misnomer the architecture in question has been called 'Norman' without a particle of proof that the Normans had anything to do with it, except in demolishing many of the most interesting ruins in the localities where they had power. If, says Mr. Keane, the reader wishes to visit the best specimens, and in greatest variety, of ancient 'Norman' buildings in Ireland, he must go to those remote parts of the country where the Normans were never known to be in occupation. Several specimens of this ancient style of architecture are found at Glendalough, in the county of Wicklow, but this is owing to the exceptional circumstance that the district, though within 25 miles of Dublin, and surrounded by the English Pale, was held by the O'Tooles, an Irish clan, who maintained possession of it with uncontrolled authority till the 17th century. Clonmacnoise also has its Norman ruins; but even to this day that district, unlike the remainder of the King's County, is inhabited by families almost exclusively Irish. 'Yet,' says Mr. Keane, 'notwithstanding the numerous ruins of Glendalough and Clonmacnoise, I think it would be found that, with the exception of Round Towers and Sculptured Crosses, a greater number of specimens of Cyclopean and so-called " Norman," but really Cuthite architecture, exists in the county of Clare and the islands Aran,

Scattery, and Iniscaltra on its coasts, than in the twenty-one counties of Leinster and Ulster. These provinces have been occupied almost entirely by English and Scotch settlers, while in Clare the inhabitants have ever been for the most part of exclusively Irish descent. . . . There are ten saints or Cuthite divinities recorded in connexion with ruins in the county of Clare. Every one of these names is found also in Ulster and in Leinster; but in these provinces, the temples with which they were associated have, for the most part, disappeared, only fragments being left to attest their former existence. Having gone to search for one of these temples in Drumholme parish, county Donegal, which the Ordnance Survey had marked as a ruin on their map, I ascertained that every vestige of it had disappeared. Meeting shortly after an intelligent farmer of Norman descent, he told me that a very curious little church had stood on his farm, with carved stones and a grave of uncommon construction, but that a short time ago he had thrown down the church, and broken the stones for draining materials. This, from his description of the ruin and locality, I believe to have been the one for which I had been searching.'

The efforts of the Government after the Reformation to put down popular superstition, to stop pilgrimages, and abolish 'Patrons,' will account for the destruction of a great many of the old temples. The policy which destroyed St. Patrick's Purgatory in Lough Derg would not spare similar shrines in less remote localities. It is strange that Dr. Petrie, Sir William Wilde, Dr. Stokes, the author of Petrie's 'Life,' and the members of the Royal Irish Academy generally, who implicitly followed that great antiquary, have not been convinced by these facts. Did it not seem to them unaccountably strange, first, that 'Norman' buildings should abound where Norman colonies never existed; secondly, that Normans, where they did rule, destroyed in a spirit of barbarism the beautiful remains of the architecture which belonged to *their own* forefathers; and, thirdly, that the native Irish, speaking their own old language, wedded to their own old customs, and hating their Norman conquerors with a perfect hatred, should nevertheless have regarded the churches they erected with impassioned veneration, and persist in going on pilgrimages to the shrines of their saints? Nothing could, in fact, be a more glaring contradiction to the national feelings on both sides. The so-called 'Norman' ruins were despised and uprooted by the Normans themselves, as instinct with the spirit of old Irish nationality, and haunted by the creations, traditions, and associations of old Irish superstition.

Thus it may be said that superstition has been literally rooted out of the soil. Nevertheless, the origin of that superstition and the people by whom it was first planted are subjects of deep interest to the historian. But unfortunately they are so completely involved in the mystery of the remote past as to baffle the inquiries of the most learned antiquaries. The Round Towers, which have existed in every part of the country, were once very numerous—always standing on holy ground, haunted by traditions which held captive the native population in a spell that nothing, even the authority of the Catholic priest, could for a long time break. Many books have been written on their origin and use; some contending that they were built long before the Christian era, and were consecrated to the worship of the Sun; others that they were Christian in their origin. The greatest advocate of the latter theory was the late Dr. Petrie, whose elaborate and learned essay on the subject obtained a special prize from the Royal Irish Academy. He contended that they were erected in the Middle Ages as Campanilia, or detached belfries, in connexion with cathedral and abbey churches; and that they were designed also to serve as fortresses for the protection of the property of the churches, and as places of defence in case of attack. He thought that the majority of them belonged to the ninth and tenth centuries, and that some of them were built so late as the twelfth century. He admitted that the *Sculptured Crosses*, which have excited admiration by their magnitude and by the beauty of the figures carved upon them, were artistic works of the same period and executed by the same kind of workmen. This may also be said of a number of ancient churches or temples, the ruins of which still survive. But in all of these cases it is hard to believe that Ireland could have produced either the men or the means for executing such works. It would require the most positive historical evidence to convince any one acquainted with the history of the country that such performances were *possible* in such a nation between the eighth century and the invasion under Henry II.

Sir John Davies, writing in the reign of James I., says:— 'Though the Irish be a nation of great antiquity, and wanted neither wit nor valour, and though they have received the Christian faith above 1,200 years since, and were lovers of poetry, music, and all kinds of learning, yet—which is strange to be related— they never did build any houses of brick or stone—some few religious houses excepted—before the reign of King Henry II., though they were lords of the isle many hundred years before and since the conquest attempted by the English; albeit, when they saw us build castles on their borders, they have only in imitation of us erected some few piles for the captains of the country. Yet I dare boldly say that never any particular person, either before or since, did build any stone or brick house for his private habitation but such as have lately obtained estates according to the course of the law of England. Neither did any of them in all this time plant any garden or orchard.' Sir William Petit, a very accurate enquirer, wrote to the same effect, saying: ' There is at this day no monument or real argument that when the Irish were first invaded by Henry II., they had any *stone* housing at all, any *money*, or any foreign trade.'

The Irish Catholic authorities fully bear out these statements: for example, Dr. O'Connor says: ' That the Irish built their houses of timber as several nations of Europe had done until very lately;' and he adds the suggestive fact, 'that durable or superb structures could not exist in Ireland, because " as the possession was *temporary*, so was the building."'[1] It is true that in the ninth century Danish settlers built castles and fortresses on the banks of the rivers to secure their conquests. But Cambrensis, writing in 1185—the period to which Dr. Petrie ascribes some of the Round Towers—testifies that, though these Danish castles were then empty and deserted, the Irish chiefs disdained to occupy them. 'For the Irish,' he said, 'built no castles;

---

[1] Sir John Davies writing to Lord Salisbury about fixing a site for the Gaol and Market in Fermanagh, said, ' For the habitations of this people are so wild and transitory as there is not one *fixed village* in all the country!' This was in the 17th century

woods served them for fortifications, and morasses for entrenchments.' The English erected castles to maintain their power and keep the natives in check. They also founded monasteries and cathedrals. And all these buildings they erected in the style of their own country, modified by inferior workmanship and by the nature of the materials, buildings of the same style being later in date in Ireland than in England. When the native chiefs and clergy began to imitate the invaders, the Bards inveighed bitterly against the innovation. 'Let us,' they cried, 'pull down those fortresses of the insidious enemy, and cease working for them by erecting any of our own. Their stratagems will assuredly wrest them out of our hands. Our ancestors trusted entirely to their personal valour, and thought the stone houses of the Gauls a disgrace to courage.'

St. Bernard, in his 'Life of S. Malachi,' quoted by the Rev. Dr. Reeves, relates that the saint's first oratory, at Bangor, county Down, was constructed of boards, but well and closely united—'a Scotic' (that is, in Irish, fabric) respectable enough; and this was a step in advance of the early structure, which probably answered the description of wicker-work, interwoven like a fence and surrounded by a ditch. Subsequently, however (in the year 1120), when foreign travel had enlarged his views, it seemed fit to Malachi 'that he build at Benchor an oratory of *stone*,' like those churches which he had seen in other countries; but when he began to lay the foundations some of the inhabitants were astonished, for no buildings of the kind were known in that land. A factious crowd gathered round him, and one who was chosen as their spokesman expressed their sentiments in these words: 'O worthy man, what is your motive for introducing this manner of work in our neighbourhood? We are Scots, not Gauls. Why this vanity? What need of a work so extravagant, so aspiring?' But the work proceeded, and subsequently received additions at various times.

Here it is distinctly stated by St. Bernard in his Life of an Irish Saint and Bishop, that there were then *no stone churches* in that land, and it was only in other countries that Malachi had seen such buildings. It is indeed admitted that there were stone edifices then in Ireland, though none used as churches. There were the Round Towers, then standing in Ulster as well as elsewhere, but those monuments seem to have been regarded very much like the rocks or the gigantic and sacred oak, as if they had grown out of the soil, or been planted there by some supernatural power. There were also, unquestionably, stone churches or temples in other parts of the country which had been for ages in ruins, and whose origin, like that of the stone Crosses, was deemed equally mysterious. However, this building at Bangor seems to have been the first well authenticated case of stone being used for the erection of a Christian Church. And as a proof that even the example of the Danes did not teach the Irish rulers to meddle with stone and mortar, we have the unquestionable historical fact that when Henry II. visited Dublin in 1171, there was no house there fit to receive him, and it was found necessary to construct a pavilion, ' with excellent workmanship and of smooth wattles after the fashion of the Irish.' Even so late as the reign of Queen Elizabeth, the better class of houses enclosed within the walls of the City of Dublin were constructed of stakes and wattles, plastered with clay mortar, and thatched with straw; their relative respectability being indicated by their size, and the neatness of the workmanship. The inferior class of houses were cabins with mud walls, such as may be seen in the outlying streets and lanes belonging to many Irish towns at the present day. The mortar was held together by a mixture of chopped straw or sedge. It is a fact, that it was not until 1331 that a bell tower of stone was erected at Christ Church, Dublin; and, as has been already remarked, what is reported by bards and others of the magnificent palace of Teamar cannot be true, for the hill of Tara itself is evidence enough to prove that there never has been a stone building upon it.

Such being the facts with regard to the architecture of the middle ages, and the peculiar habits of the Celtic people, the question to be determined is, by what race were the towers, stone crosses, and beautifully constructed temples at Cashel, Clonmacnoise, and elsewhere, built? Could it have been by the people who had no towns, but straggling villages made of wood; who had no manufactures, no foreign trade, no current coin, no mint, no iron works; who counted their property by the number of

cows and horses—whose wealth consisted in flocks and herds,
whose tribes or principalities were engaged in almost constant war
against one another, whose 'hostings' or military expeditions
consisted in burning villages which they had surprised in the
night while the inhabitants were asleep, plundering their cattle,
and destroying what they could not carry off? Yet such beyond
all question was the state of Irish society, unsettled, divided,
lawless, with life and property utterly insecure, at the period
which Dr. Petrie assigns for the erection of one of the most beautiful
stone buildings in Europe—Cormac's Chapel at Cashel. Could
that stone-roofed temple—a building that for beauty, richness,
and variety of sculpture has not been equalled by any modern
Irish edifice—have been erected only seven years after the first
essay by St. Malachi in building with stone? 'We are asked,'
says Mr. Marcus Keane, 'to believe that Cormac's Chapel was
built by an Irish provincial chief, who aspired unsuccessfully to
the sovereignty of Munster; and that he did build Cormac's
Chapel with all its beautiful sculpture more than forty years
before Henry II. erected his royal palace in Dublin, of smooth
wattles after the fashion of Ireland, and more than 200 years
before Christ Church was furnished with a bell tower of stone.'
There seems room but for one answer to this question, if we reflect
upon the habits of the Celts. This race—sometimes known as the
Gaël, the Milesians, and the Scoti, Scotia having been the
ancient name of the country—were in possession of the island
long before the Christian era, having subdued the Firbolgs or
the Belgæ, the inhabitants whom they found there. In Ireland
the Celts have preserved the characteristics ascribed to them by
the Roman historians. After five centuries of Christianity, and
at the time when it is supposed those gems of architecture, the
quiet work of years, were created, we have such records as the
following, A.D. 1041:—' The annals are too many of killing of
men, forays and battles. None can tell them wholly, but a few
among many of them.'[1] Dr. Keating, while repelling the allega-
tion that the Irish Kings were subject to the temporal jurisdiction
of the Pope, says: 'It must be confessed, notwithstanding, that
about seventy years before the English invasion, Donough, the

[1] O'Donovan, vol. ii. p. 1033.

son of Brien Boiroimhe, undertook a journey to Rome, and had a commission from the principal nobility and gentry of the island to offer themselves as *subjects* to the See of Rome, and implore the protection of the Roman Pontiff. And the reason of this act of submission was, because the petty princes of the island were continually quarrelling about the bounds of their territories, and these contests had so harassed and impoverished the island that the inhabitants chose rather to submit themselves to a Foreign Power than to be subject to the tyranny and oppression of their own kings.' What a significant passage!

Now, as the Celtic invaders of Ireland were completely an illiterate people, who had always evinced an innate dislike to the industrial arts, who learned the use of letters from the Pagans they subdued—to whom labour was degradation—who were always content to dwell in huts made of wood; whose places of worship, even the most ancient and celebrated, were constructed of the same material; whose chiefs deemed it a degradation to be lodged in stone castles, who never thought of building a stone-walled palace, even where the best materials lay thick about them; who neither quarried, nor mined, nor cut stones, nor forged weapons of war, though war was their sole profession; and as these men must be put out of the question as the builders of the ancient towers, and temples, and crosses of which so much has been written—who could those builders have been? Certainly not the Anglo-Normans, although Irish antiquaries have preposterously applied to them the term '*Norman.*'

Before the Celtic colony arrived, there existed in Ireland for more than a thousand years a mighty people who came from the East, and who were renowned for intellectual power and un-rivalled skill in the arts and sciences. The evidence of history seems to be conclusive that it was by that race the whole island was covered with Temples, Towers, Crosses, and other monuments, that have excited the wonder of posterity. This race was called the Tuath-da-Danaans, whom Dr. Petrie himself acknowledges to have been always referred to as superior to the *Scoti* or *Celts* in the knowledge of the arts. ' We learn,' he says, 'that in the traditions of the Irish the Tuath-da-Danaans were no less distinguished from their conquerors in their personal than in their mental characteristics.' These colonists were preceded by the Fomœrians and the Emedians, supposed to belong to the same Cuthic race. To that race belonged the primitive Irish language, which, intermixed with the language of their Celtic conquerors, formed the tongue which was spoken by 3,000,000 of the people half a century ago, though it is now fast dying out, even in the rudest districts of the country. However fabulous may be the Annals of the Celtic historians during the early centuries of the Christian era, there is this substratum of truth in which they all agree, viz., that the Tuath-da-Danaans were a people vastly superior to themselves in physical and intellectual power, and that their knowledge of the arts and sciences was believed to be magical. For generations after the worship of Budh had been interdicted or utterly abolished, the Bards or Priests of the fallen system continued to be the musicians, the poets, the historians, and finally the flatterers, of their warlike and uncultured masters. They corrupted history by ascribing to the Celtic chieftains the pedigrees, records, and exploits of ancient heroes, which properly belonged to their Cuthite predecessors, and thus those chiefs soon acquired a taste for long pedigrees, and imbibed the ancestral pride which so egregiously distinguished them in after times. So far was the system of flattery carried, that the very names as well as the deeds of the old heathen gods and goddesses were ascribed by the Bards to the Celtic Saints. It was the Tuath-da-Danaans that made the country a Sacred Island : in their time— the Island of Gods; in Celtic times—the Island of Saints.

'In Dr. Petrie's great work,' says Mr. Keane, 'we have illustrations of the ornaments upon the doorway and chancel arch of Cormac's Temple at Cashel. He gives about thirty of these ornaments upon the columns and capitals, all of the same general form, but different on each column, every one of them presenting a different style of decoration. The temple is small, yet more costly by far in proportion to its size than any church or cathedral ever erected in Ireland since the Conquest. It is besides, in design and construction, unlike any church in Christendom whose building can be proved to date within the Christian era. It is roofed with a thorough semi-circular arch, appearing like the interior of one of the rock temples of Hindostan; and this arch is again surmounted by another cut-stone roof, having chambers between them. Even the entwined serpents, the common ornaments of Irish stone crosses, and the ornament on the sarcophagus called the Font at the Cashel temple, have their parallels in Hindostan.

'Ireland abounds with doorways of ruined temples called churches. They have all the Cuthite or Cyclopean sloping or inclining jambs; but every so-called Norman doorway or window in Ireland has this same peculiarity, while not a single specimen of such a characteristic is to be found in any existing example of *English* Norman. The construction of windows is another point in which the ancient Irish architecture stands in direct contrast with the English Norman. Glass was known throughout England since the eighth century, and it was in general use in churches from the earliest age of "Norman" architecture. But in Ireland there is no specimen of the ancient so-called Norman window adapted to the use of glass. In respect to masonry, all the Irish windows are of the best cut stone, closed and perfectly jointed, some plain, others highly ornamented with the richest devices of the so-called Norman sculpture. They all exhibit similar characteristics, being constructed so as to admit a limited supply of light. They are not adapted to fitting of glass, and they have got slightly inclining jambs, being generally from half-an-inch to two inches wider at bottom than at top. The large double window at Kilmacduagh consists of about 200 superficial feet of beautifully-executed cut stone, used to admit about nine superficial feet of light. Mr. Parker, referring to existing examples of Early Norman architecture in England, notices a considerable degree of roughness in the masonry as characteristic of them all—the chapel of the White Tower, London, for example. Mr. Rickman, writing of the Gothic, or Early English style, says: "After the Conquest, the rich barons erected very magnificent castles and churches, the execution manifestly improved, though still with much similarity to the Roman mode debased. But the introduction of shafts, instead of the massive pier, first began to approach that lighter mode of building which, by the introduction of the pointed arch, and by an increased delicacy of execution and boldness of conception, ripened at the close of the twelfth century into the simple, yet beautiful, Early English style."' 'Now,' says Mr. Marcus Keane, 'if the best specimens of ancient *Norman* in the richest localities of England manifest a considerable degree of roughness in the masonry, compared to the styles which succeeded them, the very opposite is the case in Ireland. The so-called " Norman" ruins in Ireland are, in point of masonry and the abundance of ashlar used, as far superior to the Gothic buildings as the Gothic of England is superior to the English Norman. This anomaly has never before been attempted to be explained. Almost every church in Ireland, built within the period of authentic history, is found to be of the Pointed style, like the *English* of the same date, but *far inferior* to the English churches in point of material and execution. There are particular dates assigned to more than one hundred Gothic churches and monasteries in Ireland. The earliest are ascribed to the twelfth century, *but there is no historical record whatever of the foundation of a single one of the so-called Norman Churches.*

'In the wilds of Kerry, at the extreme west of Ireland, is the ruined church or temple of Kilmelchedor, a small building like Cormac's Chapel at Cashel, but less rich in its variety of ornament. There is a handsome Norman doorway of three orders, and the interior is lined with panels, separated by well-cut stone semi-detached semi-circular piers. It is called Teampul Melchedor, which in Irish means the temple of *the golden Molach* ; and on the inside of the soffit-stone of the doorway is sculptured in relief the head of an ox—the golden Molach himself. The presence of this emblem of Divinity is explained by the learned Bryant, who tells us that it was usual with the Ammonians (Cuthites) to describe upon the architrave of their temples some emblem of the Deity who presided there. The tradition of the common people in Kerry is that this temple was erected by supernatural agency in one night. This legend of being erected in one night is never applied to Gothic ruins, but only to Round Towers, Irish Crosses, and so-called "Norman churches." This is accounted for by the fact that after a long period of the dominion of the Celts, who had no stone buildings, these beautiful Cyclopean remains could only be explained by the peasantry as the result of supernatural agency.'

Dr. Petrie grounds his arguments as to the age of the early churches, and of the towers and crosses—all being of the same style and admittedly of the same age—on the assumption that ' the age of *Cormac's Chapel, Cashel, is definitely fixed by the most satisfactory historical evidence.*' If this be so, the question is soon settled. But what is this most satisfactory historical evidence? It is this. In the ' Annals of Innisfallen ' we read : ' 1127. Two churches were erected at Lismore, *and a church at Cashel by Cormac.*' Again, under the date 1138 : ' Donogh having built Teampul Chormaic, in Cashel, and two churches at Lismore, was treacherously murdered by Dermot Sugach O'Conor, Kerry, at the instigation of Turlough O'Brien, who was his son-in-law, gossip, and foster-child.' And again, in the ' Annals of the Four Masters,' 1134 : ' The church (at Cashel) was built by Cormac.'[1] This is the evidence. But Mr. Keane proves in the clearest manner that the Irish word *Cumdach* does not mean to *build*, erect, but to restore, repair, prop up, to keep or preserve, maintain or support, to roof, or rather cover, a building. Dr. Petrie admits this meaning, and so gives up the whole foundation of his argument. The heathen temple may have been then, for the first time, used for Christian worship, after some repairs done to the stone roof. Accordingly Dr. Keating, in his ' History,' says that Cormac's church at Cashel was then ' *consecrated.*' In fact, there never was such a superstructure raised on an assumption more baseless.

Those who are shocked with the idea that the Irish sculptur crosses could have been intended for any other than Christ' uses, or could have been made before the Christian era, can. have read much of heathen mythology, or they must shut th eyes in a determined manner against historical facts. They ou to know that the principal Hindoo temples, viz., those of Benr and Maharatta, were erected, like our Gothic cathedrals, in form of vast crosses. The cross was one of the usual sym among the hieroglyphics of ancient Egypt and India, decorat the hands of most of the sculptured images, and stamped uj the most majestic shrines of their divinities. It repeatedly occu on sacred obelisks. All the figures of Osiris and Isis bear th

[1] ' Round Towers,' p. 287.

mystic cross with a circular handle, the *circle* representing the solar disc, and when joined to a cross meant to describe the vivifying power of the sun. The visitor to the British Museum will find nearly every sculpture among the most ancient hieroglyphics of Egypt adorned with a cross. Mr. Bruce, in his travels in Abyssinia, saw the same sacred symbol universally pourtrayed amidst the ruins of Axum. The augural staff or wand of the Romans was an exact resemblance of a cross, being borne as the ensign of authority by the Augurs of Rome, who were held in such veneration that, though guilty of flagrant crimes, they could not be deposed from their offices. The Druids sought out for an oak tree, large and handsome, growing with two principal arms in the form of a cross. If they could not find one suitable, they put up a cross beam, and then the tree was consecrated. O'Brien, in his work on the Round Towers—rejected by the Royal Irish Academy—produces an immense array of authorities from ancient authors to demonstrate the Oriental origin of the Round Towers, the sculptured crosses, and the ancient crosiers. Mr. Keane adopts his views, and brings forward additional proofs from various quarters, which seem to place the matter beyond doubt to any mind that can get the better of prejudices of education and habit, which are naturally very strong in Ireland. Indeed, it seems hardly possible to examine the devices upon the Irish crosses in he magnificent work of Mr. Henry O'Neill, R.A., without being convinced that, if those crosses had been produced by Celtic artists, they could not have been the work of Christian hands; for, while they are entirely devoid of Christian symbols, they are covered with the most beautifully-wrought idolatrous representations. Colonel Wilford, in the 'Asiatic Researches,' says: 'The emblem, though not an object of worship among the Budhists, is a favourite device and emblem among them. . . . It is called the Divine Tree, the Tree of the Gods, the Tree of Life and Knowledge.' We learn that the cross was worshipped in Mexico for ages before the Spanish missionaries set foot there—large stone crosses being erected, probably to the God of Rain. Bacchus, the Babylonian Messiah, was represented with a head-band covered with crosses. And it is stated that this symbol of the Babylonian god is reverenced to this day in all the wide wastes of

Tartary where Budhism prevails. Heathen crosses were found by Stephens among the sculptures of the ruined cities in Central America.

Mr. Keane, after producing evidence that the ancient Hindoos had their victim Man, their holy Child, born of his Virgin-Mother, and at length dying upon the Cross, says:—'From the foregoing authorities I am induced to conclude that the traditional Crucifixion was the origin of these legends of the several Budhist crucifixions; that thence the figure of the Cross became the monogram or hieroglyphic of Budh; thence the Phœnician Thuath and Egyptian Thor, from which was derived the Greek Tau, the origin of our letter T.'[1]

With such a mass of evidence to prove the veneration for the Cross entertained in the ancient days of heathenism, and the primeval tradition of the Crucifixion itself, it is not surprising that crosses should be found in ancient Ireland, to which Christianity can lay no claim. Such heathen crosses abound in that country. They are even more numerous than the Round Towers; and among all, this peculiarity may be observed, that there is not on one of these ancient crosses any unquestionably Christian device which would prove it to have been made in the Christian era. An examination of Mr. O'Neill's splendid work on the 'Ancient Irish Crosses' will prove them all to have been essentially Pagan, and such as never could have been conceived for the purpose of recording the scenes in the New Testament. It is true that some scenes recorded in the Old Testament are represented on these crosses, but only those which we find from other sources to have been founded on primeval tradition, preserved among the legends of heathen nations, such as The Fall of Man, The Deluge, &c.; while, on the other hand, the sculptures abound with heathen devices, which no one has ever explained to be consistent with Bible history. Serpents in every variety of contortion, centaurs, winged quadrupeds, war-chariots, fishes and bulls presented as objects of worship; besides a number of other devices abound, such as never could have entered into the imagination of anyone acquainted with the New Testament account of the Crucifixion of Our Blessed Lord, as consistent with sacred history.'

[1] See 'The Two Babylons,' p. 322.

Aided by Mr. O'Neill's pictures, which present on a large scale exact facsimiles of the sculptures, Mr. Keane maintains the proposition with ample authorities, and illustrations from ancient heathen monuments, which cannot fail to bring conviction to any candid mind. The subject is full of interest, but space does not permit me to dwell upon it longer. One concluding remark, however, should be made upon the Irish stone crosses: the figure of a man is often found, with arms extended, in the centre of the circle, which always forms a part of the cross. This, no doubt, represents a crucifixion, but not in the Christian form. The very earliest pictures or designs of the Christian crucifixion represent the Saviour with the hands raised and *nailed* to the cross, and with the feet also pierced with nails; whereas on the Irish crosses the hands are *not* nailed and the arms are never raised above a right angle; generally they droop, forming an acute angle, and the feet, instead of being nailed, are *tied together with cords.* Another difference is that the figures on the Irish crosses sometimes have on a mural crown, as in the cross of Tuam, county Galway, and never anything like a crown of thorns. This crown resembles the ancient Oriental crown.

The mention of this cross reminds me of another important fact connected with this inquiry. There was at Tuam an ancient monastery—St. Hiarlath's or St. Jarlath's, assigned to the sixth century. It was, no doubt, one of the high places of the heathen. The cross which once stood in the market-place is the most splendid in Ireland. There was always an abbot there, and for centuries it has been the seat of an archbishop. Indeed, two archbishops sat there for 300 years, since the Reformation. Now, if that was a Christian cross, representing the crucifixion of our Saviour— venerated as it must have been in that case, like the wooden crosses set up by the Redemptorist Fathers to commemorate their missions—could it have been neglected, knocked down, mutilated, and trampled in the mire under the eyes of those two archbishops? Even if this desecration was the work of Cromwellian Iconoclasts, would not the Catholics have seized the first opportunity of restoring it to its place, or some other place worthy of its symbolic character? Undoubtedly they would. But what are the facts? Magnificent and beautiful as it was, Dr. Petrie '*discovered* it,' broken in three pieces, two of them lying in the churchyard, and the third, the pedestal, in the fish-market, covered over with a heap of stones and rubbish. The arms of this cross are supported by pillars.

With reference to the primitive Christian crosses, which were made of wood, it may be remarked further, that the designs in sculpture and fresco found in the Roman catacombs are adoptions or copies of Pagan Passion pictures and cartoons. ' How else are we to interpret the draped *fish*, standing before an altar, on which a *fire* is kindled, and presenting a dish of fruit to a *serpent*, carried on a sarcophagus, combined with the representation of incidents in the New Testament?'[1]

It is astonishing to what an extent these adaptations of heathen customs and rites were carried in England. Gregory the Great gave permission to sacrifice oxen and feast on them in the huts which the people erected around the churches during the festivals, for which he gave his reasons,—' not that they sacrificed to the devil, but to the Glory of God' (*nec Diabolo jam animalia immolent, sed ad laudem Dei*). And this was done because the minds of the people were so hard and obstinate that it was impossible to remove them at once. There was a canon enacted in the time of King Edgar against '*well*-worshippings, necromancies, and *stone*-worshippings.'[2] And so late as 1164, Reginald, a monk of Durham, records the offering of a bull to St. Cuthbert at his church on the Solway, as part of the festival of its dedication.[3]

[1] 'Journal of Brit. Archæol. Society,' vol. ii. p. 396.
[2] Lingard's 'Anglo-Saxon Church,' vol. i. p. 167.
[3] Quoted by Stuart, ' Stones of Scotland,' vol. ii. p. 9.

CHAPTER V.

PATRONS AND PILGRIMAGES.

THE first Christian Missionaries and the Founders of the Primitive Churches selected almost invariably the sites which had been resorted to from time immemorial for worship, festivals, and traffic—the central point, generally an elevated spot, being occupied by the mysterious stone cross standing on a pedestal. It was usually from ten to twenty feet high, and covered with elaborately carved figures of men, quadrupeds, serpents, trees, &c. On the same spot, or very near, rose, far above all, the majestic and still more mysterious Round Tower, popularly believed to have been erected in a night by supernatural beings, but when or for what purpose no historian could tell with certainty, although the Bards pretended to do so in their fabulous legends. The Towers and Crosses, and certain great aged trees, were regarded with such veneration, such superstitious awe, that it was only in some rare instances, antiquarians tell us, the people ventured upon the removal of any of the old monuments, not even of a small pillar stone. Their Christian teachers contented themselves with carving upon such stones the sacred names or symbols of Christianity, where they had not been preoccupied by the symbols of Idolatry. Even then in some cases the idols obtained the names of saints. The festivals of the heathen were converted into Christian solemnities and holy days. The *Beltane* and the *Samhuin* still survive in our May Day and Hallow Eve, while the bonfires of St. John's Eve represent the great national festival in honour of Baal, the god of fire, symbolised by the Sun. 'Nothing is clearer,' says Dr. O'Donovan, the learned translator of the 'Four Masters,' 'than that Patrick engrafted Christianity on the Pagan superstitions with so much skill that he won the people over to the Christian religion before they understood the exact difference between the two systems of belief; and much of this half Pagan, half Christian religion may be found not only in the Irish stories of the middle ages, but in the superstitions of the peasantry to the present day.'

St. Patrick is said to have met three stone pillars, on which he engraved the words *Jesus, Sotor, Salvator.* His followers virtually adopted the worship of the heathen in order to win over the population, hoping, no doubt, that they would be able by degrees to instruct their converts in the principles of Christianity. An illustration of what generally occurred is given by M. Dabuenot in his history of 'The Destruction of Paganism' in the West. M. Dabuenot was a learned Roman Catholic, whose work obtained the sanction of the Institute of France. He states that after the Council of Ephesus 'the churches of the East and West offered to the adoration of the faithful the VIRGIN MARY. They had received this new worship with an enthusiasm sometimes too great, since for many Christians this worship became the whole of Christianity. The heathen did not endeavour to defend their altars against the worship of the Mother of God. They opened to Mary the temples which they had kept shut against JESUS CHRIST, and confessed themselves conquered. It is true they often mixed with the adoration of Mary those heathen ideas, those vain practices, those ridiculous superstitions, from which they seemed unable to separate themselves. The Church, however, was delighted to see them enter into her bosom, because she knew well that it would be easy for her with the help of time to purify from its alloy her worship, whose essence was purity itself. . . . Among a multitude of proofs I choose only one to show with what facility the worship of Mary swept before it the remains of heathenism which still covered Europe. Notwithstanding the preaching of St. Hilarian, Sicily had remained faithful to the old worship (heathenism). After the Council of Ephesus (that which offered the Virgin Mary to the adoration of the faithful) we see its *eight finest pagan temples* become in a very short space of time churches under the invocation of the Virgin.'[1]

Such events account for the fact, of which indeed thousands of proofs present themselves in the history of Europe, that not

---

[1] Vol. ii. p. 271, quoted by Mr. Keane.

only the buildings and localities connected with the worship, but the customs and traditions of heathenism, passed over to Christian uses. Heathen feasts became saints' days; the names of heathen gods were ascribed to Christian Mythical Saints; and the localities venerated on account of their heathen associations became the favourite sites of Christian churches and monasteries. We have seen that Pope Gregory the Great sanctioned bloody sacrifices, and Theodoret recommended that to win the Gentiles they should present to them the *saints* and *martyrs* in lieu of their demi-gods. Other prudential considerations contributed materially to this change. The sites of heathen temples were centres of *authority and influence*, as well as places of general resort, where the people assembled, not only for worship and religious festivals, national games and sports, but also where they came for the transaction of business or barter in the great open space or 'Green' around the lofty stone Cross, with its symbolic circle representing the Sun, and its sculptured figures of the ox, the serpent, the fish, and other objects of worship, which made the gods, as it were, the witnesses of their bargains.

CLONMACNOISE is the most famous of the places distinguished by their mystic groups of 'Seven Churches.' With its Round Towers, its Sculptured Crosses, and ruined shrines, it is at present to the antiquary and the historian one of the most interesting places in Ireland. These magnificent ruins, standing in lonely grandeur on the banks of the Shannon, which winds its oozy way through flat, marshy ground, strike the mind with awe as they appear in the distance. The feeling of wonder and admiration is not diminished when we approach the sacred ground and examine the monuments that have stood for so many centuries in a region so desolate. Yet the aspect is not now quite of the kind that might be anticipated from reading the picturesque sketches of Cæsar Otway, who wrote:—'If ever there was a picture of grim and hideous repose, it is the flow of the Shannon from Athlone to Clonmacnoise. From this hill of Bentullagh, on which we now stood, the numerous churches, the two Round Towers, the curiously overhanging bastions of O'Melloghlin's Castle, all before us to the south, and rising, in relief, from the dreary sameness of the surrounding red bogs, presented

such a picture of tottering ruins and encompassing desolation as
I am sure few places in Europe could parallel.' I was, however, agreeably disappointed when I visited the place a few years
ago. The land about seems to have been drained and improved
since the above was written. Precautions have been taken to
arrest the progress of decay and destruction in the buildings
which are so full of historic interest, and to protect them from
wilful dilapidation. Here is the largest enclosure of tombs and
churches anywhere seen in Ireland. 'What a mixture of old
and new graves! Modern inscriptions recording the death and
virtues of the sons of little men, rude forefathers of the surrounding hamlets; ancient inscriptions in the oldest forms of
Irish letters, recording the deeds and hopes of kings, bishops
and abbots, buried a thousand years ago, lying about broken,
neglected and dishonoured.' The sculptured cross which stands
near the door of McDermott's church is, if not equal to that of
Monasteraboise, only second to it in Ireland. Harris thus
alludes to the place and its monuments:—'Before the west and
north doors of McDermott's church stood a large old-fashioned
cross or monument, much injured by time, on which was an
inscription in antique letters which nobody, that I could hear of,
could read. The west and north doors of this church, although
but mean and low, are guarded about with fine wrought small
marble pillars, curiously hewn. Another of the churches hath
an arch of greenish marble, flat wrought, and neatly hewn and
polished; and the joints so close and even set, that the whole
arch seems but one entire stone, as smooth as either glass or
crystal. The memory of St. KIERAN is yet fresh and precious
in the minds of the neighbouring inhabitants, inasmuch as they
make no scruple in joining his name with God's, both in blessing
and cursing. "God and St. Kieran after you!" is a common
imprecation when they think themselves injured. In the great
church was heretofore preserved a piece of St. Kieran's hand,
as a sacred relic. The 9th of September is annually observed
as the Patron day of this saint, and great numbers from all parts
flock to Clonmacnoise in devotion and pilgrimage.'

Chief amongst the monuments are two Round Towers, and the
existence of *two* on the same spot seems to clash with the

Christian theory concerning those buildings, defended by Dr. Petrie; for if the larger one was designed for a belfry, there could have been no use for the smaller one beside it. The larger, called O'Rourke's Tower, stands at the west side of the churchyard, rising grandly over the Shannon. It commanded the ancient causeway that was laid down across the great bog on the Connaught side, looking up and down the river over all its sweeping reaches, as it unfolded itself like a vast serpent along the surrounding bogs and 'marshes.' At whatever time this Tower was built, Dr. Petrie admits that it was repaired at a period long subsequent, the upper portion being of a coarse pointed masonry of limestone, while the greater part of it below is of *close pointed ashlar sandstone*. Besides, it is quite obvious that the Tower, when such a restoration was made, was reduced considerably in its original height in proportion to its circumference.

What then becomes of Dr. Petrie's theory that the Round Towers belonged to the '*Norman* style' of architecture? The restoration in question, of which there is no record, being beyond the reach of even monkish history, could not have taken place *later* than the time when that style flourished, if ever it flourished, in Ireland. But the original building, the unrepaired portion, instead of being of *coarse* pointed masonry of limestone, consisted of close pointed ashlar sandstone, showing traces of incomparably better workmanship. Who then were the original workmen? and who were the rulers that employed them? They must have existed many centuries before the Tower was dilapidated. McCarthy's Tower, attached to the church, retains its original proportions, being 55 feet in height and 7 in diameter, and it is peculiar in having the door level with the ground instead of being ten or twelve feet from the foundation. The workmanship of this Tower is exquisitely beautiful, so closely jointed as to appear but one mass of marble! In front of the church, called Teampul McDermott, is a magnificent stone cross, fifteen feet high, and elaborately sculptured. There is another smaller cross similarly ornamented, which leans so much off the perpendicular that its remaining in its position seems to the peasantry a standing miracle. A few perches from the principal ruins, situated on lower ground, is an architectural gem, the beautiful little temple called the *Nuns' Church*. The finely-sculptured heads and other ornaments on the arches of the doors and windows form one of the puzzles of ancient Irish architecture.

Clonmacnoise was, in the earliest Christian times—'the golden age' of Irish civilization—celebrated as a college or university. A strange place for such an institution, if the country were not different then from the dreary wastes of deep bogs and wild woods, in the midst of which those ruins stood when first seen by the Norman invaders! Yet that seat of learning was the Irish Oxford of those times; ages before Oxford had a university, or England a heptarchy. Its name imports a retreat for the sons of nobles. St. Colcha, then abbot of Clonmacnoise, visited the Continent in 791, where he received from the Emperor Charlemagne a present of 50 shekels. The establishment having eventually become an abbey of canons regular of the order of St. Augustine, Archdall says : ' It was uncommonly extensive and amazingly enriched by various kings and princes. Its landed property was so great, and the number of " cells " and monasteries subject to it so numerous, that almost half of Ireland was said to be within the bounds of Clonmacnoise.' It was believed that all persons interred within its precincts ensured to themselves an immediate ascent to heaven. On this account it was selected as a burial place by many kings and princes, who would naturally facilitate their passage to the celestial mansions, and atone for past transgressions by adding to its endowments. But its extraordinary holiness did not prevent its sanctuaries being plundered many times by royal robbers as well as marauders of a meaner sort.

KILDARE abounds in antiquities: sepulchral mounds, moats or raths, pillar stones, round towers, ruined monasteries, &c. In the 12th century, a vast circle of stones, like Stonehenge on Salisbury Plain, stood upon a similar plain in this county, called the Curragh of Kildare. There are round towers at Kildare, Castle Dermott, Old Kilcullen, Outerard, and Taghadoe ; abbey ruins at Kildare, Castle Dermott, New Bridge, and Naas ; while some of the most curious of the sculptured stone crosses have been found at Moone and several other places in the county. The town of Kildare itself was one of the most celebrated of the primitive ecclesiastical seats in Ireland. Its patroness, St. Bridgid, is stated by the annalists to have been the daughter of a prince, and to have received the veil in the fourteenth year of her age from the hands of St. Patrick. Following them, Archdall relates that she founded a nunnery in the year A.D. 484, and that an abbey was built about the same time. The nuns and monks had but one church in common, which they entered at different doors; and, strange to tell, the abbot of this house was subject to the abbess for several years after the death of the celebrated founder, which happened in 523.' Notwithstanding this anomalous rule, the sexes were separated in church by a partition. The vestal fire, for which the place was famed, was kept burning perpetually in a small stone-roofed structure which still exists, and is called the Fire House. Gerald Cambrensis, writing in the 12th century, says: 'The nuns and religious women are so careful and diligent in supplying and recruiting the fire with fuel, that from the time of St. Bridgid it hath remained always unextinguished through so many successions of years; and though so vast a quantity of wood hath been in such a length of time consumed in it, yet the ashes have never increased!'

In 1220 Henry de Londres, Archbishop of Dublin, less credulous than the historian, caused the fire to be extinguished, as a remnant of heathen idolatry; but it was afterwards rekindled and kept alive until the Reformation. Mr. Keane, in his learned work on the Towers and Temples of Ireland, states that St. Bridgid is associated with religious foundations in almost every county in Ireland. There were twelve saints of that name, which, in Irish, is sounded as if it were 'Braedh,' and answers to Braëda, the Scandinavian name for Venus. Among the Tuath-da-Danaans, Brudh was the goddess of poets and smiths.

The name of Kildare is composed of two Irish words, meaning church and oak. The oak, sacred to the Druids, abounded there from the earliest times; and there is no doubt that it was one of the great schools of ancient Ireland; but of the original church and city there are at present no remains. A Carmelite monastery, called the Grey Abbey, was founded there by

William de Vesci, in 1260. The town was repeatedly plundered and burned, first by Irish chiefs, and then by the Danes, who carried away the costly shrines of the saints. In 883 they captured the abbot himself and 280 of the clergy and monks. From that event to the beginning of the 11th century those terrible invaders visited Kildare no less than thirteen times, taking captives as well as booty; and on one occasion they made slaves of the greater part of the inhabitants. Similar calamities were endured several times subsequently; and, in 1259, Calva O'Conner, an Irish chief, stormed the castle, burned the rolls and tallies belonging to the manor, and wasted the adjacent country.

ARDMORE, in the county of Waterford, is a place which well deserves a visit, for the sake of its monuments, its cathedral ruins, its stone-roofed church called St. Declan's Dormitory, and its superb round tower. As a seat of religion, it claims an antiquity greater than the churches founded by St. Patrick, being one of the earliest of the Christian settlements on the coast; and St. Declan, its patron, has a stronger hold on the popular faith at the present day than any other primitive saint, Patrick alone excepted. The round tower, a really beautiful structure in perfect preservation, is 91 feet high, and 15 in diameter at the base, with a door 16 feet from the ground, and four windows on the topmost storey. Rising over the ruined church on the side of the hill, looking down on the bay and the coast of Waterford, and visible to a great extent on all sides, it is a grand and imposing object in the landscape. On the cliff overhanging the bay, to the right are the ruins of Dysart Church, and beside it *St. Declan's Well*, with some very old and worn stone crosses embedded in the walls. It is one of the few places in which the '*Patrons*' are still kept up, and which are resorted to by pilgrims on the anniversary day. I was there a few years ago, and the scenes that presented themselves showed that in that part of the country education has made but little change in the primitive habits and rooted superstitions of the people. I saw immense numbers of decent-looking men and women, the latter wearing heavy blue cloaks, with large hoods and handkerchiefs on the head, without any hats or bonnets, performing their penances as in old times. The 'patron' day happened to be Sunday, and the weather was fine, which favoured the pilgrims and brought them out in greater numbers. Thousands of them were assembled in and about the little town—men, women, and children, including comfortable-looking farmers and their families, brought in carts, which, with their horses and donkeys, filled the roads as at a fair; while stands for refreshments of all sorts were placed along the streets. On the previous Saturday, during the night, and Sunday morning till noon, the pilgrims were seen streaming along the cliff to the little ruined church and the holy well. On the wayside near the place were stationed beggars, disfigured in every imaginable way—blind, lame, deformed; some extending the stump of an arm without a hand, others a mutilated leg, others some hideous mark on the face, others noisome ulcers, each with beads in hand, and all praying incessantly in the loudest possible tones, and exclusively in the Irish language, while the pilgrims passed. They evidently made a good thing of it, for each pilgrim seemed to have considered it a necessary complement of his duty, or a crowning act of merit, to give coppers to these dirty and clamorous representatives of the SAVIOUR, as they deemed them to be. The penance consisted in going round the ruined chapel, saying a number of prayers at certain points, kissing certain stones, and drinking the water of St. Declan's well. Those who had 'bad legs' or other diseased parts washed them in the little stream, into which only a very small quantity of water trickled; and when I saw it, it had become quite muddy and foul.

Another and more interesting part of the pilgrimage consisted in the devotions performed around *St. Declan's Stone*, which lies upon the beach, nearer to the town. It is a concrete mass of irregular oval shape, hard as iron, and about four feet in height. It rests upon the rocks in such a way that there is an opening under it, through which a human body may pass by lying prostrate—a ceremony supposed to possess miraculous virtue for the cure of pains and aches when accompanied with prayer, the kissing of the Stone, and other forms. For the greater part of two days and a night, when the tide permitted, men and women and children were seen dragging themselves through the hole under this sacred stone, then pressing their

G

bodies against it wherever they felt the pains; while others were grouped around it, saying their prayers. I talked with several respectable-looking farmers about the town, and with two or three gentlemen whom I met at the hotel, and I found them firmly possessed by implicit faith in the legend that St. Declan's Stone, to which they ascribed such miraculous virtues, actually floated across the sea and rested in its present position, bearing with it certain things which the saint required for the celebration of Mass. I learned that the priests have exerted themselves to the utmost to put a stop to this fetish worship of the Stone; and one of them, some years ago, took up a position beside it and endeavoured to drive away the pilgrims with his whip. But he might as well attempt to keep back the tide; as soon as his back was turned they were at their devotions again.[1]

There is a large parish chapel or church at Ardmore, and when the pilgrimage was over about noon on Sunday, immense numbers crowded for admission. A charge of a penny was made at the gate, and there I saw a rather unpleasant exhibition of the working of the voluntary system. While the curate was saying Mass, the parish priest and a brother clergyman from the neighbourhood stood one at each side of the gate to see that none entered the chapel yard without payment. The former gentleman was tall and erect, with a grave and dignified aspect, such as might become a bishop; the other was very stout, with full cheeks, rubicund countenance, and a jolly expression, which showed that he was inclined to take things easy; and he did so on this occasion. But the parish priest, seeing young men forcing themselves in without depositing the coppers, on several occasions seized them by the collar and thrust them back. Some of the women seemed scandalised at this; and I heard one say to another, 'Our Father Tom would not do that!' to which her companion replied: 'Och! they'd all do it! They love the money betther than the sowls of the poor. Don't you see they keep thim boys from the Mass; and may be they haven't a penny to give.' It was not a pleasant sight.

In the afternoon the public-houses were crowded to excess,

[1] The English made a law that all persons who visited the Patrons should be publicly whipped.

the bedrooms being filled, and the gardens attached to them. There all were jolly; and flirtations were now the order of the day. Luckily, beer was the principal beverage. Formerly, the propensity to faction fights was so great, that the pilgrims would be divided into two camps, smashing each other's heads. Even now it is necessary to have several magistrates present and a strong body of constabulary, to keep the peace among the devotees.

The primitive Irish saints were fond of islands. One of the loveliest of the sacred isles in which they fixed their abodes in the earliest times is INNISFALLEN, situated in the largest of the Killarney lakes. It comprises an area of eighteen acres, having a sinuous shore-line and some bold rocks. It excites the visitor's admiration by the wonderful size and venerable age of its timber, the beauty of its foliage and its shrubs, and the inexhaustible richness of its glades of pasture. It has an air of quietude and of holy tranquillity which belongs to no other island in the lakes or in the kingdom. We are not surprised, then, to learn that in very ancient times the Abbey of Innisfallen was esteemed a paradise and secure sanctuary, where the most valuable treasures belonging to the churches of the surrounding country were deposited for safety. Nor can we avoid being horrified at reading that the O'Donaghues and McArthys violated this sanctuary, carrying off the treasures and slaughtering the monks. We find it difficult to believe that the foot of the sacrilegious spoiler could ever have stained the sod of so holy a place, especially when that spoiler was neither a Pagan, a Dane, nor a Norman, but one of the native chiefs of the Island of Saints. This was one of the retreats, however, in which the early Christians had their nests made and feathered for them by their Pagan predecessors. For there is no doubt that Innisfallen is associated with the remotest antiquity, and that it contained a temple of Sun-Worship. There are remains of this temple a few yards to the right of the landing-place. Most of the building now in ruins was a restoration; but the round-headed doorway at the west end, the window in the eastern wall, and some remains of the walls at the north side are in a style of architecture of the most ancient type, while the other buildings on the island are of the rudest early Christian style;

from which it would appear that, although greatly venerated as an ancient religious foundation, and highly esteemed as a burying-place, it never acquired any ecclesiastical importance since the English Conquest. The abbey, however, is supposed to have been founded by St. Finian in the sixth century, and here were compiled the ' Annals of Innisfallen,' of which a copy exists in the Bodleian Library, Oxford. It professes to be a history of the *World*, and is written in the Irish language, intermixed with Latin.

When engaged in suppressing or punishing 'the Desmond Rebellion,' a body of English troops came to Killarney. Pelham, their leader, reported that he had hanged a priest in the Spanish dress, and that otherwise ' they took small prey, and killed less people, though they had reached many places in their travels.' At Killarney they found the lakes full of salmon. In one of the islands there was an abbey, in another a parish church, in another a castle out of which came to them a fair lady, the wife of Lord Fitzmorris. Even the soldiers were struck with the singular loveliness of the scene. ' A fairer land,' one of them said ' the sun did never shine upon ; pity to see it lying waste in the hands of traitors.' Mr. Froude, in a generous mood, makes this comment upon the remark :—' Yet it was by those traitors that the woods, whose beauty they so much admired, had been planted and fostered. Irish hands, unaided by English art or English wealth, had built Mucross, and Innisfallen, and Aghadoe, and had raised the castles on whose walls the modern poet watched the splendour of the sunset.' It is a mistake to say the natives '*planted*' the woods—their planting and growth were Nature's unassisted work ; even the arbutus flourished without man's help. Innisfallen, from whatever cause, did not become a place of pilgrimage. It had no patron saint whose fame attracted the devout from remote regions. Perhaps it was too beautiful for a place of penance. Not so another little island in a northern lake, the celebrated *Patrick's Purgatory.*

LOUGHDERG, in the county of Donegal, presents the greatest possible contrast to the lakes of Killarney, in the dreariness of the surrounding scenery. It was nevertheless the only one of the Irish lakes which was well known throughout Europe in the middle ages. It is situated about five miles from the little town of Pettigo, and covers an area of 2,140 acres. It contains a number of islands, the largest of which, now called 'Station Island,' is almost completely covered by two chapels and other buildings connected with the pilgrimages, which are still held there annually, from June 1 to August 15, attracting many thousands of devotees, who are guided in their devotions by a 'prior' and several priests, who are engaged incessantly in hearing confessions and imposing penance. This consists chiefly in going on the bare knees on the stones a certain number of rounds, by which indulgences are obtained, and cures are supposed to be effected. Some of the pilgrims are lodged in houses on the island, but many sleep in the open air, having brought with them provisions and bed-clothes. They are ferried across from the mainland, and even now a Protestant landlord derives an income of some hundreds a year from the ferry-boats. When I visited the island alone, I found the prior, a handsome and comparatively young man, exceedingly courteous. As he moved about among the pilgrims, showing me the chapels—very rude buildings— several of them seized the opportunity to implore his blessing, falling on their knees and kissing his hand. Station Island is not the famous St. Patrick's Purgatory. This lies away about a mile in the lake, and the prior kindly ordered a boat to take me there. A few stunted trees decaying from age, some loose stones, and the fragment of a wall, are all that remain of the structure and surroundings which inspired so much awe in the pilgrims who went there from the Continent of Europe for the expiation of sins deemed otherwise unpardonable. In 1632 the Government ordered Sir James Balfour and Sir William Stewart ' to seize unto his Majesty's use this Island of Purgatory,' and accordingly Sir William proceeded to the island, and reported that he found there an abbot and forty friars, and that there was a daily resort of 450 pilgrims, who paid eightpence each for admission to the island. Sir William further informed the Privy Council, that, in order to hinder the seduced people from going any longer to this stronghold of purgatory, and wholly to take away the abuse hereafter, he had directed the whole to be defaced and utterly demolished. 'Therefore the walls, works, foundations, vaults, &c.,

he ordered to be rooted up; also the place called St. Patrick's bed, and the stone on which he knelt. These and all other superstitious relics he ordered to be thrown into the lough.' The destruction was complete, and so far as that island is concerned St. Patrick's Purgatory is clean gone for ever. But the superstition still flourishes on another island, and the resort of pilgrims is still great, having, unlike those at Ardmore, the sanction and guidance of the clergy, who regard it in the light of a 'retreat' for the people.

It is certainly difficult to find a spot more appropriate for an entrance to the Infernal Regions—the shores, the mountains, the accompaniments of all sorts, present 'the very landscape of desolation.' The waters expand in their highland solitude, amidst a wide waste of moors, without one green spot to refresh the eye, without a house or a tree, all mournful in the brown hue of far-reaching bogs and the grey uniformity of rocks, never rising boldly from hills without elevation or grandeur.

I went there alone, supposed to be an Englishman led only by curiosity, not having received a note of introduction to the prior promised me by a priest. My Irish jaunting-car could not proceed beyond a point nearly an English mile distant from the ferry. I made my way with difficulty through bogs and rocks. At the ferry-house, a rude building like a stable, were three young men with carts, waiting to take away some of the pilgrims with their goods. Near the place was a hill covered with a plantation of Scotch fir. No human habitation was visible—none within miles of the spot. With an opera-glass I watched the movements of the pilgrims on the island, expecting a boat to come over every minute, but none started for two hours. All the time the men with the carts eyed me with what appeared to be a suspicious scrutiny. I was quite in their power; they might have killed me as a Protestant spy, and disposed of my body in the lake or the forest, with apparent safety. When the boat came and discharged its freight of pilgrims, I had the greatest difficulty in persuading the ferryman to take me over, as I had no pass, and it was contrary to his orders. However, he consented, provided I did not attempt to land without the express permission of the prior. This was readily obtained on sending him my card; but while on the island he did not allow me to be a moment out of his presence. He politely insisted that I should not return with the pilgrims, but ordered a special boat to take me round by the old St. Patrick's Purgatory. To that desolate spot I was rowed by a man and a boy; and if they had thought proper to leave me there to die of starvation, what was to hinder them, and how were my friends in Dublin to know what became of me? I exposed myself in a similar manner at Dunbrody Abbey, allowing two strange peasants to help me over the high wall that I might examine the ruins inside. From aught that appeared, these men might have robbed or murdered me with impunity. English readers, constantly reading stories of Irish assassinations and religious fanaticism, will no doubt think I was very rash to expose myself in this manner. Perhaps I was; but what astonishes myself now, while looking back upon those adventures here in London, is the fact, that at the time *the idea of danger never once entered my mind.*

The Seven Churches of Glendalough were among the most famous in Ireland for the miracles wrought by the supposed relics of St. Kevin. I saw an immense multitude at the Patron. Its fame was heightened by Moore's Melodies; but miners and pic-nic parties and improving landlords have somewhat changed the aspect of the scene. *Beds,* as well as *basins,* are found in the rocks of many holy places in Ireland; indeed, in most of them, 'the bed of the saint,' the stone coffin, or the shrine, is held in high veneration, and people are still found who lie in those stone beds in the hope of finding a husband or a wife within a certain time, or of being made prolific, or of being cured of certain diseases. St. Finian's Bed, at Innisfallen, Killarney, is well known; but the most celebrated of them all is St. Kevin's Bed, at Glendalough. The glen is about three miles in length, bounded on the south by the mountains of Derrybawn and Lugduff (2,176 feet high), and on the north by three other mountains, the highest 2,196 feet. It contains two lakes, as the name imports—the glen of the two loughs; but the lower one is very small. The upper lake is a mile in length, and about a quarter of a mile in breadth. The mountains rise abruptly, casting deep shadows on the still waters, excluding the sun, and thereby, perhaps, accounting for the absence of the skylark, alluded to in Moore's melody—'The lake which skylark never warbled o'er.' Everyone knows the legend of St. Kevin and Kathleen. In a hole in a rock, which hangs twenty-five feet perpendicularly over the dark, deep lake, the saint is said to have made his bed. In that bed, so difficult of access, in a spot so lonely and desolate, he expected to be safe from woman's charms; but even there the young and handsome anchorite was followed by 'Kathleen's eyes of most unholy blue.' Starting from a horrible dream, in which the tempter presented her lovely form between him and the gate of heaven, he saw her there actually gazing upon him in the flesh, and in a fit of divine frenzy he flung her into the lake, and so got rid of the temptation for ever.

The impression of the whole scene of Glendalough is, to thoughtful minds, very saddening, however the romantic spots about may be enlivened by the merriment of pic-nic parties. The aspect of the surrounding mountains is in keeping with the ruins scattered over the valley, which speak of power, of art, of piety, and of oriental civilisation existing in ages so remote, that history affords no authentic records of their origin. The gloomy lake and the cold sterile mountains seem to be in a sort of mysterious communion with the ivy-clad towers, and broken arches, and sculptured ornaments of the ruined temples, still haunted by human associations, which produce a painful sense of desolation. The Round Tower rises to the height of 110 feet, and is one of the finest structures of the kind. It is surrounded by time-worn monuments of the dead. There were many sculptured crosses in the cemetery, but they have all been thrown down, broken, and the fragments scattered about. One, however, remains, made out of a solid block of granite, eleven feet high, with the usual mystic circle at the top. Other stones, elaborately sculptured, have been found lying around the Abbey or Priory of St. Saviour, with curious symbolical devices. They are so beautiful in an artistic point of view, and represent animals and the human figure with such wonderful distinctness, that it is hard to believe they were produced in the times of confusion, destructive warfare, and barbarism, to which they have been generally ascribed. About a quarter of a mile west of the Ivy Church is the supposed site of the ancient 'city' of Glendalough. For the reasons already given, it is not likely that there was a large population permanently dwelling in this valley; but the fact that no traces of private houses have been found there is no proof to the contrary, because Irish 'towns,' or villages, as they would now be called, were then built of wood, and most of them were many times literally 'burnt to the ground.' Those towns, however, were so numerous in primitive times, that the land attached to them has formed the basis of the *Ordnance Survey*, and also of local taxation, the first division being '*town lands*.' Most of them still bear the names of the old Irish clans. We learn from the Annalists that during the period when it was alleged that '*Norman*' architecture prevailed, the city of Glendalough was repeatedly burned. Thus we read that in the years 1020, 1044, 1061, 1071, and 1084, the city of Glendalough was 'reduced by fire to a heap of ashes.' Again the abbey was destroyed by fire in 1163; and only six years later, Dermott McMurrough, King of Leinster, destroyed it once more; so that the capital of the O'Tooles' principality must have been very like a phœnix, springing up from its ashes as often as it was consumed. It was through the valley thus desolated that King Dermott conducted the forces of Strongbow to the siege of Dublin; and in the year 1176 Glendalough was once more plundered by the Anglo-Norman adventurers. Other desolating acts followed from time to time.

Now it should be recollected that this capital of the tribes which had possessed those glens for thousands of years is twenty-five miles from the metropolis, the seat of the English Government, and yet they continued to defy its power, unconquered, for four centuries. When, therefore, we consider the succession of calamities the O'Tooles endured from the violence of their enemies, our wonder should be, not that the ecclesiastical buildings erected in more modern times had fallen into ruins, but that one stone remained upon another, when the clan was finally subdued. Nor should we wonder that, to the Celtic imagination, the mist-enveloped mountains, which witnessed the glories of the past, should appear wrapt in mourning; or that the dark waters should seem a dead lake - a reservoir of tears—wept by a suffering people, who had struggled for so many ages, bravely, constantly, and faithfully, against their destiny.

Bangor, in the county Down, was honoured by the title of 'The Mother of Monasteries.' It was said to have had 4,000 students at one time. No doubt the numbers are exaggerated in those ancient records, or traditions. But we must recollect that during the summer half-year they were accustomed to dwell in tents, and that they lived much in the open air. It was also their habit to bring with them provisions and other contributions to the common stock of the community. At any rate, this was one of the most celebrated of the Irish monasteries. It was easily reached by foreigners, as the passage from Scotland to the neighbouring town of Donaghadee is only twenty-one miles. In the course of time it became rich enough to attract the cupidity of the Danes, and of native robbers—Christians in name, but not less cruel than the Pagans. We have already noticed the fact that the first monastery in Ireland built of stone was at Bangor. During the three centuries that elapsed between that time and the Reformation, the Abbot of Bangor became very powerful and wealthy; and the church there seems to have deserved her title as a Mother. The last of the line was found, in the thirty-second year of Henry VIII., to be possessed of thirty-one townlands in Ards and Upper Clandeboye, the Grange of Earbeg, in the county of Antrim, the two Copeland Islands, the tithes of the Island of Raghery, three rectories in Antrim, three in Down, and a townland in the Isle of Man. The abbey, some of the walls of which still remain adjoining the parish church, was built early in the twelfth century. We are informed by Archdale that it had so gone to ruin in 1469, through the neglect of the abbot, that he was evicted by order of Pope Pius II., who commanded that the friars of the third order of St. Francis should immediately take possession of it, which was accordingly done, says Wadding, by Father Nicholas of that order. The whole of the possessions were granted by James I. to James Viscount Clandeboye.

CHAPTER VI.

THE CHURCH OF THE PALE AND THE REFORMATION.

WHY did the Celts make no social progress in Ireland for a thousand years? Was it likely they would make none if let alone for ten thousand years? Is this due to their race, or to their institutions? If to the latter, why did they not reform their laws and customs? And how did it happen that Christianity did not correct propensities incompatible with the peace and order of society? Mommsen, in his 'History of Rome,' says:— 'Such qualities—those of good soldiers and bad citizens—explain the historical fact that the Celts have shaken all States and have founded none. . . . They were dispersed *from Ireland* and Spain to Asia Minor; but all their enterprises melted away like snow in spring, and they nowhere created a great State, or developed a distinctive culture of their own.' Niebuhr had written to the same effect:—' An inherent incapacity of living under the dominion of law distinguishes them as barbarians from the Greeks and Italians. As individuals had to procure the protection of some magnate in order to live in safety, so the weaker tribes took shelter under the patronage of a more powerful one; for they were a disjointed multitude. . . . The houses and the villages, which were very numerous, were mean, the furniture wretched— a heap of straw covered with skins served both for bed and a seat; they did not cultivate corn save for a very limited consumption, for the main part of their food was the milk and the flesh of cattle.'

The annals of Ireland, from first to last, bear out this description, and no Celt seems ever to have thought of a radical cure for those social evils. In Ireland they had (all to themselves) for 2,000 years one of the richest countries in the world; and from century to century the land remained uncleared, uncultivated, unenclosed, unfenced—no man having a field he could call his own, while families fought about the ridges of their petty cultivation, and tribes about the boundaries of the districts, ' countries,' or ' regions.' Dr. Keating says :—' It was the misfortune of the Irish that they were *never free from intestine divisions, which contributed to their ruin.* And so implacable was the spirit of discord among them that they would *often join with the forces of the Danes to bring slavery on the country.* About this time (A.D. 984), the Primate of Armagh assisted the foreigners who lived in Dublin, and by that means Ugaire, the son of Tuathal, King of Leinster, was surprised and taken prisoner.' The same author informs us that Brien Boiroimhe had the honour of his country so much at heart ' that by his authority he expelled all the Danes throughout the island except such as inhabited the cities of Dublin, Wexford, Waterford, Cork, and Limerick, whom he permitted to remain in the country for the benefit of trade; for these foreigners were a mercantile people, and by importation supplied the kingdom with commodities that served for pleasure, &c., and by this means were a public advantage to the whole nation.' No doubt of it, and they would have been a still greater advantage if they had not been so often robbed, and if the natives had followed their example, and given up war for industry. But how could the descendants of kings for forty generations stoop to shopkeeping? Their high mission was to consume, waste, and burn the fruits of the earth, and kill as many as possible of the ignoble producers. They could fight, and plunder, and feast, and sing, and dance, and hurl, and play at football, and jump, and run races, hunt for game, and catch fish, but they would not work. They would not use the spade, or the hammer, or the trowel, nor hew wood, or draw water. They had neither trades nor shops. They never developed their own abundant resources. What Christianity found them in the fourth or fifth century, they remained in all social circumstances to the twelfth century. Aptness for organisation, and method, and system they had none. Laws indeed they had, but they had no regular courts to enforce them, and when passion was roused they were brushed away like a spider's web.

' So stationary was the character of this race,' says Mr. Prendergast, 'that when the companions of Strongbow landed, in the reign of Henry II., they found a country existing beyond the current of Roman conquest and civilisation, such as Cæsar found in Gaul 1,200 years before. A thousand years had passed over the island without producing the *slightest social progress*. . . . The British Celts had been disciplined by 400 years of Roman government and civilisation. The French Celts had enjoyed still greater advantages from the same source, with a larger admixture of energetic Teutonic blood from the North; but Ireland was never embraced in the Roman Empire, and the Northmen kept aloof in their Irish settlements, and never amalgamated with the natives. Consequently the Irish Celts remained still divided into tribes, on the system of clansmen and chiefs without a common government, suddenly confederating, suddenly dissolving, with Brehons, Shannahs, Minstrels, Bards, and Harpers, in all unchanged, except that for their ancient Druids they had got Christian priests'[1] The Milesian kings and chiefs were tyrants too. Under their despotism, says Mr. D'Arcy Magee, it was high treason to record the actions of the conquered race, so that the Irish Belgæ fared as badly in this respect at the hands of the Milesian historians as the latter fared in after times from the chroniclers of the Normans. We only know that such tribes were, and that their numbers and physical force more than once excited the apprehension of the children of the conquerors.' Mr. Haverty, another Irish Catholic historian, laments the oppression of the mass of the people, while those who boasted of descent from the Spanish hero would have considered themselves degraded were they to devote themselves to any less honourable profession than that of soldiers. Hence the cultivation of the soil and the exercise of the mechanical arts were left almost entirely to the vanquished people. 'These were ground down by high rents and the exorbitant exactions of the dominant race.' As to the fighting propensities, they continued in full force after the English invasion. It was not fighting for an idea, nor for a principle, nor for the country. As an Irishwoman would join in the *keene* when she met a funeral, and then ask 'Who is dead?' so an Irishman would join in a fight, and when it was all over,

[1] 'Cromwellian Settlement,' Introduction.

enquire what was the quarrel about. The Rev. Matthew Kelly, of Maynooth College, translator of *Cambrensis Eversus*, having observed that from 722 to 1022 only twelve Irish kings died a natural death, says :—' It appears from the Irish and English Annals that there was *perpetual war* in Ireland during more than 400 years after the invasion. It could not be called a war of races, except, perhaps, during the first century ; for English and Irish are constantly found fighting under the same banner, according to the varying interests of rival lords. *This was the case even from the commencement.*' [1] No wonder the Pope said that the nation would be exterminated by mutual slaughter. There is little doubt that such a fate would have been the end of the Celtic race in Ireland if there had been no invasions. And although the first Norman chiefs became more Irish than the Irish themselves, there is no doubt that they contributed materially to prevent that catastrophe and to introduce elements of civilisation. The Geraldines of Kildare and Desmond, and the De Burghs of Galway, were able to extend protection to life and property more effectually and over a larger area than the old kings, and their example was followed by some of these, particularly the O'Briens of Thomond, and the O'Neills in Ulster. At all events it was during the two or three centuries that followed the invasion that all the monasteries, which were the glory of the country, and which the Reformers laid in ruins, were erected. And during a period as long as from the Reformation to the present time those great institutions, ruled by their mitred abbots, lords of Parliament, were the only asylums of religion, learning, and skilled industry throughout the country, the only refuges for the weak and oppressed. They were schools, colleges, hospitals, courts of justice, free hotels, brotherhoods and sisterhoods of mercy, in those times of violence and reckless wrongdoing. Yet the lawlessness of the chiefs became so uncontrollable that an English priest residing at Limerick in 1566 says :—' Of late they spare neither churches nor hallowed places, but thence also they filled their hands with spoil.'

In the Colonial system which the Anglo-Irish established in Dublin there was a perfect union of civil and ecclesiastical

[1] Vol. i. p. 216.

power. Bishops were not only chancellors, viceroys, and lords justices; but occasionally they acted the part of generals, and led the English forces against the 'Irish enemy.' In these military expeditions the native clergy fared no better, if they fell into the hands of the clerical commander, than the rest of the vanquished; nor was there much scruple about the plundering and burning of churches and monasteries. The Anglo-Irish Parliament, in which the clergy had paramount influence, enacted laws imposing the severest penalties on any of the English who consorted with the Irish in the way of business, in hospitality, or even in religion, though both professed the same faith and had the same sacraments. The appeal of an Irish Catholic to a Catholic of the pale, 'Am I not a man and a brother?' would be as scornfully repelled as a similar appeal made by an American negro to his white master. The 'statute of Kilkenny' was passed so late as the year 1367, when the English had been a century in the country. By this it was enacted, that alliances with the Irish by marriage, fostering, or gossipred, was high treason. The Brehon law, which was the law of the land amongst the natives, was declared to be 'wicked and damnable,' and all the English who submitted to it were denounced as traitors. If any Irishman, no matter how religious, was found within the pale not shaved and dressed in the English fashion, or unable to speak the English language, he was to be punished by confiscation of lands and goods, and if he had no property he was cast into prison. No Irish ecclesiastic, however eminent, could get a benefice within the pale, and no religious house was permitted to receive any Irishman into its community. Hence, as Dr. Todd remarks, 'his blood was his crime,' and so great was the crime that it excluded him from Christian fellowship as effectually as if he were tainted with the vilest heresy; and from society, as if he were covered with leprosy as white as snow. Three archbishops and five bishops, having their jurisdiction from Rome, were consenting parties to this Anti-Christian and Anti-Social Enactment, and they pledged themselves to denounce the spiritual sentence of excommunication against all its violators. In those times the Pope nominated many of the Anglo-Irish prelates and other ecclesiastics, and he was always ready to fulminate his thunder against the king's Irish enemies. Hence it is, says Sir John Davis, that in all the parliamentary rolls that are extant from the fortieth year of Edward III., when the statutes of Kilkenny were enacted, to the reign of Henry VIII., we find the degenerate and disobedient English called '*rebels*,' but the Irish which were not in the king's peace are called 'enemies.' After referring to a number of statutes passed in the reigns of Henry IV., Henry VI., Edward IV., and Henry VIII., he proceeds:—' All these speak of " English rebels " and " Irish enemies " as if the Irish had never been in the condition of subjects, but always out of the protection of the laws; and they were indeed in a worse case than aliens of any foreign realm that was in enmity with England. For, by divers heavy penal laws, the English were forbidden to marry, to foster, to make gossips with the Irish, or to have any trade or commerce in their markets or fairs. Nay, there was a law made, no longer since than 28 Henry VIII., that the English should not marry with any person of Irish blood, though she had got a charter of denization, unless she had done both homage and fealty to the king in Chancery, and were also bounden by recognisance and sureties to continue a loyal subject, whereby it is manifest that such as had the government of Ireland under the crown of England did intend to make a perpetual separation of enmity between the English and the Irish.'

In later times the phrase '*Irish enemy*' was represented by the word '*papist*,' which became synonymous with '*traitor*.' The plantation of Ulster, ages after this time, was based upon the same principle of the separation of races; and so deep was the hold that the idea got upon the minds of the English, that even in our own day an eminent statesman, whose wisdom obtained for him the title of 'the Nestor of the House of Lords,' declared in his place in Parliament, after thirty years of the Union, that the Irish Catholics were '*aliens* in blood, language, and religion.' That a race inhabiting Ireland before the Romans set foot in England, subject to the British crown for seven centuries, and said to have enjoyed 'the blessings of the Constitution' for two or three centuries, should be thus denounced by such a man in such a place is a fact that may well excite the wonder of the future historian.

Not less surprising will it be that the system of mutual destruction, of deadly hatred between race and race, tribe and tribe, clan and clan, with old quarrels bequeathed from 'bleeding sire to son,' should have existed among a people who were exclusively Catholic when no Protestant was yet in existence. The old wounds between Catholic factions began to heal only when the King of England quarrelled with the Pope, and finally broke his connection with Rome. This was a breach which affected something more than faith and morals in the estimation of the Papal Court. It put a stop to the flow of 'Peter's Pence' from Ireland. It cut off the 'provisions,' the rich livings, and various ecclesiastical preferments enjoyed by the hangers-on of that foreign Court. It was, therefore, in every sense the interest of the Pope to espouse the cause of the Irish enemy against the English colony. The thunders of the Vatican were no longer fulminated against the Celts as schismatic, contumacious, vile, and barbarous. On the contrary, they became objects of special interest to the Sovereign Pontiff as victims of persecution, martyrs for the faith, devoted, self-sacrificing children of the Church. The apostolic Nuncio, or the prelates who flaunted the *pallium* conferred by the hands of the Pope, no longer directed the councils of the lords of the Pale in the framing of barbarous statutes, which set man against man, Christian against Christian, and fanned the flames of fierce international animosity between peoples whom they should have embraced with equal charity in the common fold. These apostolic emissaries of a foreign Power were thenceforth 'on the other side,' availing themselves with all their wit and cunning of the old nationality, whose perpetual fire they had laboured for centuries to trample out and extinguish for ever. Now, on the contrary, they were ready to apply the mighty ecclesiastical bellows, and blow it into the desolating conflagration of civil war.

Nor should we be surprised that the Irish nation eagerly and gratefully accepted this foreign support. Religious persecution of the most ruthless character had come in the train of extirpating conquest. The native priests were chased away; no Irish-speaking minister was permitted to open his mouth in any pulpit; no mass could be publicly celebrated; no Catholic school could be opened. The deserted churches, if not demolished on account of

H

their Popish ornaments, were allowed to fall to ruin; the nobility and gentry were exiles. In such a state of things the intervention of the Pope, with his Spanish and his French adventurers, was welcomed as affording the only hope of deliverance, to which the nation, exhausted and bleeding, clung as its last refuge from utter annihilation. The old native Church, indeed, had been almost entirely destroyed by the internecine war of four centuries. It received the *coup de grâce* from Elizabeth. Until the time of the Reformation, there had been the Papal Church of the Pale, which came in with the English colony, and kept up its communion with Rome and Canterbury; and there was the national Church of the Irish, which never could be brought into complete subjection to the Papacy. This independent, monastic Church now ceased to exist, with the clans to which it adhered, and from which it drew its support. From that time the Church of the Pale became Protestant, following the destiny of England, while the Irish natives gradually obtained from Rome a new priesthood—strictly Papal in its origin, foreign in its education, intensely and inveterately anti-English in its spirit and teaching. Hating England for her heresy and tyranny—recruited more and more from the ranks of the subjugated race, and therefore, full of its animosity and vindictiveness, while heroically devoted to the interest of an oppressed people—the Irish *Roman Catholic* priesthood imbibed in its inmost core the spirit of disaffection, which English policy continued to inflame, from the Reformation to the Union. This, in brief, is the natural history of the 'Irish difficulty,' which half a century of concession and conciliation has not been able to remove, though Mr. Gladstone has laid the axe to the root of 'the Upas tree.'

Let us, however, return to the internal history of the Anglo-Irish Church as it existed within the narrow limits of the Pale, which at the Reformation did not extend beyond three or four counties. The Danes who occupied Dublin and the seaports, with territory along the eastern coast, had refused to acknowledge the jurisdiction of the Irish Abbots, and had looked to the English Primate for the consecration of their Bishops long before the English conquest by Henry II., so that there was an old animosity, a confirmed schism when the English arrived; and it was, as we have seen, most zealously maintained ever afterwards. Of twenty-eight prelates who occupied the see of Dublin, from Donatus to the Reformation, a period of 600 years, there were only seven who were not Englishmen, or Northmen of some other country; and of these seven, the greater number seem to have been educated in England. A great effort was made, however, in the year 1152, by the Pope through Cardinal Papero, to bring all the Irish churches into a state of uniformity and subjection to the Papal See. It is recorded that on that occasion the principal personages of Ireland, bishops, abbots, princes, and chiefs, with 3,000 ecclesiastics, assembled for this purpose at Drogheda, or Mellifont, or at Kells—certainly not at Dublin or Armagh. But, wherever they held their meetings, their decrees remained a dead letter to a great extent, until Henry II. became the Pope's auxiliary, guaranteeing the collection of his tribute, in consideration whereof his Holiness gave his assent to the ' pious and praiseworthy desire ' of the King to subject the wild Irish to the Church's laws, enforcing her rights and extirpating vice, by which service his Majesty was to obtain from God ' an accumulation of eternal rewards, and on earth a glorious fame for ages.'[1] In

[1] The following is the text of this Bull as it appears in Keating's History of Ireland:—' Adrian the Bishop, the servant of the servants of God, to his most dear son in Christ, the noble King of England, sends greeting and Apostolic benediction. You have been very careful and studious how you might enlarge the Church of God here on earth, and increase the number of saints and elect in heaven, in that as a good Catholic King you have, and do by all means, labour and travail to enlarge and increase God's Church, by teaching the ignorant people the true and Christian religion, and in abolishing and rooting up the weeds of sin and wickedness. And whereas you have and do crave, for your better furtherance, the help of the Apostolic See (wherein more speedily and discreetly you proceed), the better success, we hope, God will send; for all they, who of a fervent zeal and love in religion, do begin and enterprise any such thing, shall no doubt in the end have a good and prosperous success. And as for Ireland, and all other islands where Christ is known and the Christian religion received, it is out of all doubt, and your excellency well knoweth, they do all appertain and belong to the right of St. Peter, and of the Church of Rome; and we are so much the more ready, desirous, and willing to sow the acceptable seed of God's word, because we know the same in the latter day will be most severely required at your hands. You have, our well beloved son in Christ, advertised and signified unto us, that you will enter into the land and realm of Ireland, to the end to bring them to obedience unto law, and under your subjection, and to root out from among them their foul sins and wickedness; as also to yield and pay yearly out of every house, a yearly pension of one penny to St. Peter, and besides also will defend and keep the rights of those churches whole and inviolate. We therefore, well allowing and favouring this your

1162, nine years before the landing of Henry in Ireland, Lawrence O'Toole, son of the Chief of Imaile, became Archbishop of Dublin. He was the first of its bishops who did not go to Canterbury for consecration, and thenceforth the custom was entirely abandoned. He became the patron saint of Dublin, and his anniversary is still celebrated on account of his nationality. But, although connected with an Irish sept which always fiercely and obstinately resisted the English power, it is a fact that Archbishop O'Toole worked harmoniously with Strongbow, Fitzstephen, and Le Gros, who co-operated with him in the enlargement of Christ Church Cathedral, the erection of the choir, the steeple, and two chapels. It was in this cathedral that the remains of Strongbow, the proud invader, were peacefully laid, with the Church's blessing. St. Lawrence O'Toole also assisted Cardinal Vivian as the Pope's legate, at a Council held in Dublin six years after the visit of Henry II., and this Council confirmed the King of England in his claim to the sovereignty of Ireland. The saint afterwards went to Rome, where he obtained a bull from the Pope, subjecting not only Glendalough, but Kildare, Ferns, Leighlin,

godly disposition and commendable affection, do accept, ratify, and assent unto this your petition, and do grant that you (for the dilating of God's Church, the punishment of sin, the reforming of manners, the planting of virtue, and the increasing of Christian religion) do enter to possess that land, and there to execute, according to your wisdom, whatsoever shall be for the honour of God and the safety of the realm. And further also we do strictly charge and require, that all the people of that land do with all humbleness, dutifulness, and honour, receive and accept you as their liege lord and sovereign, reserving and excepting the right of Holy Church to be inviolably preserved, as also the yearly pension of Peter pence out of every house, which we require to be truly answered to St. Peter and to the Church of Rome. If, therefore, you do mind to bring your godly purpose to effect, endeavour to travail to reform the people to some better order and trade of life, and that also by yourself and by such others as you shall think meet, true and honest in their life, manners, and conversation, to the end the Church of God may be beautified, the true Christian religion sowed and planted, and all other things done, that by any means shall or may be to God's honour and salvation of men's souls, whereby you may in the end receive of God's hands the reward of everlasting life, and also in the meantime, and in this life, carry a glorious fame and an honourable report among all nations.' *

---

* 'Adrianus Papa quartus, natione Anglus, vir sapiens et pius, Hiberniam insulam Henrico secundo regi Anglorum concessit ea conditione, ut in ea insula virtutes plantaret et vitia eradicaret, ut a singulis domibus quotannis denarium Sancto Petro pendi curaret, et ut jura ecclesiastica illibata servaret.' Extat diploma T. XII. Cardinalis Baronii.

and Ossory to his metropolitan authority. Subsequently, however, he was found not sufficiently tractable in the hands of his royal master, and he was banished to Normandy, where he died in a monastery; hence, no doubt, his canonisation. He must, indeed, have been a great troubler of the Pale, for he is said to have sent nearly two hundred of his clergy to Rome to seek absolution for notorious sins, among which was their Norman repugnance to celibacy. It thus appears that Archbishop O'Toole was a very useful servant to the Pope, for those numerous clerical penitents must have brought a great deal of money into the coffers of his Holiness. This rigid discipline, however, must have called forth loud complaints against him to the King from those who smarted under the blows of his crosier. Perhaps, too, his nationality had something to do with their complaints. Father Malone, a candid historian of our own time, laments that the Church of the Pale became a 'close borough.' All healthy competition being set aside, laziness and ignorance resulted—breeding in and in, transformed an hereditary priesthood into a caste; the Anglo-Irish Church promised to be only an eyesore, a scandal to the Church of God. So careful was this family party to keep all the good things to themselves that their Parliament, in which the Prior of Christ Church always held a seat, passed a law in 1380, that no native should be suffered to profess himself in that institution—an enactment so strictly observed that, excepting in the reign of James II., no Irishman was admitted even as Vicar Choral of Christ Church, until John A. Stevenson was enrolled among the pupils of its music school, late in the eighteenth century! Even at a time when there was a great dearth of ministers, the Anglo-Irish in Dublin shut the sanctuary against the native talent and zeal.

Thus the gloomy background of the Irish social picture, which we deplore to-day, the national animosity, the sectarian bigotry, the chronic dissension, the uncontrollable tendency to division, existed 800 years ago in colours far darker than at the present time. In fact the unprejudiced student of Irish history can trace amidst all the wars and revolutions that have swept over this country *a steady progress towards* NATIONAL UNITY. And this progress has been greater during the last fifty years than during all the centuries that preceded, even from the time of St. Patrick to the Reformation!

The See of the metropolis is not the metropolitan See of Ireland. Armagh has long enjoyed that prerogative. It was, however, in dispute for several centuries; and although the Pope had decided in favour of Armagh, it was not definitely and legally established till the reign of Charles I., when Lord Strafford devoted several days to the investigation of the long-vexed question and confirmed the Pope's decision. Consequently, while the Archbishop of Dublin was admitted to be 'Primate of Ireland,' the Archbishop of Armagh was declared 'Primate of *all* Ireland,' and to have the right to raise his crosier in each of the other three provinces. Armagh may be said to be the Canterbury of Ireland, and in each the claims of antiquity have withstood the claims of political power and State influence. The Archbishop of Dublin, far more than the Bishop of London, played continually a great part in history as a State functionary. He was not only honoured by a seat in the King's Privy Council in *England*, where he used to attend his Majesty in many weighty consultations, but also had within his 'Liberties of the Cross' the rights of a Prince Palatine, with power of even condemning to death criminals offending therein. For their execution a gallows was erected at Harold's Cross, and his seneschal, down to a recent period, held a court and had a prison for confining debtors. He had the regulation of the police in the Manor or Liberty surrounding the parish of St. Sepulchre, and likewise the right of a market in Patrick Street. But these were small matters to him. In many instances the Archbishop of Dublin was the Grand Justiciary or Lord Deputy of the English monarch, and sometimes he led in that capacity the military forces of the Pale against the Irish enemy.

Christ Church, Dublin, was governed by the Prior of the Augustinians under monastic rules from the year 1163 to 1538, when Henry VIII. issued a commission to enquire into the condition of this church among others, and in pursuance of the recommendation of the Commissioners he changed the constitution, making it a cathedral. By an instrument dated September 12, 1539, he acknowledged Christ Church as the Archiepiscopal See and the second metropolitan church in Ireland. Payneswick, the Prior, was appointed first Dean; the Sub-Prior, Precentor, and so on; the Canons being made Vicars Choral. In 1541 a new Charter was obtained, constituting the corporation under the title of Dean and Chapter of the Church of the Holy Trinity, Dublin. In 1521 the Pope appointed Hugh Inge to the Archbishopric. He was succeeded by John Allen, formerly Chaplain to Cardinal Wolsey, and an active agent in the dissolution of the English monasteries. He too was confirmed in his See by the Pope. Having rendered himself obnoxious to the Geraldines, he tried to escape from the city in a boat; but, betrayed by the pilot, he was stranded near Clontarf. Feeble from age and sickness, kneeling in his shirt and mantle, bequeathing his soul to God, his body to the traitor's mercy, he was brutally murdered in the presence of Lord Thomas, commonly known as Silken Thomas, who had just renounced his allegiance, exasperated by the report of his father's execution in the Tower of London. Allen was the last of the Papal Archbishops. His successor was George Brown, Provincial of the Augustinians in London. He was invested with a pall, and consecrated by Archbishop Cranmer and two other English Bishops. He had a very difficult task set to him in Ireland by the King—to root out all that the Pope had planted in the portion of the vineyard committed to his care, and throughout the land generally. His successor, Hugh Curwen, on the contrary, was sent over by Queen Mary to pluck up everything of the King's planting, and to restore the Roman Catholic worship in all its pomp. He was dutiful to Queen Mary, but not less dutiful to her sister Elizabeth, who rewarded him handsomely for his zeal in the cause of Protestantism. The next Archbishop was a very young man—Adam Loftus—who had been consecrated as Archbishop of Armagh by Hugh, Archbishop of Dublin. Consequently, says Harris, 'the Irish Protestant Bishops derived their succession through him without any pretence of blemish or opening for cavil, for he was consecrated by Curwen, who had been consecrated in England according to the forms of the Roman Pontifical in the third year of Queen Mary.'

A few of the public acts of the State at this time of ecclesiastical transition will show how easily the Catholic Church of the Pale was transformed into the Protestant Church of England established in Ireland; and how the King succeeded the Pope as its head. On Easter Sunday, 1551, the Liturgy in the English language was read for the first time at Christ Church, in the presence of the Lord Deputy St. Leger, Archbishop Brown, and the Mayor of Dublin. On the accession of Mary, the Roman Catholic worship was reinstated; but in 1559 it was again suppressed by Elizabeth. On the 13th of August in that year the Earl of Sussex, Lord Deputy, came to Christ Church, where he was sworn in; and the Te Deum was sung in English, at which the trumpets sounded. In January following, the Parliament sat in that church, when it passed the Act of Uniformity and several other laws. This year orders were sent to Thomas Lockwood, Dean of Christ Church, 'to remove out of his church all Popish relics and images,' and to paint and whiten it anew, putting sentences of Scripture on the walls in lieu of pictures or other the like fancies, which orders were observed, and men set to work accordingly. On the 25th of May, 1559, the Archbishop of York sent to Christ Church and St. Patrick's a large Bible to each, to be placed in the middle of their 'quires,' 'which two Bibles, on their first setting up to the public view, caused a great resort of people thither on purpose to read therein.'

It is in virtue of such authorities that the advocates of the late Established Church pretended to be exclusively the lineal descendants of those who introduced Christianity into Ireland in the fifth century, and that they alone had a just and rightful claim to the tithes, ecclesiastical estates, cathedrals, and churches, which their predecessors had enjoyed from time immemorial. 'In fact,' says the Rev. T. W. Roe, 'the State did little more than merely continue those Bishops with their clergy in possession of the property which they had enjoyed previous to the improvements they had been instrumental in effecting in the doctrines and discipline of the National Church, and which were never in the possession of the troublesome and ever-encroaching Romish sect.'

It was very easy, no doubt, for the conquerors to take possession of the tithes, estates, and buildings, but not so easy to convert those who were despoiled, nor to remove the plague of ungodliness from the Church of the Pale, which had now enlarged her borders and strengthened her stakes. But the Rev. Dr. Todd has shown how absurd it is to claim tithes in virtue of being successors of St. Patrick, for the tithe system was not introduced into Ireland till the twelfth century, and then it was introduced by the foreign settlers. Elizabeth's Establishment got everything but *the people*,—the property, the buildings, the dignity, and worldly state; but until the hour of its abolition the people were utterly estranged. Indeed, nothing could be more futile than the argument founded on an alleged Episcopal succession. Even if spiritual authority, the right to preach the Gospel and administer the Sacraments, depended on the authenticity of diocesan records, only an enemy of Christianity could wish to rest its claims upon such a shadowy foundation, if his mind had not been deluded by strange misconception. Yet we find the Archdeacon of Dublin, the learned Dr. Lee, Regius Professor of Divinity in the University, in a consecration sermon preached before the Archbishop, seriously and solemnly asserting this claim as an all-sufficient ground for the exclusive authority of the Episcopal Establishment in Ireland. This ground has been pronounced by Mr. Froude 'the most impudent falsehood in all history.' It is pretended that the Irish Bishops accepted the Book of Common Prayer for the Mass-book, and took the oath of allegiance to Elizabeth as the Head of the Church, and thus became the legitimate channels of Divine grace, flowing from the Apostles through the Pope and St. Patrick; and this, although the primatial See was occupied for 200 years by laymen, and the records of the Middle Ages must have passed miraculously through a thousand conflagrations.

The subject is thus referred to in a note by Mr. Froude in his 'History of England' (vol. x. p. 481):—'I cannot express my astonishment at a proposition maintained by Bishop Mant and others, that the whole hierarchy of Ireland went over at the Reformation with the Government. Dr. Mant discovers that the Bishop of Kildare and the Bishop of Meath were deprived for refusing the oath of supremacy. The rest he infers must have taken the oath, because they remained in their places. The English Government, unfortunately for themselves, had no such opportunity as Dr. Mant's argument supposes, for the exercise of their authority. The Archbishop of Dublin, the Bishops of Meath and Kildare were alone under English jurisdiction when Adam Loftus was made Archbishop of Armagh. The primacy became titularly Protestant; but Loftus resided in Dublin, the See was governed by a Bishop in communion with the Pope, and the latter, not the former, was regarded in Ireland even by the correspondents of the English Government as the lawful possessor of the See. In a survey of the country supplied to Cecil in 1571, after death and privation had enabled the Government to fill several Sees with English nominees, the Archbishops of Armagh, Tuam, and Cashel, with almost every one of the Bishops of the respective provinces, are described as Catholics. The Archbishop of Dublin, with the Bishops of Kildare, Ossory and Ferns, are alone reckoned as Protestants.' Even in the cities of the Pale a Spaniard, Don Diego Ortes, could see in the people two virtues —fidelity to the Catholic Church, and hatred to the English. 'They all looked to Spain to deliver from tyranny, to save their souls, and give them back the blessed mass; the mass, indeed, they everywhere still used in their own houses. In Youghal there are yet two monasteries, a Franciscan and a Dominican. The friars are much troubled by the English. When their persecutors are near, they flee to the mountains, or hide in their cellars. When the coast is clear again, they return to their houses. Everywhere, both in the cities and in the country, there is a universal desire for the appearance of a Spanish Armada to deliver them from slavery, and to restore their churches to them. There is an English proverb in use among them, which says:—

> He who would England win,
> In Ireland must begin.'

Mr. Froude remarks truly, that 'but for the question of religion the towns would have been loyal; for their prosperity depended on the maintenance of order; while the native chiefs, however turbulent, would never have seriously desired to transfer their allegiance to Spain, for Philip, they well knew, would have been as intolerant of anarchy as the English viceroy in Dublin. The suppression of the Catholic service, enforced wherever the English had power, and hanging before the people as a calamity sure to follow as the limits of that power were extended, created a weight of animosity which no other measure could have produced, *and alone perhaps made the problem of Irish administration hopelessly insoluble*. Notwithstanding the fair speeches of the Mayor of Waterford, neither that city nor any other in Ireland, except Dublin, would receive an English garrison. When they admitted the English Prayerbook it was with a reluctance which was nowhere concealed.' The same writer further remarks that the ' *intrusive religion* was not recommended by the brilliancy of its moral influences. The spiritual disorganisation of the country was even greater than the social. Whatever might have been the other faults of the Irish people, they had been at least eminent for their piety. The multitude of churches and monasteries which in their ruins meet everywhere the stranger's eye witness conclusively to their possession of this virtue; for the religious houses in such a state of society could not have existed at all, unless protected by the consenting reverence of the whole population. But the religious houses were gone, and the prohibition of the mass had closed the churches, except in districts which were in armed and open rebellion. For many years, over the greater part of Ireland public worship was at an end. The Reformed clergy could not venture beyond the post towns, and in these they were far from welcome.'[1]

Mr. Froude often speaks of the *Irish nature* as the cause of the evils that have afflicted the country. But if so, the Irish nature is not the result of race or blood, but the outcome of the soil and climate. If the natives are prone to rebel, it is not because they are Celts,—not even because they are Catholics. For in describing the state of things under Elizabeth, after the Reformation, this writer says:—' *The English settlers became everywhere worse than the Irish in all the qualities in which the Irish were most in fault.* No Celt hated England more bitterly than the transported Saxon. The forms of English justice might be introduced, but juries combined to defeat the ends for which they were instituted, and every one in authority, English or Irish, preferred to rule after the Irish system.'

Well, if they had let the Irish system alone, backward as it

[1] Vol. x. pp. 534–5.

was, the case would not have been half so bad. In those troubled times, the monasteries seem to have been a social necessity. For travellers they were free hotels; for the poor they were hospitals, centres of charity, and refuges from oppression; and upon them even depended a portion of the work now done by grand juries. All these means of civilisation were recklessly abolished by the Reformers. For, as Mr. Froude testifies, 'the bridges—the special charge of the religious orders—fell into ruin; the chiefs took possession of the Church lands, the churches fell in and went to ruin, and the unfortunate country seemed *lapsing into total savagery.*'

These are the hideous facts of history that cannot be explained away. Elizabeth strove in vain to suppress Popery. But she succeeded too well in disorganising society and demoralising the people of both nationalities. How different is this state of things from the rose-coloured pictures so complacently presented by Prelates, dignitaries, and other champions of the late Establishment! These writers describe the native Bishops, clergy, and people as quietly transferring their allegiance to the Queen, and making themselves her willing instruments in purifying the Church, restoring it to its primitive simplicity, eagerly and almost unanimously casting off the galling yoke of the Pope! It is astonishing to what an extent these gross perversions of Irish history, made by men of learning and eminence, have succeeded in deluding both the clergy and the laity of the late Established Church.

A majority of the Marian Bishops may have outwardly conformed when Elizabeth, in her short and decisive way of ending disputes about religion, put before them the alternative—'sign or resign'—'submit or quit'—'refuse to swear if you dare.' And it is possible that a couple of the Irish Bishops assisted Curwen in consecrating those whom the Queen subsequently appointed. We leave the bewildering arguments about the succession to the several Irish Sees, because they have nothing to do with the real question at issue. That many of them did submit to the Queen's supremacy, and in words repudiated the Pope, there is no doubt. But for what purpose? Why, manifestly that they might deceive the Government and be in a position to alienate the property of the Church, which they saw passing into the hands of their enemies. For perjury committed with this object, they could easily have got the Pope's dispensation. And they would have done what the Queen required the more readily, as they daily expected to hear of her assassination or deposition, to make way for Mary Queen of Scots, who was determined to restore the Roman Catholic worship in Ireland and walk in the footsteps of her Royal namesake. Indeed this fact is admitted by the highest authorities. Archbishop Bramhall, in a work vindicating the consecration of Protestants, asserts that 'the old Bishops complied, and held their places, and joined in such ecclesiastical acts (as consecration) *until they had made away to their kindred all the land belonging to their Sees.*' And Cox, in his History of Ireland, says: 'The very Popish Bishops did assist at the consecration of most of the Protestant Bishops, and complied with the Government, and kept their Sees, until they had sacrilegiously betrayed the Church and alienated much of its possessions.' With this agrees the testimony of Jeremy Taylor, who, in a sermon preached at the consecration of Archbishop Bramhall, said: 'At the Reformation the Popish Bishops and Priests seemed to conform, and did so, that, by keeping their bishoprics, they might enrich their kindred and dilapidate the revenues of the Church.'

Doubtless the Roman party thought that this was a case, if ever there was one, in which the end sanctifies the means; for the property in question was not English or Protestant property, but Irish and Catholic, bestowed by Irish Catholics for the support of their own religion, from which purpose it would otherwise have been alienated by their conquerors and oppressors. Nor should we fling against those old conforming Bishops the charge of perjury without due consideration of times and circumstances. Were their English accusers in a position to cast stones at them, as being without sin in this matter? It would only show gross ignorance of history to suppose that the sanctity of official oaths was more binding three centuries ago than at present. We know how common false swearing is in England; and a Roman Catholic might quote Mr. Buckle and Sir William Hamilton for the fact that England is pre-eminent among nations for perjury; and Oxford is pre-eminent in England for the same crime.

It is, however, easy enough to find pleas for persecution if men once adopt the barbarous principle that religious opinion is a crime to be punished by the civil magistrate. That principle is still more detestable if it be enforced as an excuse for plunder, effected by means of the law.

CHAPTER VII.

A CRUSADE AGAINST THE REFORMATION.

THE celebrated Hugh O'Neill, King of Ulster, published in November 1599 a manifesto to the Catholics of the towns in Ireland, warning them of 'the great calamity and misery into which they were likely to fall by persevering in the damnable state in which they had been living.' If they did persevere, he told them, he should use means to despoil them of their goods and to dispossess them of their lands, because the towns were the means whereby wars were maintained against the exaltation of the Catholic faith. Contrariwise, if they joined him, he assured them upon his conscience that he would employ himself to the utmost of his power in their defence, 'as well as for the extirpation of heresy, the planting of the Catholic religion, the delivery of the country from infinite murders, wicked and detestable policies by which this kingdom was hitherto governed, nourished in obscurity and ignorance, maintained in barbarity and incivility.' Therefore he thought himself in conscience bound to use all means for the reduction of that poor afflicted country to the Catholic faith, which never could be brought to any good pass without either the destruction or the helping hand of the Catholics of the *towns*. He protested that he did not want their lands or goods, nor would he plant any in their places, if they would only join him. He declared 'upon his salvation' that he chiefly and principally fought for the Catholic faith to be planted throughout all their poor country, as well in cities as elsewhere, protesting that 'if he had to be King of Ireland without having the Catholic religion established, he would not the same accept.' He exhorted them to follow the example of 'that most Catholic country, France, whose subjects, for defect of Catholic faith, did go against their most natural king, and maintained wars till he was constrained to profess the Catholic religion, duly submitting himself to the Apostolic See of Rome, to the which, doubtless, he might bring his country, the Catholics of the towns putting their helping hands with him to the same.' He thus concluded: 'As for myself, I protest before God and upon my salvation I have been proffered oftentimes such conditions as no man seeking his own private commodity could refuse; but I, seeking the public utility of my native country, will prosecute these wars until general religion be planted throughout all Ireland. So I rest, praying the Almighty to move your flinty hearts to prefer the commodity and profit of your country before your own private ends.'[1]

In those times, when religious wars had been raging on the Continent, when the whole power of Spain was persistently employed to exterminate Protestants with fire and sword and every species of cruelty, it is not at all surprising that a Chief like O'Neill, leading such a wild, warlike life in Ulster, should persuade himself that he would be glorifying God and serving his country by destroying the Catholic inhabitants of the towns, that is, all the most civilised portions of the community, because they would not join him in robbing and killing the Protestants; but it is not a little surprising that a learned and liberal Catholic priest, writing in Dublin in the year of our Lord 1868, should give his deliberate sanction to this unchristian and barbarous policy. Yet Father Meehan, while publishing this document for the first time, writes: 'But no; not even the dint of that manifesto, *with the ring of true steel in its every line, could strike a spark out of their hearts, for they were chalky.*'

With such documents before them, however, and others of a similar kind, it was only natural that the English Government should act upon the same principle of intolerance, especially when they could urge the plea of State necessity. Still, they did not go the length of exterminating Catholics in the style with which O'Neill threatened his peaceable and industrious co-religionists in the towns. All they required was that the Catholics should cease to harbour their priests, and should attend the

[1] 'Fate and Fortunes of the Earls of Tyrone and Tyrconnel,' by Rev. P. C. Meehan, M.R.I.A., p. 34.

Protestant churches. Remarking upon the proclamation of the Lord Deputy Chichester to this effect, Mr. Meehan says: 'Apart from the folly of the King, who had taken it into his head that an entire nation should at his bidding apostatize from the creed of their forefathers, the publishing of such a manifesto in Dungannon, Donegal, and elsewhere was a bitter insult to the Northern chieftains, whose wars were *crusades*, the natural consequence of faith stimulated by the Roman Pontiff, assisted by Spain, then the most Catholic kingdom in the world.' Does not Mr. Meehan see that crusading is a game at which two can play? And if wars which were crusades were *the natural consequence of the Catholic faith, were stimulated by the Roman Pontiff's, and assisted by Spain for the purpose of destroying the power of England* everywhere as well as in Ireland, and abolishing the Reformation, does it not necessarily follow that the English Government must in sheer self-defence have waged a war of extermination against the Irish priests as its mortal enemies? No better plea for the English policy in Ireland was ever offered by any Protestant writer (not even by Mr. Froude) than this language, intended as a condemnation by a very able priest of strong national proclivities in our own day. It was, no doubt, extreme folly for the King of England to expect that a nation or a single individual should apostatize at his bidding; but it was equal folly in the King of Spain to expect Protestants to apostatize for no better reason than the Royal command. It was still greater folly in the Earl of Tyrone to expect the Catholic denizens of Munster to join him in the bloody work of persecution. It was, then, the Spanish policy, stimulated by the Pope, that was the standing excuse of the cruel intolerance and rancorous religious animosity which have continued to distract Irish society down to our own time. Persecution is alien to the Irish race. The malignant virus imported from Spain poisoned the national blood, maddened the national brain, and provoked the terrible system of retaliation that was embodied in the penal code, and which is still defended by the old plea—the intrusion of a foreign power striving to over-rule the government of the country.

Mr. Buckle has a suggestive passage on religious persecution which he might have abundantly illustrated from the history of Ireland:—' To punish even a single man for his religious tenets is assuredly a crime of the deepest dye; but to punish a large body of men, to persecute an entire sect, to attempt to extirpate opinions which, growing out of the state of society in which they arise, are themselves a manifestation of the marvellous and luxurious fertility of the human mind'—this is ' not only one of the most pernicious, but one of the most foolish, acts that can possibly be conceived. Nevertheless it is an undoubted fact that an overwhelming majority of religious persecutors have been men of the purest intentions, of the most admirable and unsullied manners.' He shows that the best of the Roman Emperors were the greatest persecutors of the Christians; that the most cruel of the Spanish Inquisitors were men of strict integrity and great humanity; and he might have added, from Mr. Froude's pages, that the most ruthless slayers of Irishwomen and children who had the misfortune to be born Catholics, were the most gentle, the most generous, the most refined of the English commanders. If men once get possessed by the delusion that ' heretics ' on the one hand, or ' Papists' on the other, are more dangerous to society than wolves, then the more earnest their convictions, and the more ardent their humanity, the less will they be disposed to spare those whom conscience commands them to destroy.

Mr. Buckle, viewing the matter in the most favourable light, justly ascribes this fearful perversion of the mind to ignorance. ' It is,' he says, ' to the diffusion of knowledge, and to that alone, that we owe the comparative cessation of what is unquestionably the greatest evil men have ever inflicted on their own species. For, that religious persecution is a greater evil than any other, is apparent not only from the enormous and almost incredible number of its known victims, as from the fact that the unknown must be far more numerous, and that history gives no account of those who have been spared in the body in order that they might suffer in the mind. . . . It is this which is the real curse of religious persecution. For in this way, men being constrained to mask their thoughts, there arises a habit of securing safety by falsehood, and of purchasing impunity with deceit. In this way *fraud becomes a necessary of life*; insincerity is made a daily custom; the whole tone of public feeling is vitiated, and the gross amount of vice and of error fearfully increased. Surely, then, we have reason to say that, compared to this, all other crimes are of small account; and we may well be grateful for that increase of intellectual pursuits which has destroyed an evil that some among us would even now willingly restore.'[1]

We may say with the Apostle Paul, 'The times of this ignorance God winked at, but now commandeth all men everywhere to repent;' to repent of the spirit of persecution that may still lurk in their churches or in their hearts. Allowing all due weight to the plea of ignorance, sincerity, and good intention, it is hard to read without burning indignation the blood-stained records of persecution. Persecution in Ireland grew by feeding upon human sacrifices, to such monstrous proportions that the dragon opened its jaws to devour a whole nation! This proved to be an impossibility, for which we might suppose that every Christian, whatever his church may be, would devoutly thank God. What, then, are we to think of a modern historian who, in this age of 'sweetness and light,' loudly applauds the attempt, and deeply deplores the failure? —

> Who would not laugh if such a man there be?
> Who would not grieve if Atticus were he?

Since the defeat of the Spaniards at Kinsale, the Catholics had consoled themselves with the assurance that Philip III. would send another expedition to retrieve the honour of his flag and avenge the humiliation he had sustained. Clement VIII. pressed this upon him as a sacred duty which he owed to his co-religionists in Ireland, whose efforts to free themselves from Elizabeth's tyranny that Pontiff pronounced to be 'a crusade against the most implacable heretic of the day.' Hugh O'Neill, however, had submitted to the Queen's mercy, imploring her gracious commiseration in the most abject terms, vowing everlasting loyalty, abjuring all foreign power, renouncing all manner of dependency upon the King of Spain, promising to fight against him, and resigning all claim and title to any lands but such as should now be granted to him by her Majesty. 'And I will,' he said in conclusion,

[1] 'History of Civilization in England,' vol. i. pp. 171, 172.

'endeavour for myself and the people of my country to erect civil habitations such as shall be of greater effect to preserve us against thieves and any force but the power of the State.' After this he accompanied the Lord Deputy Mountjoy to Dublin, and the day after James was proclaimed he repeated the absolute submission which he had made at Mellifont Abbey.

The accession of James I. produced a delirium of joy in the Catholics of the South. Their bards had sung that the blood of the old Celtic monarchs circulated in his veins; their clergy told them that, as James VI. of Scotland, he had received supplies of money from the Roman Court, and, above all, that Clement VIII. had sent to congratulate him on his accession, having been solicited by him to favour his title to the crown of England, which the Pope promised to do on condition that James should not persecute the Catholics. The consequence was that the inhabitants of the southern towns rose *en masse* without waiting for authority, forced open the gates of the ancient churches, re-erected the altars, and used them for public worship. The Lord Deputy was startled by intelligence to this effect from Waterford, Cork, Limerick, Kilkenny, Clonmel, Lismore, Wexford, &c. The cathedrals, churches, and oratories were seized by the priests and people—Father White, Vicar-Apostolic of Waterford, being the leader in this movement, and going about from city to city for the purpose of hallowing and purifying the temples which the Protestants had desecrated and defiled.

The mayors of the cities were rebuked by Lord Mountjoy as seditious and mutinous in thus setting up the public exercise of the Popish religion, and he threatened to encamp speedily before Waterford, 'to suppress insolences and see peace and obedience maintained.' He kept his word, and on May 4, 1603, he appeared before that city at the head of 5,000 men, commanded by Sir R. Wingfield, who had distinguished himself in Tyrone's war. There is among the family pictures of Powerscourt, says Mr. Meehan, 'a portrait of this distinguished old warrior, whose lineal descendant, the present noble lord, has always proved most generous to his Catholic tenantry.' The rev. gentleman gives an amusing sketch of the logical combat between him and Father White, who came forth to the camp under safe-conduct, wearing his clerical habit, and preceded by a cross-bearer. The soldiers jeered at the sacred symbol, and called it an idol. Father White indignantly resented the outrage, when Wingfield threatened to put an end to the controversy by running his sword through the Vicar-Apostolic. The Lord Deputy Mountjoy relied on other weapons. He was a bit of a theologian and a bookish man—at one time inclined to Catholicity—and he listened quietly to the priest on the right of resisting or disobeying the natural prince, producing authorities from the works of St. Augustine. But Mountjoy caused to be brought to him out of his tent the identical volume, and showed, to the amazement of the bystanders, that the context explained away all that the priest had asserted. The triumphant theologian then turned upon White, and told him that he was a traitor, worthy of condign punishment for bringing an idol into a Christian camp, and for opening the churches by the Pope's authority. Later in the day Father White appeared a second time in the camp, greatly humbled; and, falling upon his knees before the Lord Deputy, he begged for liberty of conscience, free and open exercise of religion—protesting that the people would be ready to resist all foreign invasion were that granted; and, finally, beseeching that some of the ruined churches might be given to the Catholics, who were ready to rebuild them, and pay for them a yearly rent into his Majesty's exchequer. But all the Deputy would grant was permission to the priests to wear clerical costume and celebrate Mass in private houses. He then entered the city, received the Oath of Allegiance from the chief inhabitants, and made over all the churches to the small section of Protestants. At the same time he sent despatches to other towns, ordering the authorities to evict the Roman Catholics from the ecclesiastical buildings they had presumed to occupy. Then proceeding to Cork, and thence through Cashel to Dublin, he restored Protestantism everywhere—'leaving, perhaps, to future statesmen, living above the atmosphere of prejudice, the duty of restoring to the Catholics of Ireland those grand old temples which were never meant to accommodate a fragment of its people.'

So wrote Father Meehan on the eve of the disestablishment of the Irish Church; but his expectations were not realised by Mr. Gladstone, for, though there were two cathedrals in Dublin, both were left in possession of the Protestant Episcopalians—St. Patrick's being recognised as the 'National Cathedral,' to be kept in repair by the State. However, Mountjoy having put down, North and South, all resistance to the King's authority, and having received O'Neill's solemn submission, the latter was induced to accompany him to England, travelling under the King's protection. On the way from Chester to London, wherever the great Irish chief was recognised, in city or hamlet, the populace, notwithstanding their respect for Mountjoy, the hero of the hour, pursued him with bitter insults and stoned him as he passed along. The Welsh and English women also assailed him with loud invectives. And not unnaturally, 'for there was not one among them but could name some friend or kinsman whose bones lay buried far away in some wild pass or glen of Ulster where the object of their maledictions was more often victor than vanquished.' The King, however, gave him a gracious reception, having issued a proclamation that he had restored him to his favour, and that he should be 'of all men honourably received,' to the intense disgust of English officers who had been engaged in the Irish wars. Sir John Harrington, writing to a bishop, said:—'I have lived to see that damnable rebel Tyrone brought to England, honoured and well liked. O what is there that does not prove the inconstancy of worldly matters! How I did labour after that knave's destruction! I adventured perils by sea and land, was near starving, and ate horse flesh in Munster, and all to quell that man, who now smileth in peace at those who did hazard their lives to destroy him; and now doth Tyrone dare us, old commanders, with his presence and protection.'

The favour of the King, however, went to an excess fatal to its object, by conceding to the Ulster chiefs powers incompatible with his own sovereignty, while exciting mortal enmity in those who were charged with the government of Ireland. The Earl of Tyrone received power to execute martial law upon any offenders who lived under him, 'the better to keep them in obedience,' and it was ordered that the King's garrisons should not meddle with him or his people. The O'Donel also was restored to all the lands and rights of ancient time belonging to his house, excepting abbeys and other spiritual livings, the castle and town of Bally-

Shannon, and 1,000 acres adjoining the fisheries there. He was formally installed as Earl of Tyrconnel, in Christ Church Cathedral, in the presence of Archbishop Loftus and a number of high officials.

But Tyrone was dogged by spies in London, suspected of intriguing with Jesuits. In the meantime the correspondence of Sir George Carew and others in authority in Ireland was loaded with complaints that the country ' so swarmed with priests, Jesuits, Seminarists, Friars, and Romish Bishops, that, " if speedy means were not used to free the kingdom of this wicked rabble which laboured to draw the subjects' due obedience from their prince, much mischief would burst forth in a short time." ' For, said Carew, ' there are here so many of this wicked crew that are able to disquiet four of the greatest kingdoms in Christendom. It is high time they were banished from hence, and none to receive, or aid or relieve them. Let the judges and officers be sworn to the Supremacy. Let the lawyers go to church and show conformity, or not plead at the Bar, and then the rest by degrees will shortly follow.'

Sir Arthur Chichester succeeded Carew as Lord Deputy. Descended from a family in Devon, and having served with great success in several posts of importance in Ireland, he proved to be one of the ablest and most successful administrators that ever represented the royal authority in that country. He was a great organiser and reformer; earnest and determined in his efforts to establish law and order throughout the country. He sent Judges of Assize throughout Munster and Connaught, reducing the ' countries ' or ' regions ' into shiregrounds or counties; abolishing ' cosheries, spendings,' and other customary exactions of the chiefs, by which a complete social revolution was effected. He issued a proclamation, by the King's order, commanding all Catholics, under penalties, to assist at the Church of England service; proscribing priests and other ecclesiastical persons deriving authority from the See of Rome; forbidding parents to send their children to seminaries beyond the seas, or to keep as private tutors others than those licensed by the Protestant archbishop or bishop. If any priest dared to celebrate Mass, he was liable to a fine of 200 marks and a year's imprisonment; while to join the Romish Church was to be a traitor and to be subject to a like penalty. Churchwardens were to make a monthly report of persons absent from church, and to whet the zeal of wardens and constables, they were for each conviction of offending parties to have a reward of 40s. levied out of the recusant's estates and goods. Catholics might escape these penalties by quitting the country and taking the oath of abjuration, by which they bound themselves to abjure the land and realm of James King of England, France, Scotland, Ireland, to hasten towards a certain port by the most direct highway, and diligently to seek a passage and tarry there but one flood and ebb. According to one form, quoted by Mr. Meehan, the oath concluded thus—' And unless I have it (a passage) in such a place, I will go every day into the sea up to my knees, essaying to pass over—so God me keep and His holy judgment.'

The Lord Deputy, finding some of the chief Dublin citizens refractory, summoned sixteen of them before the Privy Council, censured them for recusancy, and imprisoned them in the castle during pleasure; inflicting upon six the fine of 100*l*. each, and upon three 50*l*. each. The King, who was fond of divinity, was delighted with this method of extending the Reformed Religion in Ireland. Congratulating his Deputy, he expressed a hope that many, by such means, might be brought to conformity who would hereafter 'give thanks to God for being drawn by so gentle a constraint to their own good.' This gentle constraint was imposed in all directions. The Privy Council decreed that none but a member of the Church of England could hold any office under the Crown. The old Catholic families humbly remonstrated, and their chief men were flung into prison. Sir Patrick Barnwell, their agent, was sent to London to petition for them, and was forthwith committed to the Tower for contempt. Henry Ussher, then Archbishop of Armagh, carried out the system of exclusion in his own diocese, which included the territories of Tyrone, who was forbidden to have Mass in his own house. Against this he protested as a violation of the Royal word, promising that the people might have liberty to worship in their private houses. The answer was decided and imperative. His Majesty had made up his mind to disallow liberty of worship, and his people, whether they liked it or not, must repair to their parish churches. Bishop Montgomery of Derry met Tyrone one day at Dungannon. The Earl said, ' My Lord, you have two or three bishoprics, but yet you are not content with them, but seek the lands of my earldom.' ' My Lord,' replied the Bishop, ' your earldom has swollen so big with the lands of the Church that it will burst if it be not vented.' The Bishop was particularly anxious that O'Neill should have no territory in the country of O'Cahan, whom he claimed as a tributary, because O'Cahan was of great power ' to offend or benefit the poor city of Derry ; its new bishop and people cast out from the heart and head into the remotest part of Ireland where life would be unsafe until the whole region was well settled with civil subjects. If this be not brought to pass, we may say, " *Fuimus Troes—Fuit Ilium*." '

This was done very soon after. For O'Neill and O'Donel, being charged with a conspiracy to murder the Viceroy, and with plotting and preparing for a Spanish invasion, and being closely beset on every side by enemies among the Protestant settlers, they at length lost confidence in themselves and in their destiny, and secretly fled from the country. They embarked with their families at Lough Swilly, in a ship under French colours, and after being tempest-tossed for three weeks, they dropped anchor in the harbour of Quillebœuf, in France, having narrowly escaped shipwreck, and their remaining provisions being one gallon of beer and a cask of water. They proceeded first to Brussels, thence to Louvaine, and found their final resting-place at Rome, where they were placed upon the Pope's civil list. Tyrconnel died in 1608. ' Sorrowful it was,' say the ' Four Masters,' ' to contemplate his early eclipse ; for he was a generous and hospitable lord, to whom the patrimony of his ancestors seemed nothing for his feastings and spendings.' Eight years after Sir Francis Cottington wrote from Madrid—' The Earl of Tyrone is dead at Rome ; by whose death this King saves 500 ducats every month, for so much pension he had well paid him. Upon the news of his death I observed that all the principal Irish entertained in the several parts of this kingdom are repaired unto this court.'

Thus ended the first attempt to overthrow the Reformation, and restore the Pope in Ireland. And thus the way was providentially cleared for the long-desired settlement and plantation of Ulster by the final expatriation of a dynasty which had lasted for 2,000 years.

CHAPTER VIII.

THE PLANTATION OF ULSTER BY JAMES I.

SIR JOHN DAVIS, the Irish Attorney-General, a man of extraordinary ability, who took a most active part in bringing about the great changes of this revolutionary time, writing to the English Prime Minister, Lord Salisbury, stated that the fugitive Earl Tyrone could never be reconciled in heart to the English Government, because 'he ever lived like a free prince, or rather like an absolute tyrant. The law and the ministers thereof were shackles and handlocks unto him. After the Irish manner he made all the tenants of his land villeins. Therefore, to evict any part of that land from him was as grievous unto him as to pinch away the quick flesh from his body. . . . Besides,' he added, 'as for us that are here, we are glad to see the day wherein the countenance and majesty of the law, as civil government, hath banished Tyrone out of Ireland, *which the best army in Europe and the expense of two millions sterling pounds did not bring to pass.* And we hope his Majesty's happy government will work a greater miracle in this country than ever St. Patrick did; for St. Patrick did only banish the poisonous worms, but suffered the *men* full of poison to inhabit the land; but his Majesty's blessed genius will banish all that generation of vipers out of it, and make it, ere it be long, a right fortunate island.'

Certainly St. Patrick did not kill or banish the inhabitants of the country—he came to convert and civilize, not to destroy; neither did he bring an army of foreigners to take possession of the soil and divide it among themselves. It never entered into his head, though living in a barbarous age, that the proper way to evangelize a country was to starve or transport the human beings that lived there; nor to regard men, made in the image of God and redeemed by His Son, as a generation of vipers. The 'blessed genius' of his immaculate Majesty James I., however, was capable of nobler and holier things than were dreamt of in the Christian philosophy of the great Apostle.

At any rate it appears that ideas of a mundane kind entered into the policy of his chief advisers. Sir Geoffrey Fenton, one of these, writing to Lord Salisbury at the same time, said:— 'And now I am to put your lordship in mind what door is open to the King, if the opportunity be taken and well converted, not only to pull down for ever these two proud Houses of O'Neill and O'Donel, but also to bring in colonies to plant both countries to a great increasing of his Majesty's revenues, and to establish and settle the countries perpetually in the Crown; besides, that many well-deserving servitors may be recompensed in the distribution, a matter to be taken to heart, for that it reaches somewhat to his Majesty's conscience and honour to see these poor servitors relieved, whom time and the wars have spent even unto their later years, and now, by this commodity, may be stayed and comforted without charges to his Majesty.'

Salisbury approved the idea of the Plantation, but wished that there might be a *mixture* in it, the natives being made his Majesty's tenants in part, the rest to be divided amongst those who would *reside*; and in no case should a planter receive more than he could well *manure*. He said that this was an oversight in the plantation of Munster, where 12,000 acres were commonly allotted to bankrupts and country gentlemen who never knew the disposition of the Irish. This was wise and just. But Davis had no great faith in the mixture; for he compared the Irish to *weeds* which would grow apace and choke the wheat. Lord Bacon, too, deriving his impressions from the reports of English adventurers hungering for Irish estates, recommended that some of 'the chiefest of the Irish families should be transported to England, and have recompense there for their possessions in Ireland till they were cleansed from the blood, incontinency, and theft which were not the relapses of particular persons, but the very laws of the nation.'

But if the people were to continue quiet and submissive, how was it possible to get possession of their land in any legal form;

and, above all, how was it possible to get rid of the priests, who abstained from politics and quietly devoted themselves to their clerical duties? There was only one way, and that was proposed to the Prime Minister, as the result of the deliberations of the English servants of the Crown in Ireland at that critical time, by the Lord Deputy. He wrote thus :—' If I observed anything during my stay in this kingdom, I may say *that it is not lenity and good works that will reclaim the Irish, but an iron rod and severity of justice for the restraint and punishment of those firebrands of sedition, the priests; nor can we think of any other remedy but to proclaim them and their relievers and harbourers,* TRAITORS.'

Fatal words for the Irish race! But how were the ' traitors' to be got rid of? Great armies and the expenditure of 2,000,000*l.*, equal to about 6,000,000*l.* in our day, had failed to accomplish the philanthropic purpose of exterminating the inhabitants of Ulster. In view of this difficulty the Lord Deputy writes again :—' I have often said and written it is FAMINE *that must consume the Irish,* as our *swords* and other endeavours work not that speedy effect which is expected. Hunger would be a better, because a speedier, weapon to employ against them than the sword.' Speedy as that Christian plan might be, however, he did not wait for it. Jehovah gave the Israelites of old a choice of plagues. But the blessed genius of James I., working by his ' godly' statesmen in the seventeenth century, visited the unfortunate Irish with all the plagues at once—the sword, famine, and pestilence. We have seen that English armies in Munster spent weeks in the diligent destruction of corn and cattle, the burning of houses and the killing of men, women and children, and every living thing they met on their march, just like ancient Arabs; and here in Ulster we find the Viceroy reporting with exultation his progress in the same evangelistic work. He says :—' I burned all along the Lough [Neagh] within four miles of Dungannon, and *killed* 100 *people, sparing none, of what quality, age, or sex soever; besides many burned to death. We killed man, woman, and child; horse, beast, and whatsoever we could find.*'

This was beating St. Patrick with a vengeance! But, immediately after the flight of the Earls, it was feared that they would be able to rouse the Catholic Powers on the Continent to interpose for the protection of their brethren in Ireland. Consequently a policy of conciliation was ostentatiously proclaimed and circulated far and wide, lest the maddened people, inspired by a gleam of hope, would rise and turn upon the ruthless exterminators. The inhabitants of Ulster were, therefore, solemnly assured that they had nothing whatever to fear; that his Majesty would secure to them their lands and goods without trouble or molestation from his officers, so long as they lived as dutiful and obedient subjects. 'His Majesty will graciously receive all and every of his loyal subjects into his own immediate safeguard and protection, giving them full assurance to defend them and every of them by his kingly power from all violence or wrong which any loose persons among themselves or any foreign force shall attempt against them.' Notwithstanding the treason of their chiefs, the King would 'extend such grace and favour to the loyal inhabitants of their territories that none of them should be impeached, troubled, or molested in their own lands, goods, or bodies, they continuing in their loyalty, and yielding unto his Majesty such rents and duties as shall be agreeable to justice and equity.' These gracious promises, however, were forgotten as soon as the danger was over. O'Dougherty, the chief of Innishowen, who had been brought up as a loyal subject, and trained in all knightly accomplishments, was unfortunately persuaded by evil advisers to revolt. Having surprised Culmore Castle, on the banks of the Foyle, and also the city of Derry, the governor of which he brutally murdered, committing many other atrocities, and reducing the town to a heap of ashes, in which Bishop Montgomery's valuable library was destroyed; and having been himself killed soon after, his vast territory was added to the regions already forfeited to the Crown. The insurgent leaders and the dangerous kerne were now effectually cleared off in various ways by the English troops, aided by treacherous Irishmen; and the whole country was overrun by the King's troops. Sir Arthur Chichester, with a numerous retinue, including the Attorney-General Davis, sheriffs, lawyers, provosts-marshal, engineers, and 'geographers,' made a grand progress, and penetrated for the first time the district of Innishowen, which was to become the inheritance of his family, the great house of Donegal. 'As we passed through the glens and forests,' wrote Sir John Davis, 'the wild inhabitants did as much wonder to see the King's Deputy as the ghosts did to see Æneas alive in hell.' In this exploring tour a thorough knowledge of the country was for the first time obtained. And as the result, the Attorney-General reported that 'before Michaelmas he would be ready to present to his Majesty a perfect survey of six whole counties which he now hath in actual possession in the province of Ulster, a greater extent of land than any prince in Europe hath in his own hands to dispose of.' O'Cahan, the chief of a very fertile district lying between the Foyle and the Blackwater, having committed himself like the rest, was a prisoner in Dublin Castle when a Royal Commission met in his house at Limavaddy for the purpose of enquiring into the extent of the lands forfeited in all the Ulster principalities. It consisted of the Primate Ussher, Montgomery, Bishop of Derry, and Sir John Davis. It soon went abroad that it was determined to remove the native population, in order that those fine tracts of territory should be planted with Protestant colonists from England and Scotland. The Catholic inhabitants ventured to recall to the recollection of the new rulers the Royal promises made to them through the Lord Deputy, that they should be protected in the enjoyment of their lands and goods; but they were bitterly disappointed. They ventured, however, to hope that, so much of the summer being spent before the Commissioners came down, 'so great cruelty would not be showed as to remove them upon the edge of winter from their houses, and in the very season when they were employed in making their harvest.' Sir Toby Caulfield, ancestor of the Earl of Charlemont, relates that they held discourse among themselves that, if this course had been taken with them in war time, it had had some colour of justice; but, being pardoned and their land given to them, and they having lived under law ever since, and being ready to submit themselves to the mercy of the law for any offence they can be charged withal since their pardoning, they concluded to be the greatest cruelty that ever was inflicted upon any people.'

The general opinion of Christendom, and of all the civilised world beyond Christendom, would agree that this conclusion of the poor Catholic peasantry of Ulster was perfectly right; and, save Mr. Carlyle and Mr. Froude, all historians have concurred in the same conviction. Only such historians as these, if there be any more such, would ascribe to natural depravity and Celtic perversity, or Popish idolatry, the fact to which Sir Toby Caulfield testified, when he said 'there is not a more discontented people in Christendom; the hearts of the Irish are against us; we have only a handful of men in entertainment, so ill paid that every one is out of heart, and our resources so discredited by borrowing and not repaying, that we cannot get up 1,000l. in twenty days if the safety of the kingdom depended upon it. The Irish are hopeful of the return of the fugitives or invasion from foreign parts.' Can we wonder that they should turn for relief from such cruel oppression to any quarter under heaven where a single gleam of hope was visible?

The Ulster plantation was committed in the first instance to the city of London. King James, in proposing it, placed before them the most laudable objects. He said: 'We therefore, deeply and heartily commiserating the wretched state of the said province, have esteemed it to be a work worthy of a Christian prince and of our royal office to stir up and recall the same province from superstition, rebellion, calamity, and poverty, which heretofore have horribly raged therein, to religion, obedience, strength, and prosperity.' His beloved and faithful subjects, 'the mayor and commonalty, and citizens of our City of London—burning with a flagrant zeal to promote such our pious intention in this behalf'—had undertaken a considerable part of the said plantation in Ulster, and were making progress therein. . . . He was not ignorant how much the real accomplishment of the plantation concerned the future peace and safety of that kingdom, but if there was no reason of State to press it forward, he would yet pursue and effect that object with the same earnestness, merely for the goodness and morality of it; esteeming the settling of religion, the introducing of civility, order, and government among a barbarous and unsubjected people to be acts of piety, and glory, and worthy also a Christian prince to endeavour.

This would have been all very well if the barbarous and unsubjected people had been allowed to enjoy their houses and lands, and civil rights, as he had promised; and if the new settlers had laboured in a Christian spirit to instruct and civilise them, treating them as fellow-subjects on the principle of civil and religious equality—a principle which was as good then as it is now, and would then have been tenfold more fruitful of loyalty and morality than it has proved in our day, when the Roman Catholics have been alienated, and hardened and prejudiced by centuries of misgovernment. But the policy adopted was a policy of the *sternest exclusion*, which thrust the native population entirely out of the pale of civilisation.

I have to do with the Plantation here, however, only so far as it bears upon the religious history of the province. The plantation scheme was said to be the work of the Privy Council of Ireland, and submitted by them for adoption by the English Government. It was arranged that the lands escheated in each county should be divided into four parts, whereof two should be subdivided into proportions of about 1,000 acres each, a third part into proportions of 1,500 acres each, and a fourth into proportions of 2,000 acres. Every proportion was to be made into a *parish*; a church was to be erected on it, and the minister endowed with glebe land, the endowment varying according to the proportions, that is, 60, 90, and 120 acres; while the whole of the tithes and duties of every parish should be allotted to the incumbent as well as the glebe. The Primate's share in the county of Armagh was 2,400 acres; the glebes comprised 4,650 acres; the Dublin University got 1,200 acres, and the Free School at Armagh 720. After these deductions, and allowances to two Irish chiefs—Sir T. MacHenry and Sir Henry O'Neill—there remained for the undertakers in this county 55,620 acres, making in all forty-two proportions.

But Derry, henceforth called Londonderry, was the headquarters of the plantation. The London Companies, who had undertaken the work, did not carry it on in a satisfactory manner. They had committed the management to a representative body, called the 'Irish Society,' and they were so far from carrying out the ideas of James I., that sixteen years after they had been invested with their estates, powers, and privileges, his son Charles I.

found it necessary to bring them into the Star Chamber in 1631. He said, 'Our father, of blessed memory, in his wisdom and singular care, both to fortify and preserve that country of Ireland from foreign and inward foes, and also for the better establishment of true religion, justice, and civility and commerce, found it most necessary to erect British plantations there, and to that end ordained and published many politic and good orders; and, for the encouragement of planters, gave them large proportions and privileges. Above the rest, his grace and favour was most enlarged to the Londoners, who undertook the plantation of a considerable part of Ulster, and were specially chosen for their ability and professed zeal to public works; and yet advertisements have been given from time to time, not only by private men, but all succeeding deputies and commissioners sent from hence, and chosen there and being many of them of our council—that the Londoners for private lucre have broken and neglected both their general printed ordinances and other particular directions, given by us and our council here, so as if they shall escape unpunished, all others would be heartened to do the like, and in the end to expose that our kingdom to former confusions and dangers,' &c.

This proceeding on the part of the Crown was ascribed to Bishop Bramhall of Derry, who had come over with Lord Strafford as his chaplain. The result was, that in the year 1632 the whole county of Londonderry was sequestrated, and the rents levied for the King's use, the bishop being appointed receiver, and authorised to make leases. The Lord Chancellor, with the concurrence of the other judges, decreed 'that the letters patent should be surrendered and cancelled.' This decree was duly executed.

Cromwell, however, reinstated the Londoners in their possessions, and Charles II. granted a new charter to the same Companies. It was founded on a system of *protection and corporate exclusiveness*, the most perfect and the most thorough that ever existed in the three kingdoms, except at Bandon—the Derry of the south. The grants made to the Irish Society in the name of the Companies included the city of Derry with 4,000 acres of land around it, besides bog and barren mountains; also a large tract of land about the town of Coleraine, with all the fishing, hawking, fowling, &c., in all the places, shores, and coasts, at their will and pleasure. The grants were most comprehensive, and they were made without any reservation in favour of the tenants or the old inhabitants, saving some portions of land given by letters patent by James I. to certain Irish gentlemen who were made freeholders under a small yearly rent. The 'Londoners' obtained the most extraordinary privileges as traders. They had free quarters in every port throughout the kingdom; they were to be at home everywhere, while they treated all but the members of their own body as '*foreigners.*' By royal charter they were to be 'for ever quit and free, and all their things throughout all Ireland, of all tolls, wharfage, murage, anchorage, beaconage, pavage, pontage, piccage, stallage, passage, and of all other tolls and duties.' The 'foreigners,' that is, all the rest of his Majesty's subjects in Ireland, were forbidden to buy or sell, or practise any trade in this sanctuary of freedom and head-centre of civility, or the suburbs and liberties thereof. The 'foreigners' about the city could not even buy or sell from one another, but must bring their commodities to pay toll within the wharves of the Londoners. Similar exclusive privileges were conferred upon the Corporation of Coleraine. Such was the system established by the enlightened city of London, about the middle of the seventeenth century, in its model communities in Ireland. Such were its model schools of freedom, its fountains of civilising and Christianising influences which were to reclaim and convert the barbarous and superstitious natives into industrious citizens and loyal Protestants. What the natives beheld in Londonderry was, in fact, a royal organisation of selfishness, bigotry, and monopoly of the most intensely exclusive and repulsive character. In one sense, the Londoners in Derry showed that they prized very much indeed the blessings of civilisation, for they kept them all to themselves, as a miser keeps his gold. Unlike the miser, they displayed their treasures in the most tantalising manner. The golden fountain was flowing before the thirsty Irish, but they were to apply their lips to it at their peril. Fines which no Irishman was able to pay must be the penalty for every attempt at civilisation. From the very beginning, indeed, every possible care was taken to keep out the natives. The citizens were forbidden to take Irish apprentices, and to meet their wants poor children were brought from Christ's Hospital in London and elsewhere. These became the originals of the ''Prentice Boys of Derry,' who won so much glory during its memorable siege.

It is very instructive to observe how utterly the exclusive and protective system failed in its object in keeping out the natives, and keeping down the Roman Catholics. It was there as '*thorough*' as thorough could be. The wall of prejudice—the moral and social barrier—seemed to be as thick and strong and as well guarded as the wall that surrounds the city, and stands to this day an enduring monument of the old exclusiveness. In 1622 Sir Thomas Phillips made a muster roll, in which he gave 110 as the number of settlers in the city of Derry capable of bearing arms, and the list included but two *Irish* names, McSwine and Dogherty. So late as the year 1708 the Derry corporation considered itself nothing more or less than a '*branch of the city of London*.' In the memory of persons still living, there was no Catholic house within the walls, and Catholic servants were obliged to sleep outside the sacred enclosure. Yet, strange to say, the favoured population did not increase very fast. In 1626 they were only 109 families in the city; and Archbishop King stated that ' in 1690 the whole population of the parish was about 700.' But the irrepressible Irish increased and multiplied around the walls with alarming rapidity. 'The tide of native population rose steadily against the ramparts of exclusion, and could no more be kept back than the tide in the Foyle. The census of 1821 showed that the city had a population of 9,313 within the walls. The religious census of 1834 gave the following results:—Population of the Established Church, 3,314; Presbyterians, 6,083; Roman Catholics, 10,299. The figures in 1861 were—Roman Catholics, 12,036; Protestants of all denominations, 8,839; showing a majority of Irish and Catholics in this branch of the city of London, with its famous motto of ' No surrender!' amounting to 3,197. This very nearly equals the total number of Church people which the exclusive system, with all its protection, its bounties and its privileges, its endowments and its monopolies, could produce in the course of two centuries! What an instructive fact!

Viewing these results, Mr. Froude would, perhaps, confidently appeal to an American audience, and ask 'what better could the English have done for their Church and for the natives during the seventeenth and eighteenth centuries in their exercise of dominant power in Ireland?' It might be answered, that if the Roman Catholics had been admitted within the pale of English civilisation, if they had been instructed in the industrial arts by the settlers, if the Gospel had been preached in their own language in the spirit of Bishop Bedell, if their rights as British subjects had been respected—the results with regard to religion would have been very different. The priesthood would not have been driven for protection to Foreign Powers; the civil wars thence arising would not have desolated the land; the Established Church would have grown by degrees into a really national institution, and men of the Celtic race would have been among its most zealous and efficient ministers. As it was, the Church of Rome has proved incomparably the greatest gainer by coercion, and her advocates have derived from it their most powerful pleas, and a moral force which Protestantism has found irresistible.

CHAPTER IX.

FOUNDATION OF THE PRESBYTERIAN CHURCH.

ONE of the first of the Scottish ministers who came over with the settlers gives a graphic account of their character and of the state of the province at that time. It is very instructive and interesting, enabling us to realise the change that has been effected by the plantation. He remarks that 'the English had been more tenderly bred and entertained in better quarters than they could find in Ireland. They were very unwilling to flock here except for the good land such as they had before at home, or to good cities where they might trade; both of which in these days were scarce enough here. Besides that the marshiness and fogginess of this island was still found unwholesome to English bodies, more tenderly bred and in better air; so that we have seen in our own time multitudes of them die of a flux called here the country disease at their first entry. These things were such discouragements that the new English came but very slowly, and the old English were become no better than the Irish.' He adds, that the king being himself a Scotchman had a 'natural love to have Ireland planted with Scots, as being, beside their loyalty, of a middle temper between the English tender and the Irish rude being, and a great deal more likely to plant Ulster than the English, it lying far both from the English native land, and more from their humour, while it lies nigh to Scotland, and the inhabitants not so far from the ancient Scots manners; so that it might be hoped that the Irish untoward living would be met both with equal firmness, if need be, and be especially allayed by the example of more civility and Protestant profession than in former times had been among them.'

Between the two races, however, the face of the country was soon changed. The decayed and deserted towns were rapidly replenished with inhabitants, the lands were gradually cleared of the woods, marshes were drained, substantial houses were erected by the farmers on their allotments, the chief undertakers being required to reside and build houses surrounded by ' bawns ' strong enough to protect their cattle against the plundering incursions of the expelled natives, who issued from their fastnesses in the woods. These hungry ' woodkernes ' often swooped down upon their prey with great audacity. Thus Sir Toby Caulfield's people were driven every night ' to lay up all his cattle as it were in ward; and do he and his what they could, the wolf and the woodkerne within culver's shot of his fort had oftentimes their share. Even in the old English Pale Sir John King and Sir Henry Harrington, within half a mile of Dublin, had to do the like, for those fore-named enemies did every night survey the field to the very wards.'

Notwithstanding these difficulties, proofs were everywhere exhibited of industry, order, and peace within the border of the colony. It was then that some of the greatest of the noble houses of Ulster were founded. Sir Hugh Clotworthy obtained the lands of Antrim ' both fruitful and good, and invited thither several of the English, very good men.' ' Chichester,'[1] a worthy man, had an estate given him in the county of Antrim, where he improved his interest, built the prospering mart of Belfast and a stately palace at Carrickfergus. Conway[2] had an estate given him in the county of Antrim, and built a town, afterwards called Lisnagarvie (now called Lisburn), and this was planted with a colony of English also. Moses Hill had woodlands given him, which woods being thereafter demolished left a fair and beautiful country where a late heir of the Hills built a town called Hillsborough.'[3] All these lands, and more, were given to the English gentlemen, worthy persons, who afterwards increased and made noble and loyal families in places where formerly there had been nothing but robbing, treason, and rebellion.'

The same old writer adds, that of the Scots nation there were

[1] Now represented by the Marquis of Donegal.

[2] To Conway, who left no issue, succeeded the Seymours, whose representative was the late Marquis of Hertford, now, happily for the tenantry, succeeded by Sir William Wallace, Bart.

[3] He founded the House of Downshire.

the families of the Balfours, of the Forbeses, of the Grahams, two of the Stewarts, and not a few of the Hamiltons. The MacDonnells founded the earldom of Antrim, the Hamiltons[1] the earldom of Strabane. There were besides many knights of that name—Sir Frederick, Sir George, Sir Francis, Sir Charles, his son, and Sir Hawk, all Hamiltons; for they prospered above all others in this country after the first admittance of the Scots into it. The territory of the Irish chief Con O'Neill became the property of Montgomery of Ards and Hamilton of Clandeboye. 'But land without inhabitants is a burden without relief.' The Irish were gone, the ground was desolate, rents must be paid to the king, and of tenants there were none to pay them. Hence the lords shared their lands with their friends and countrymen who became freeholders under them. Then came Scots in great numbers, becoming tenants and subtenants to their countrymen, whose manner and way they knew. As the colony multiplied they built towns nearly all on a uniform plan, with the market square, the town hall, the church, the meeting-house, and the school. Thus originated the towns of Donaghadee, Grey Abbey, Bangor, Newtown Ards, Killeleagh, Lisburn, Belfast, Antrim, and many others. The parliament now repealed the barbarous laws which had been passed to prevent the English inhabitants of the kingdom from intermarrying or associating with either the Scotch or the Irish. The latter were in many cases permitted to occupy the poorer land in the midst of the new settlers, and to assist them with their labour. They were no longer branded by statute as the 'natural enemies' of the Government, whom it was felony to marry or to employ as nurses. These Presbyterian settlers were subsequently joined by many of the Puritans from England; and some of them being promoted to bishoprics and other ecclesiastical dignities, they gave a Low Church temper to the Established Church, which it always retained.

It seems there was much need of this leaven of Puritanism, from the character of the settlers who came from the Land of Cakes. The contemporary chronicler just quoted, a clergyman named Stewart, describes a state of things more like the morals and manners of the Restoration than of the Commonwealth. From

[1] Represented by the Duke of Abercorn.

Scotland came many, from England not a few, yet all of them generally the scum of both nations, who, from debt, or breaking, or fleeing from justice, or seeking shelter, came hither, hoping to be without fear of man's justice in a land where there was nothing, or but little yet, of the fear of God. And in a few years there flocked such a multitude of people from Scotland that these northern counties of Down, Antrim, Londonderry, &c., were in a good measure planted which had been waste before. Yet most of the people were void of godliness, who seemed rather to flee from God in this enterprise than to follow their own mercy. Albeit, as they cared little for any church, so God seemed to care as little for them.' The good Scotch minister goes on to say that they were entertained merely with the relics of Popery, under a sort of anti-Christian hierarchy, by a number of careless men. 'Thus on all hands atheism increased, iniquity abounded, with contention, fighting, murder, adultery, &c. Their carriage made them to be abhorred at home in their native land, insomuch that *going for Ireland* was looked on as a miserable mark of a deplorable person—yea, it was turned into a proverb; and one of the worst expressions of disdain that could be invented was to tell a man that *Ireland would be his hinder end.*' [1]

This account is confirmed by other contemporary writers, and it shows that the character of Ulster as the model province of Ireland is not to be ascribed to the purity of the stock of men with which it was first planted, but to the religious and moral culture and discipline brought to bear upon them by the Presbyterian Church through the ministry of the Bruces, the Blairs, and Livingstones, and others of that stamp. They were powerfully aided by the influence of some of the lords of the soil, thoroughly good men, among whom the Hamiltons had honourable mention, particularly Sir James Hamilton, the ancestor of Earl Dufferin, now Governor-General of Canada—who had been ennobled by the title of Lord Clandeboye. 'To my discerning,' says Livingstone, 'he was the man who most resembled Jesus Christ in all his carriage that ever I saw, and was so far reverenced of all, even by the wicked, that he was oft troubled with that Scripture "Woe to you when all men speak well of you."' His descendant

[1] 'History of the Presbyterian Church in Ireland,' by J. S. Reid, D.D., vol. i. p. 91.

at the present day might well be troubled for the same cause, for who is there that does not speak well of Lord Dufferin? Sir Hugh Clotworthy, ancestor of Lord Masserine, also exerted himself as a religious and social reformer, and was a man of much influence. Through their exertions and those of the eminent ministers they induced to settle in the country, a great and permanent improvement was effected among the people.

According to Dr. Reid, the learned historian of the Presbyterian Church, most of the northern clergy in possession of the parish churches were at this period Nonconformists both in principle and practice. They conformed only just so far as was requisite for their security and maintenance under the protection of the legal establishment. In some of the dioceses this was all the bishops required. When succeeding prelates became more strict in exacting uniformity, the clergy generally yielded, though with reluctance, the canonical obedience required by their superiors. But in the seclusion of the parishes they continued to observe the Presbyterian forms so congenial to the habits and prejudices of their people. A more searching intolerance was soon after enthroned in high places. The good Primate Ussher was not disposed to molest them, but when the Lord Deputy Wentworth arrived, a policy of persecution was carried out with relentless severity. The consequence was that a number of the Nonconformist ministers were suspended by the bishops. Blair, one of the most eminent of the sufferers, went to London to appeal to the king, Charles I., armed with letters from noblemen and gentlemen to their friends at Court. Lord Stirling, then Secretary of State, promised to forward his suit, at which the good minister was so overjoyed that he said 'I did literally exult and leap. But when the timorous man did see my forwardness, he, fearing Bishop Laud more than God, did faint, and break his promise.' Another minister laid the petition before the king, who returned a gracious answer directed to Lord Strafford, who had not yet arrived in Ireland; for, although appointed Lord Deputy in January 1632, he did not enter upon his government until the July following. Mr. Blair lost no time in waiting upon him in Dublin; but his reception from that imperious churchman was anything but encouraging. He reviled the Kirk of Scotland and rebuked the petitioner, bidding him come to his right wits and then he should be regarded. 'With this intelligence I went to Archbishop Ussher, which was so disagreeable to him that it drew tears from his eyes; but he could not help us.' All hopes of relief were thus blasted, and in the tone and manner of the Deputy they discerned the storm that was gathering blackness throughout the kingdom.

By the 'Graces' of Charles I., it had been stipulated that all Scottish men, 'undertakers' in Ulster and other places, should be made free citizens of Ireland, and that no advantage for want of denization should be taken against the heirs or assigns of those that were dead. The king consented to the calling of parliament to give the sanction of law to those 'Graces'; but he did not keep his word. When the Irish parliament assembled in July, 1634, having voted an extraordinary supply, the Commons presented a remonstrance to the king urging the ratification of the 'Graces.' But Lord Strafford refused to transmit this remonstrance to his royal master, for which unconstitutional proceeding the latter was peculiarly grateful. Writing soon after, the king said, 'Your last public despatch has given me a great deal of contentment, and especially for keeping off the envy of a necessary negative from me of those unreasonable " Graces " that that people expected from me.' Subsequently, however, as already intimated, the Irish parliament passed an Act for the naturalization of all the Scottish nation which were born before his late Majesty King James's accession to the throne of England and Ireland. Those persons having been regarded by the laws as 'foreigners,' being made capable of legally acquiring or holding property within the realm, the king was assured in the preamble that 'the grievance in question was a sad discouragement and disheartening unto many of his subjects of Scotland that would otherwise have planted themselves here for the further civilising, strengthening, and securing this realm against rebels at home and all foreign invasion.'

The truth of this was so obvious, and the condition of the English colony was often so critical, that it seems almost unaccountable that the Scottish settlers were not received from the first joyfully, and invested with all the rights of British subjects. But the Irish parliament was composed exclusively of Episcopalians and ruled by the Bishops, and by the peers who were their relatives and intimate friends, and by whom the members for the House of Commons were for the most part nominated. All this hateful exclusiveness was most detrimental to the country, and so degrading to the king, on whom it imposed a policy of evasion and treachery, meanness and duplicity, that it must have exposed him to the contempt of all honest men.

CHAPTER X.

THE ESTABLISHED CHURCH UNDER CHARLES I., LAUD, AND STRAFFORD.

Now let us see what was the spiritual state and the social and civilising utility of the ecclesiastical body for which those sacrifices were made. Archbishop Laud was a reformer after his fashion,—a restless, energetic man, irritable and arbitrary, with the highest possible notions of sacerdotal power; and he was naturally very much provoked at the prevalence of Puritanism in the Irish Church. Lord Strafford was a man after his own heart in this respect, being at the same time utterly unscrupulous as to the means he employed to carry out his purposes. Carried out they must be, no matter what obstacle stood in the way. He instituted enquiries, and found that throughout the greater part of the country, owing to the neglect of the bishops, the parish churches, and even the cathedrals, were in a wretched state of dilapidation, a great part of the church revenues having been alienated and appropriated to the aggrandisement of their own families. The Ecclesiastical Courts were mere engines of oppression and extortion,—engines which were worked with the most ruinous effect. Bishop Burnet, in his Life of Bedell, says: 'Bribes went about almost barefaced, and the exchange they made of penance for money was the worst sort of simony, being, in effect, the very same abuse which gave the world such scandal when it was so indecently practised in the Church of Rome.' Bishop Bedell himself sent to Laud a sketch of the religious condition of the kingdom. His own cathedral, together with the bishop's house, were 'down to the ground.' The parish churches were all in a manner ruined, unroofed, and unrepaired. The clergy, being Englishmen, had not the 'tongue of the people,' and could not converse with them or perform for them any divine offices. Many of them held two, three, or four or more vicarages each. This account was corroborated by Bramhall, an English prelate of a very different stamp, whom Oliver Cromwell called the Canterbury of Ireland, from his resemblance to Laud. In a letter to that primate he wrote—'It is hard to say whether the church be more ruinous and sordid, or the people more irreverent.' I found one of them in Dublin, a parish church, converted to the Lord Deputy's stable; a second, to a nobleman's dwelling-house; the choir of a third to a tennis court, the vicar acting as the keeper. In Christ Church, the principal church in Ireland, whither the Lord Deputy and Council repaired every Sunday, the vaults, from one end of the minster to the other, are made into *tippling rooms* for beer, wine, and tobacco, let all to *popish recusants*, and by them to others,—much frequented in time of Divine service! The inferior sort of ministers, Bramhall described as below all degrees of contempt in respect to their poverty and ignorance. He then proceeds: 'The boundless heaping together of benefices by *commendams* and dispensations in the superior courts is but too apparent; yea, even often by plain usurpations and indirect compositions made between the patrons as well ecclesiastical as lay, and the incumbents; by which the least part, many times not above 40 shillings, rarely 10*l.* in the year, is reserved for him that should serve the altar; insomuch that it is affirmed that by all or some of these means one bishop in the remoter parts of the kingdom doth hold three-and-twenty benefices with cure! Generally their residences are as little as their livings. Seldom any suitor petitions for less than three vicarages at a time.'

This is the way in which those English shepherds used the church property they had seized at the Reformation for the purpose of converting and civilising the wild Irish! This was the example of honesty they set to an impoverished people denounced for their thievish propensities! This is the way in which the new Anglican nobility, shooting up from the Church establishment, struck its roots into the Irish soil and derived its sap from the fat of the land. But the ecclesiastical reformers who began their work under Charles I. had as little idea of justice and fair dealing, or fidelity to public trust, as the aristocratic hierarchy which they undertook to correct. Lord Strafford went to Dublin with the express intention of making his master 'the most absolute sovereign in Europe;' and Archbishop Laud set to work with the no less determined purpose to make the Church *sacerdotal and dominant over the State.* Henceforth, therefore, all Irish Sees, as they became vacant, were filled by High Churchmen of the Laud stamp, in whose eyes there was nothing in human depravity so abominable as schism. The Lord Deputy required the aid of such men to carry out his schemes of absolutism, and he found ready instruments in most of the prelates.

He had ordered a Convocation of the Clergy to meet simultaneously with the Parliament to adopt the Articles of the Church of England, so that the Irish Articles and Canons, as savouring of Puritanism, might become a dead letter. The Convocation went to work conscientiously, digesting the canons, &c., to the best of their judgment and ability; but Strafford finding that they were not doing what he wanted, sent for the Chairman, directing him to bring the Book of Canons noted in the margin together with a draft he was to present that afternoon to the House. The spirit of the man is admirably displayed in the letter to Laud, in which he describes exultingly the manner in which he snubbed the Convocation, and how that brow-beaten, well-whipped body servilely obeyed his lordly dictation, in framing laws for their Church, and especially that sacred bond of union by which it has been alleged the English and Irish episcopalians were made the united Church of England and Ireland. The Book of Canons was brought to the Lord Deputy as he had ordered; but he said : ' When I came to open the book and run over the *deliberandums* in the margin, I confess I was not so much moved since I came into Ireland. I told him certainly not a Dean of Limerick, but an Ananias, had sat in the chair of that Committee: however, sure I was an Ananias had been there in spirit if not in body, with all the fraternities and conventicles of Amsterdam—that I was ashamed and scandalized with it above measure.'

The Dictator immediately issued orders to the Lord Primate, the Bishops of Meath, Kilmore, Raphoe and Derry, with Dean Leslie, the Prolocutor, and the whole Committee, to wait upon him next morning. They obeyed, and he publicly rebuked them for acting so unlike churchmen; told them that a few petty clerks had presumed to make articles of faith without the privity or consent of State or Bishop, 'as if they purposed at once to take away all government and order forth of the church. But those heady and arrogant courses he would not endure, nor would he suffer them either to be mad in the Convocation or in their pulpits.' He gave them strict injunctions as to what the Convocation should do and should not do. Their sole business was to say content or not content to the Articles of England, and not to discuss them. He directed the Primate to frame a canon on the subject. This did not please him, so he took up his pen and wrote one himself, whereupon his Grace came to him instantly and said, 'he feared the canon would never pass in such a form as his lordship had made, but he was hopeful it might pass as he had drawn it himself. He therefore besought the Lord Deputy to think a little better of it.' This was too much for the Viceroy's patience; and he thus describes what followed: 'But I confess having taken a little jealousy that these proceedings were not open and free to those ends I had my eye upon; it was too late now to persuade or affright me. I told his lordship I was resolved to put it to them in those very words, and was most confident there were not six in the house that would refuse them, telling him, by the sequel we should see whether his lordship or myself better understood their minds on that point, and by that I would be content to be judged; only, for order's sake, I desired his lordship would vote this order first in the Upper House of Convocation, and so vote it and pass the question beneath also. He adds that he enclosed the Canon to Dean Leslie, which accordingly was that afternoon unanimously voted, first by the bishops and then by the rest of the clergy.' This was the first Irish Canon.

The letters of this overbearing and insolent tyrant tell very frankly how the union of the two Churches was effected, and by what Christian means the Irish Establishment received its constitution. Surely a more humiliating spectacle was not presented in the whole course of ecclesiastical history than by the Irish Convocation—the hierarchy—with the venerable Primate Ussher at its head, thus abjectly submitting to the dictation of the secular power, not merely *circa sacra*, but in the most spiritual affairs of their Church. The Viceroy, however, continued to carry out his policy with a high hand; and in order more effectually to accomplish his object, he established in Dublin a 'High Commission,' to support the ecclesiastical courts and officers. The objects of this Commission were two: first, to bring the people to a conformity of religion; and second, to raise a good revenue for the Crown.

The first work to which the High Commission directed its attention was to exterminate the Presbyterians in Ulster. The new Bishop of Down, Henry Leslie, a Scotchman, was the most vigorous agent of this policy. He was unrelenting in the persecution of his countrymen who had been officiating in that diocese. So severe were his measures, that a number of ministers and people prepared to emigrate to the wilds of America; but the vessel proving unseaworthy, and being caught in a storm, they were obliged to put back; and so the scheme of colonization was abandoned at that time, and the fugitives took refuge in the west of Scotland. Bramhall, Bishop of Derry, was equally active in that part of the country. No one dared to resist or remonstrate; if he did, he was immediately brought into the Dublin Star Chamber, where the High Commission sat, and this was ruin. Consequently, subordinate officials tortured and plundered the Nonconformists without restraint wherever they had an opportunity. The Bishop of Down was authorized to arrest and imprison during pleasure the Presbyterians of his diocese. Many were incarcerated, many fled to Scotland; but the majority, bending before the storm, yielded a reluctant conformity while cursing Prelacy in their hearts. Bishop Leslie was not satisfied with the powers conferred upon him; rather, he complained that the civil authorities interfered to prevent their due exercise, and would not give effect to his excommunications. Consequently, those whom he had forced into conformity revolted. He therefore complained to the Lord Deputy, who replied that if he would give him a list of the offenders, with their places of abode, he would have them brought into the Ecclesiastical Courts by his own pursuivants. He did so, and by that means several of the best families in the country were ruined.

But those powers were not comprehensive enough to carry out the policy of Strafford and Laud. A new measure was adopted, more sweeping, more comprehensive in its reach, more tremendous in its effects than all the rest. This is what was called the ' *Black Oath.*' This oath bound those who took it not only to bear true allegiance to King Charles, but to submit in all due obedience to all his royal commands—to renounce and to abjure all covenants, oaths, and bonds whatsoever contrary to this oath. In vain did the leading Royalists of Ulster entreat that a qualifying phrase might be inserted, such as, 'just commands,' or 'commands according to law.' Implicit submission to everything the king enjoined, whether political or religious, was absolutely demanded. A return was made of all the Scots in each parish; they were assembled in their meeting-houses, and, in presence of the military, each congregation was compelled to take the oath kneeling, their minister setting the example. Women were also obliged to take it; the only class exempted being Roman Catholics. Upon the Presbyterians who refused, the highest penalty short of death was unsparingly inflicted, without distinction of age, rank, or sex. A summary of those atrocities was laid before the Long Parliament in a petition presented by Sir John Clotworthy. From that statement it appeared that the most godly and learned ministers were by the bishops and the commissaries silenced and deprived for not conforming and subscribing to an unlawful canon; that through the hotness of the persecution they were forced to flee the land, and their places were supplied by men unsound in doctrine, profane in life, and cruel in persecution, the bishops conferring the livings upon their own children and retainers *studendi gratiâ*—four, five, six or more benefices to each; that the king's officers were required to execute the bishop's writs, casting honest men and women into prison until they were forced to free themselves by heavy composition; that they usurped with a high hand the judicature of civil causes, imposed fines beyond all bounds, and imprisoned at their pleasure, whereby many were utterly undone; that divers of the prelates did jointly frame and wickedly combine with the

Earl of Strafford that most lawless and scandalous oath imposed upon the Scottish-British among us, who were Protestants, for receiving all commands indefinitely; that very many, as if they had been traitors in the highest degree, were apprehended, examined, reviled, threatened, imprisoned, fettered by threes and fours in iron yokes, some carried up to Dublin in chains and fined in the Star Chamber in thousands beyond ability, and condemned to perpetual imprisonment; divers women were arrested, threatened, and terrified, on the eve of childbirth; others of them, two or three days after their confinements, were so narrowly searched for, that they were fain to fly out of all harbour into woods, mountains, caves, and cornfields, and many days and nights together absent themselves, to the injury of their health, to the death of several, and to the loss of the goods which the enemy at their pleasure made havoc of. 'These, with many more inexpressible, have been the woful result of the yoke drawn up by advice of the prelates, and so unjustly pressed by the authority of the Earl of Strafford.'

Sixteen of the charges against Strafford related to his government of Ireland, and amongst these was his imposing the Black Oath without authority of Parliament. The case of Henry Stewart and his family produced a deep impression on the house. For refusing to take the oath he was fined in the sum of 5,000*l.* (equal to 20,000*l.* of our money); his wife in a similar sum; his two daughters 2,000*l.* each, and his servant 2,000*l.*—a sum of 16,000*l.* levied off one family, equal to about 80,000*l.* in our day. The whole were imprisoned in Dublin at their own charges till the fine should be paid. The petition further stated that the prelates had taken possession of the best lands in every county, pretending that they were church lands, so that there was scarcely a gentleman of any worth whom they had not bereaved of some part of his inheritance, few daring to oppose the unjust commands, and if they did, there was none equal to maintain their rights against that power and oppression. By these means it was stated they had ruined many families, 'destroyed and cast away thousands of souls, and, moreover, in their own persons been a scandal to the Gospel, and a stumbling-block even unto the common enemy by their swearing, cursing, drunkenness, Sabbath breaking, &c.; and by having such servants usually in their families as were the most profane in the kingdom, few others being countenanced by them but such; and if any seemed to be of a holy life, he was scorned and persecuted by them.'[1]

Two things are to be noted in connection with this appalling picture of the Episcopal Church at this time. The first is that while the Presbyterians of Ulster, the industrious hardworking people who were reclaiming the country, increasing its resources, adding to the revenue, and presenting to the natives an example of a peaceful and well-ordered community, were thus cruelly persecuted by their fellow Britons and their fellow Protestants, the Roman Catholic priesthood and people were treated with indulgence and favour. The victims of this ruthless persecution at the hands of Englishmen in Ireland in the seventeenth century were a thoughtful, educated, self-reliant, honest, law-respecting, Bible-reading, God-fearing people; the people to whose industry, and skill, and perseverance, and good conduct, and loyalty, has been truly ascribed the prosperity of Ulster, presenting as it does such a striking contrast to the backward state of the other provinces.

The second point to be noted is that the Protestant clergy and people who were unfortunately involved in the 'Massacre of 1641,' which followed those proceedings, were not the sort of clergy or people which we should regard as martyrs for their religion. As to the bishops and clergy—covetous, greedy, dishonest, usurping, intolerant, cruel, regardless of their professional duties, violators of their solemn trust, irreligious, profane, and abandoned to all sorts of worldliness and licentious indulgence—they demand pity indeed for their sufferings, but deserve little sympathy as Irish Protestants, placed in the country to war with spiritual weapons against ignorance, superstition, and barbarism. The laity, indeed, with their families, their wives, and their children, must be regarded in a different light, because they were left without instruction, without pastoral care or spiritual oversight, by the faithless and rascally men that were paid for preaching the Gospel to them. Besides it has not been sufficiently considered that the rapacious and unscrupulous conduct of the

[1] Read's 'History,' vol. i. p. 275.

Earl of Strafford, in seeking out what he called defective titles, incarcerating and fining sheriffs and juries who would not do his bidding in robbing Catholic gentlemen of their estates which had been confirmed to them by kings and parliaments, was the principal exciting cause of the Revolution of 1641. That the promotion of the Reformed Religion was not his object is plain enough, from the fact that the Roman Catholics, as we have seen, were unmolested, while the Presbyterians were tortured. Their bishops, priests, fraternities, schools and colleges, all flourished until they were betrayed into that disastrous revolt; and we find Bishop Bedall complaining that every parish had its priest and the Catholic hierarchy ' exercise full jurisdiction, and his Majesty is now with the greater part of this country—as to the heart of his subjects; King but at the Pope's discretion!' The Presbyterians were not so completely surprised by the rebellion of 1641 as the Episcopalians. The havoc produced by this outbreak of fanaticism was fearful. The Established Church was now overthrown and desolate. Few of her clergy, and only two of her prelates, remained in Ulster.

CHAPTER XI.

THE MASSACRE OF 1641.

THE English Puritans and the Scottish Covenanters who engaged in the civil war against Charles I. were determined never to lay down their arms till they had made an end of Popery in Ireland. Pym, their celebrated leader, was said to avow that the policy of his party was not to leave a priest alive in the land. Rumours were spread abroad that similar sentiments and purposes had been uttered in Dublin by the Lords Justices, Sir John Parsons, and Sir John Borlase. It was generally believed the former had said, that in twelve months no more Romanists should be seen in the country. Meantime the Irish chiefs were busy intriguing at Rome, Madrid, Paris, and other Continental capitals, clamouring for an invasion of Ireland to restore Catholicity, and to expel the English heretics from the forfeited lands. Philip III. of Spain, an intensely bigoted Catholic, favoured these aspirations, and he kept up an Irish legion under the command of Henry O'Neill, son of the fugitive Earl of Tyrone. It was reported that in 1630 there were in the service of the Archduchess in the Spanish Netherlands alone, 100 Irish officers able to command companies, and 20 fit to be colonels, with many others at Lisbon, Florence, Milan, and Naples. They had in readiness 5,000 stand of arms laid up at Antwerp. The banished Irish ecclesiastics at the same time formed an efficient diplomatic corps at every Catholic Court of Europe. Religious wars, grand expeditions for the extermination of heretics, were popular in those times, for heresy was considered not only a crime in itself—treason against the King of Kings—but a monstrous iniquity pregnant with all sorts of damnable abominations. Hence a crusade against the English Protestants in Ireland was received with general favour on the Continent, and the religious motive was, of course, the one urged loudly and incessantly by the exiled bishops and priests. But with the Irish chiefs, the strongest stimulus was the desire to get possession of their homes and their lands. The most active among these was Rory O'Moore, a man of high character and great ability, with a handsome person and fascinating manners. With him were associated Macguire, two McMahons, two O'Neills, and Magennis. O'Moore visited the country, went through the several provinces, communicated with the remaining chiefs personally, and organised a grand conspiracy to expel the British, and recover the kingdom for Charles II. and the Pope.

The plan agreed upon by the confederates was, that they were to rise when the harvest was gathered in, to make a simultaneous attack upon all the English fortresses, to surprise Dublin Castle (said to contain arms for 12,000 men), bringing with them for these objects all possible aid from the Continent in officers and munitions of war. The opportunity seemed favourable; Dublin Castle was then guarded by only a few pensioners and forty halberdiers. The rising took place on the night of October 22, 1641, but the lords justices had got information of the plot through an informer, just in time to take measures for the defence of the city.

The chief command of the insurgents was taken by Sir Phelim O'Neill, one of the 'Irish gentlemen' who, by a royal favour, were permitted to retain some portion of their ancient patrimony. He was at this time the owner of thirty-eight townlands in the Barony Dunganon, estimated to be then worth 1,600*l.* a year. He might therefore have been content with his position, so far as property was concerned. But, setting aside patriotism, ambition, and religion, it is likely that he distrusted the Government, and feared the doom that had overtaken the other chiefs of his race in Ulster. He began by issuing a proclamation, in which he stated that the insurrection was in no wise intended against the king nor to hurt any of his subjects, either English or Scotch, but only to defend the liberties of the Irish people; promising reparation for any damage that had been done, and that the severest punishment should be inflicted upon the offenders. The insurgents seized in succession the forts of Charlemont and Mountjoy, the towns of Dunganon, Newry, Carrickmacross, Castle Blaney, and Tanderagee, while the O'Reilleys and Maguires overran their own territories in Cavan and Fermanagh. Sir Carvill Magennis wrote from Newry to the heads of the Government in Dublin, saying: 'We are for our lives and liberties. We desire no blood to be shed; but if you mean to shed our blood, be sure we shall be as ready as you for that purpose.' Blood was indeed shed abundantly on both sides, and shed too with the utmost barbarity. However well-disposed insurgent chiefs may be; however humane and honourable, they cannot possibly answer for the consequences when arms are put into the hands of a tumultuous mass of excited, vindictive, drunken men, whose passions are inflamed by a religious fanaticism.

However, the notion common among Protestants, repeated by historians, and credited by learned and eminent men, even in our own day, seems to have no foundation in fact, viz., that the insurgent chiefs planned and designed a *nocturnal massacre of all the Protestant inhabitants*. Mr. Prendergast quotes contemporary authorities, which seem to be decisive upon this point. In the same year was published by 'G. S., a minister of God's Word in Ireland,' '*A Brief Declaration of the Barbarous and Inhuman Dealings of the Irish Rebels, written to excite the English Nation to relieve our poor wives and children that have escaped the Rebels' savage cruelties.*' The account which this writer gives of the plan was this—' On Saturday the rebels were to disarm all the English; on Sunday to seize all their cattle and goods; on Monday, at the watchword " skeane," they were to cut all the English throats.' And then, he adds, ' the former they executed; the third only, (that is, the *massacre*) they failed in.' Though this is stated by an anonymous writer, it is confirmed by the contemporary official documents, which certainly would not diminish or extenuate, however naturally they might exaggerate, the atrocities which the enemy had treacherously perpetrated. The lords justices, in their proclamation of February 8, 1642, more than three months after the alleged event, stated expressly that the massacre had failed. Many thousands had been robbed and spoiled, dispossessed of house and lands, and many murdered on the spot. But 'the chief part of their plots, amongst them *a universal massacre, had been disappointed.*'

'But,' says Mr. Prendergast, 'after Lord Ormonde and Sir Simon Harcourt with their forces, in the month of *April* 1642, had burned the houses of the gentry in the Pale, and committed slaughters of unarmed men; and the Scotch forces in the same month, after beating off Sir Phelim O'Neill's army at Newry, drowned and shot men, women, and priests in that town, who had surrendered on condition of mercy; then it was that Sir Phelim O'Neill's wild followers, in revenge and in fear of the advancing army, massacred their prisoners in some of the towns in Tyrone. The subsequent cruelties were not on one side only, and were magnified to render the Irish detestable, so as to make it impossible for the king to seek their aid without ruining his cause utterly in England.' 'A True Relation of the Proceedings of the Forces in the North of Ireland,' published in 1642, states, that, on May 5 the common soldiers, without orders, took some eighteen of the Irish *women* at Newry, stripped them naked, threw them into the river and drowned them, shooting some in the water; and more had suffered so, but that some of the soldiers were punished.' Another writer, the author of 'A Levite's Lamentation,' published at the same time, says : ' About the 4th May, we put forty of them to death upon the bridge of the Newry, amongst which were two of the Pope's pedlars, two seminary priests; in return for which they slaughtered many prisoners in their custody.' In Dublin, the Bishop of Meath, preaching in Christ Church Cathedral, pleaded for mercy to the Irish *women and children*; but an English officer present was so offended at this clemency, that he threw up his commission in disgust. Such was the bloodthirsty spirit of the times !

From depositions made at the time it would be easy for the historian to collect soul-harrowing descriptions of the atrocities perpetrated against the Protestant families, if that could serve any good purpose. But it must serve a very bad purpose if the deplorable facts are not fairly presented—if, on the one side, the cruelties are thrown into the shade and the sufferings and virtues made prominent in the light of a brilliant rhetoric ; and if, on the other side, the sufferings and virtues are thrown into the shade, and the *cruelties* made prominent in the same strong light. In this way the truth of history is sacrificed, and, however unconsciously this may be done by the writer, he is fairly chargeable with culpably misleading his readers and creating or strengthening unjust prejudices against a class of his fellow subjects. This is unfortunately what Mr. Froude has done in his 'English in Ireland.' On a passage of Irish history, which of all others required judicial treatment, he has shown himself an impassioned advocate, writing in a state of violent excitement, piling up horrors with all the rhetorical art of which he is a master. He carefully excludes every consideration—every fact, which could by possibility extenuate the guilt of the Irish Catholics; and he grounds his charges upon evidence which he must know would be regarded as utterly worthless in a court of justice at the present day.

For English Protestants it is difficult to sympathize with Irish mothers and children who, according to state papers and official correspondence published by him in his ' History of England,' were from generation to generation treated like reptiles or vermin, shot down like foxes or wolves, burned in their cabins, or butchered by the soldiery, wherever they were met in their long days' marches through the country which they often found smiling with cornfields and comfortable homes, but which they left behind them a blasted desert. As to the mass of affidavits preserved in the library of Trinity College, which Mr. Froude relies upon as ' an eternal witness ' of the massacre, I will only observe that any one acquainted with the current history of our own enlightened times, with the daily scrutiny of the press on each side, knows how easily affidavits are got for almost any object, and how thoughtlessly persons sign what is placed before them if the interest of the cause demands it. This is especially the case where the passions are violently excited by party spirit, and factious contentions, or by actual fighting and bloodshed. Let us take a few familiar illustrations. In the case of the Jamaica insurrection, suppose the evidence on behalf of Governor Eyre had been taken in affidavits, and that many of them contained mere hearsay evidence, including stories alleged by some one to have been told by the negroes themselves; and suppose some historian met with these documents 200 years hence, and took them as true witnesses of the facts, what sort of history would that be? Last year there was civil war in the streets of Belfast, considered to be the most enlightened and the most religious town in Ireland. The war lasted several days in the presence of the magistrates and the troops. The result was, that from one district the Roman Catholics were obliged to remove their furniture and fly to another district, to avoid being burnt out or shot; and, in like manner, the Protestants were compelled to fly from Roman Catholic districts. Some were killed, and many wounded in these encounters. Now suppose the friends and leaders of each party prepared affidavits for the victims to sign, could they be relied on as a correct statement of facts? could they stand a cross-examination in a court of justice? would the stories be more likely to be true if the victims had to fly to Dublin, or Derry, wounded and terror-stricken? Before a Royal Commission which sat in Belfast to enquire into a similar war, the evidence of the belligerents was point blank contradictory. Again, let us look at the contradictory swearing at the trial of an election petition in Ireland—the celebrated Galway case, for example. The witnesses in such cases include clergymen, magistrates, lawyers, highly respectable witnesses of all classes. Yet who would be so weak as to take the sworn testimony on either side as a true statement of facts, 'an eternal witness' of the truth of the case of the prosecution or the defence? In any such conflict of evidence, arising from prejudice, passion, revenge, and strong worldly interest, it would be easy to take the documents on one side only, and work up a case tremendously sensational, making the opposite party look very black and vile. This is just what Mr. Froude has done in relating the Protestant story of 1641. When he comes to deal with the numbers alleged to have been killed, finding them to be absurdly exaggerated and so incredible as to destroy the effect of the testimony of his witnesses, he puts in a reflection calculated to obviate this difficulty, like a skilful advocate. It would have been more fair if he had done this in connexion with the horrifying details of the cruelties and atrocities which he works up with such artistic effect. But then this would weaken the impression he wanted to produce—namely, that the Irish were '*not even human savages, but ferocious beasts.*'

Sir John Temple, Mr. Froude's chief authority, though he

was afterwards ashamed of his own reports, and wished he had not made them, stated that the number of lives destroyed by the rebels was not less than 300,000 in two years. A more moderate estimate gave the destruction as 200,000 Protestant lives in six months. At Lord Maguire's trial—a judicial proceeding—the number was sworn to be 152,000. But though the historian had as good evidence for these figures as he had for the cruelties, he finds they cannot be sustained, for the simple reason that some of the estimates exceed the whole Protestant population in Ireland when the rebellion began, which was only 160,000. Of these, thousands fled to England and Scotland, while in one generation after the war the proportion of Protestants to Roman Catholics was higher than in 1861. The numbers, as given by Sir Wm. Petty in 1672 were, Protestants, 300,000, Roman Catholics, 800,000. Clarendon reduced the number of Protestants that perished in the outbreak to 40,000, and Sir Wm. Petty to 37,000. These numbers are far too high, as we shall see. But, meantime, let us take Mr. Froude's caution, which he should have applied to the wild sensationalism of the affidavits made, or signed rather, by the fugitives. Owing to the fearful excitement, he says—'*the balance of reason was overturned.*'

That was, no doubt, the fact with many of those sufferers, who were witnesses; but what a pity the historian did not think of this sooner! He may have been colouring up the horrific visions of frenzied panic-insanity. Some of the affidavits were indeed, little better; for they contained accounts of the bodies of the victims appearing frequently after burial in the rivers into which they had been thrown, and floating upwards against the current,—with other miraculous manifestations.

Surely the sober truth about those deplorable occurrences was bad enough; and Mr. Froude might well have offered as mitigating circumstances some facts which he himself records. First Strafford, ' seeing Ireland with the eye of a born ruler,' and wanting money for the king, resolved to confiscate all the estates held by Irishmen in Connaught, and to clear out that province for Protestant settlers, as Ulster had been cleared. Jurymen, who failed to find for the crown, he sent ' to meditate on their *misdemeanours* in the county gaols.' ' Never till then,' says Mr. Froude, ' had *spoliation* so direct and unprovoked been attempted.' Again, in May, 1641, the Lords Justices wrote: 'This country is fearfully robbed and harassed by the soldiers in every part where they come. They go six or seven miles from their garrisons, and rob houses, and take all they meet with in their way; and do all the mischief that can be. We have not had a penny these four weeks to give them' (p. 93). In view of these facts, and of the 'free use of shot and halter' made by Sir Charles Coote and others, is it fair of the historian to say that 'the Catholics were indulged to the uttermost, and *therefore* rebelled,'—that they had 'too much liberty of conscience, and *that* made them rebel'? Is it fair to complain, under these circumstances, that 'a knot of Irish barristers—patriots of the familiar type—put themselves forward as the spokesmen of Irish grievances'? Is it wise to speak of the chiefs of the Irish people, representing families who inherited their lands from ancestors that flourished before the Heptarchy, as 'men supported by others' toil,—drudges and victims of those who think it scorn to work,—who, calling themselves rulers, were, *in no point, morally superior to their own wolves;* and had nevertheless usurped to themselves the name of the Irish nation' (p. 120). Hence, adds Mr. Froude, 'the Irish proprietors had become intolerable; they were dismissed, and their room was supplied by better men' (p. 131).

We may grant that those Milesian chiefs were a useless set of consumers of the fruits of the earth. But the people acknowledged their rights; and we may ask, Did these better men *work?* did they relieve the earth-tillers from their drudgery? did those English landlords who replaced the Irish wolves in human shape, prove themselves tender and careful shepherds? Would it be surprising that the Irish peasantry of to-day should apply to their present landlords the language which the English historian applies to those old proprietors who were chased away to make room for them,—or that, when noticed 'to quit' and evicted— they should say that their new masters 'are in no point morally superior to wolves'? If ignorant, angry men, smarting under a sense of wrong, should think they find in the pages of Mr. Froude a plea for agrarian outrage, it would be very deplorable, but by no means astonishing.

Returning, however, to the painful subject of the 'massacre,' it should be observed that Mr. Froude admits that 'a universal massacre appears at first to have been nowhere deliberately designed.' He says, without any proof, 'the *order* was to drive them (the Protestants) from their houses, to strip them—man, woman, and child—of their property, strip them even of their clothes upon their backs.' He admits also that some families were sent with escorts to the sea. It is to be regretted that he did not notice the beautiful episode in this history of horrors, presented at Kilmore, in the county of Cavan, where an English Bishop, an eminent Protestant, an ardent enemy of Popery, a keen controversialist, but a just and benevolent man—Dr. Bedell—was so revered by the chiefs and people, that his house and his church and its precincts became an asylum to a multitude of Protestant refugees, including another bishop, and that they remained quite safe under the protection of that venerable prelate, a case which shows in a striking light what Englishmen might have done in Ireland if, like Bishop Bedell, they had been actuated by the spirit of CHRIST, and not by the spirit of Cromwell.

For my own part, I believe the truth about the massacre has been conveyed to us by several impartial and conscientious authors. The first of these is the Rev. Mr. Warner, a Protestant, who, in his History of Ireland, says: 'It is easy enough to demonstrate the falsehood of the relation of every Protestant historian of this rebellion. Their first intention went no further than to strip the English and the Protestants of their power and possessions, and, unless forced to it by opposition, not to shed any blood.' Warner examined the depositions on which the story of the massacre was based, and found the estimates of the victims to have been enormously exaggerated. He calculated the number of those killed, upon evidence collected within two years after the rebellion broke out, at 4,028, besides 8,000 said to have perished through bad usage. To the same effect is the testimony of Dr. Leland, who says: 'Resistance produced some bloodshed; and, in some instances, private revenge, religious hatred, and the suspicion of some valuable concealment, enraged the triumphant rebels to insolence, cruelty, and murder. So far, however, was the *original scheme* of the conspiracy at first pursued, that *few fell by the sword, except in open war and assault.*'

Dr. Curry, in his valuable History of the *Civil Wars in Ireland*, gives in the following summary a fair statement of the facts. He says: '" The report that his Majesty's Protestant subjects first fell upon and murdered the Roman Catholics, got credit and reputation, and was openly and frequently asserted," says Jones, Bishop of Meath, in a letter to Dr. Borlase, in 1679. And Sir Audley Mervin, Speaker of the House of Commons, in a public speech to the Duke of Ormonde, in 1662, confesses, " that several pamphlets then swarmed to fasten the rise of this rebellion upon the Protestants; and that they drew the first blood." And, indeed, whatever cruelties may be charged upon the Irish in the prosecution of this war, " their first intention, we see," says another Protestant voucher, " went no further than to strip the English and the Protestants of their power and possessions, and, unless forced to it by opposition, not to shed any blood." Even Temple confesses the same; for mentioning what mischiefs were done in the beginning of this insurrection, " certainly," says he, " that which these rebels mainly intended, at first, and most busily employed themselves about, was the driving away the Englishmen's cattle, and possessing themselves of their goods."

' In a MS. journal of an officer in the king's service, quoted by Mr. Carte, wherein there is a minute and daily account of everything that happened in the North of Ireland, during the first weeks of the insurrection, there is not even an insinuation of any cruelties committed by the insurgents on the English or Protestants; although it is computed by the journalist, " that the Protestants of that province had killed near a thousand of the rebels in the first week or two of the rebellion." And on the 16th of November, 1641, " Mr. Robert Wallbank came from the North, and informed the Irish House of Commons, that two hundred of the people of Coleraine fought with one thousand of the rebels, slew six of them, and not one of themselves hurt. That in another battle sixty of the rebels were slain, and only two of the others hurt—none slain." Nor do we find in this account the least mention of cruelties then committed by the Irish; but much of the success and victory of his Majesty's Protestant subjects, as often as they encountered them.

' It is worthy of particular notice that a commission of the

Lords Justices, Parsons and Borlase, dated so late as December 23rd, 1641, was sent down to several gentlemen in Ulster (where it is agreed on all hands that these cruelties and outrages were chiefly committed), in virtue of which commission, Temple and Borlase confess, " several examinations were afterwards taken of murders committed by the rebels, and the perpetrators of many of these murders were discovered." Yet the commission itself, though it authorises these gentlemen to call upon all those who had then suffered in the rebellion, and all the witnesses of these sufferings, to give in examinations of the nature of them, and of every minute circumstance relating to them, expressly and particularly specifying every other crime usual in insurrections, and then committed in this—viz., plunder, robbery, and even traitorous words, actions, and speeches; yet, I say, there is not a syllable mentioned of any murders then committed, in this commission, nor any express power given by it to make inquiry into them. From whence it seems necessarily to follow, either that few or no such cruelties had been committed by the insurgents before the 23rd of December, 1641, or that these Lords Justices deemed murders and massacres less worthy of their notice, of being strictly inquired after, than even traitorous words and speeches.

'That a great number of unoffending Irish were massacred in Island-Magee by Scottish Puritans, about the beginning of this insurrection, is not denied by any adverse writer that I have met with. An apology, however, is made for it by them all, which, even if it were grounded on fact, as I shall presently show it is not, would be a very bad one, and seems at least to imply a confession of the charge. These writers pretend that this massacre was perpetrated on those harmless people in revenge of some cruelties before committed by the rebels on the Scots in other parts of Ulster. But as I find this controversy has been already taken up by two able Protestant historians, who seem to differ about the time in which that dismal event happened, perhaps, by laying before the reader the accounts of both, with such animadversions as naturally arise from them, that time may be more clearly and positively ascertained.

'A late learned and ingenious author of a history of Ireland has shifted off this shocking incident from November, 1641 (in which month it has been generally placed), to January following, many weeks after horrible cruelties (as he tells us) had been committed by the insurgents on the Scots in the North. "The Scottish soldiers," says he, "who had reinforced the garrison of Carrickfergus were possessed of an habitual hatred of Popery, and inflamed to an implacable detestation of the Irish, by multiplied accounts of their cruelties. In one fatal night they issued from Carrickfergus into an adjacent district called Island-Magee, where a number of the poorer Irish resided, untainted with the rebellion. If we may believe one of the leaders *of this party*, thirty families were assailed by them in their beds, and massacred with calm and deliberate cruelty. As if," proceeds the historian, "the incident were not sufficiently hideous, Popish writers have represented it with shocking aggravation."'

Mr. Froude said to his hearers in New York: 'Read Temple, whatever else you read, if you would form an independent opinion.' But, in giving this advice, the following important document, published in 1770, must have escaped his notice. If produced in a court of justice, the counsel would say to Temple: 'You may go down.' It has been produced by Mr. John Mitchell; and we learn from it that in the year 1674 Lord Essex was soliciting from the English Government a considerable grant for Temple— five hundred pounds a-year, 'on the forfeited estates.' And the ministry seems to have made the republication of Temple's History an objection against the grant, which objection Lord Essex, on the part of his friend, thus endeavours to remove:—

Extract of a letter from the Earl of Essex, Lord-Lieutenant of Ireland, to Mr. Secretary Coventry.

'I am to acknowledge the receipt of yours of the 22nd of December, wherein you mention a book that was newly published, concerning the cruelties committed in Ireland at the beginning of the late war. Upon further inquiry, I find Sir J. Temple, Master of the Rolls here, author of that book, was this last year sent to by several stationers of London, to have his consent to the printing thereof. But he assures me that he utterly denies it; and whoever printed it, did it without his knowledge. Thus much I thought fit to add to what I formerly said upon this occasion, that I might do this gentleman right, in case it was suspected he had any share in publishing this new edition.'

Hence it appears that Temple himself was ashamed of 'the eternal witness of the truth,' which to Mr. Froude's mind is so conclusive. His strongest desire respecting his own book was that it should be buried and forgotten.

CHAPTER XII.

THE CATHOLIC CONFEDERATION.

THE Irish Government lost not a moment in taking the most effectual measures for crushing the rebellion. Lord Ormonde, as Lieutenant-General, had soon at his disposal 12,000 men, with a fine train of field artillery, which had been provided by Strafford for the campaign in the north of England. The King, who was then in Scotland, got 1,500 men sent into Ulster, and authorised Lords Chichester and Clandeboye to raise regiments among their tenants. These together formed the Scottish army. The Irish, on the other hand, were ill provided with arms and ammunition; they had not time to make pikes enough for the occasion. The military officers who were to drill them did not make their appearance. Rory O'More had never seen service; Sir Phelim O'Neill was only a civilian when he assumed the high sounding title of 'Lord General of the Catholic Army in Ulster,' taking also the style and title of The O'Neill. It was not likely that such a man could do much in the way of organising an army and providing a commissariat. It was not so with the Protestants. The English soldiers who happened to be in Ireland in those times, if not taken quite by surprise, regarded an outbreak of rebellion with feelings of satisfaction, rather with joy, very much resembling what officers feel at the commencement of a war in some country where plenty of prize money can be won, where the 'looting' will be rich, and the promotion rapid. Relying with confidence on the power of England and the force of discipline, they knew that the defenders of the Government would be victorious in the end, and that their rewards would be estates. The more rebellions, the more forfeited territory, and the more opportunities for implicating, despoiling, and ruining the principal men of the hated race. The most sober-minded writer, dealing with such facts, cannot help stirring men's blood while recording the deeds of the heroes who founded the English power in Ireland and planted there her feudal system on the basis of confiscation.

The immediate prospect of forfeitures, therefore, roused the ambition and cupidity of every man who was in a position to turn the troubles to account for his own advantage. In Munster, the aged Earl of Cork, still insatiable as ever for other men's possessions, worked with the president of Munster, St. Leger, for this end. He prepared 1,100 indictments against Roman Catholic proprietors in his district, which he sent to the Speaker of the Long Parliament, with an urgent request that they might be returned to him with authority to proceed against the parties named as *outlaws*. In Leinster, 4,000 similar indictments were found in the course of two days, by the free use of the rack with witnesses—one aged gentleman having been subjected to this torture. When such proceedings took place before the tribunals in peaceable cities, we may imagine what must have been the excesses of the excited soldiery in the open country. Lord Muskerry and other leading Catholics, who had offered their services to maintain the peace of Munster, were driven by an insulting refusal to combine for their own protection. The 1,100 indictments of Lord Cork soon swelled their ranks, and the capture of the ancient city of Cashel by Philip O'Dwyer announced the insurrection of the south. Waterford, Wexford, and Kilkenny—old strongholds of the Pale—declared for the Catholic cause. In the mean time Sir Charles Coote's troops in Wicklow and elsewhere were slaughtering the inhabitants in such a way as had not been equalled since the days of the Pagan Northmen. They did not spare the women, and little children were carried aloft and tossed about on the points of their spears, the gallant commander jocosely remarking 'that he liked such frolics.' In Ulster, by the end of April, there were 19,000 regulars and volunteers in garrison or in the field. The rebels were driven from Newry, Down, and Monaghan, while Sir Phelim O'Neill burned the towns of Armagh and Dungannon, and took his last stand at Charlemont. Lord Ormonde routed a large body of rebels in the county Kildare, leaving 700 men and a number of officers dead on the field. For this victory the Long Parliament voted him a jewel worth 500*l.*

Refusing to trust the King with the control of the English forces in Ireland, the Long Parliament took the work of subjugation into their own hands. Having already confiscated 2,500,000 acres of Irish land, they offered it as security to 'adventurers' who would advance money to meet the cost of the war, and there was no lack of offers by well-affected Englishmen to raise forces at their own charge 'against the rebels of Ireland, and afterwards to receive their recompense of the rebels' estates.' Under the Act for 'the Speedy Reducing of the Rebels,' the adventurers were to carry over a brigade of 5,000 foot and 500 horse, and to have the right of appointing their own officers. They were to have estates given them at the following rates:—1,000 acres for 200*l.* in Ulster, for 300*l.* in Connaught, for 450*l.* in Munster, and for 600*l.* in Leinster. The nature of the war, and the spirit in which it was conducted, may be inferred from the sort of weapons issued from the military stores. They included scythes with handles and rings, reaping hooks, and whetstones, intended for cutting down the growing corn, that the inhabitants might be starved into submission or compelled to quit the country. Bibles also were issued to the troops, one Bible for every file, that they might learn from the Old Testament the sin and danger of sparing idolaters. The texts upon that subject seem, indeed, to have been well studied, and not without fruitful results. The rebellion in Ulster had almost collapsed before the end of the year. The tens of thousands who had rushed to the standard of O'Neill were now reduced to a number of weak and disorganised detached parties of armed men, taking shelter in the woods. The English garrison scoured the neighbouring counties with little opposition, and where any was encountered they gave no quarter. Sir William Cole proudly boasted of his achievement in causing 7,000 Roman Catholics to be starved to death, within a circuit of a few miles of his garrison.

The cause of the insurgents in Ulster seemed now all but lost. Sir Phelim O'Neill had proved himself utterly incapable as a general; but there was another man of that name, who had learned the art of war, and seemed born to be a great general.

He had been treated with favour at the English Court, and he had doubtless now the opportunity of winning honours and titles if he had, like many of his kinsmen, been false to his country and his race. This was Colonel Owen Roe O'Neill, the same to whom Mr. Froude refers when he says, 'if you treat a wolf as a dog, he will be a wolf still.' If, however, he had been a Pole or a Venetian, or a brave patriot of any other oppressed nation, who had hastened to his country's standard in the hour of peril, and said—

> Oh give but a hope, let a vista but gleam
> Through the gloom of my country, and mark what I'll feel—

he would, doubtless, be celebrated by the English historian as a hero of the noblest type. But give to an Irish patriot the highest culture, and let him yield to the instinct which has prompted in all ages to acts the most heroic and heart-thrilling, and what is he at best but a tamed wolf? However, when the national cause seemed hopeless, when the Celtic population in Ulster were meditating a wholesale emigration to the Scottish highlands, ' a name that seemed to have a magic power was whispered on the coast, and like electricity it ran from Donegal to Donaghadee, and from Derry to Kinsale.' Owen Roe O'Neill had arrived with a single company of veterans, 100 officers, and a quantity of ammunition. He landed at Doe Castle, proceeded to the fort of Charlemont, met the heads of the Clans at Clones in Monaghan, was elected General-in-Chief of the Catholic forces, and at once set about organising an army. Meantime the Catholics of the whole kingdom had joined in a 'confederation' which held its meetings at Kilkenny. A general assembly was convened there for October 23, 1642, the Catholic peerage being represented by fourteen lords and eleven bishops. A general was appointed for each of the provinces—Preston for Leinster, Barry for Munster, and Burke for Connaught.

The Catholic Confederation was from the first distracted and weakened by sources of division, which have proved fatal to every national combination in Ireland. With the Anglo-Irish members, the war was *Catholic*, and its object simply religious liberty. They had no animosity or antipathy to the English, being the descendants of Norman adventurers. The Pope's Nuncio was there, thinking only of the interest of his master, having the prelates on his side. Next there were the chiefs representing the old Irish, either deprived of their lands or likely to become so. At the same time the King, then at Oxford, was importuned by the Confederation on the one side, and the Puritans on the other —the former petitioning for freedom of worship, the latter demanding the suppression of Popery. Pending these appeals, there was a cessation of hostilities between the Irish belligerents. Months were spent in Dublin with Ormonde in negotiations for a permanent peace and settlement. Charles, out of patience with the delay, sent over the Earl of Glamorgan, son of the Marquis of Worcester, and son-in-law of the Earl of Thomond. He belonged to a family which was said to have contributed no less than 200,000*l.* to the Royal cause in England. His religion, his rank, his Irish connections, as well as the enjoyment of the King's confidence, pointed him out as likely to be a successful ambassador. He arrived in Dublin, where Ormonde managed to detain him for ten weeks in discussions on the Articles relating to Religion, and it was not till November 12 that the celebrated Glamorgan Treaty was concluded. This treaty conceded all the most essential claims of the Irish—equal rights as to property, equal rights in the army, in the universities, and at the bar. It gave Roman Catholics seats in both Houses of Parliament and on the Bench, and it declared that the independence of the Parliament of Ireland on that of England should be decided by a declaration of both Houses agreeably to the laws of the kingdom of Ireland. In short, it gave to the Irish Catholics in 1646 all that was subsequently obtained either for the country or the church in 1782, 1793, and 1829.

The Catholic Confederation was a singular episode in the history of the country. The greatest personage that figured in it was the Pope's Nuncio, John Baptist Rinuncini, Archbishop of Fermo, who was there to look after the interests of the Court of Rome. He was in a state of very feeble health, and from Limerick to Kilkenny, where the Confederation sat, he was carried in a litter, escorted by a guard of honour. We read that the pomp and splendour of his public entry into the Catholic capital was a striking spectacle. Five delegates from the Supreme Council accompanied him. A band of fifty students mounted on horseback met him on the way, and their leader, crowned with laurel, recited to him congratulatory Latin verses, while a vast multitude of people crowded along the road cheering with all their might. At the city gate he was lifted from the litter, and mounted a horse richly caparisoned. Here he was met by a procession of the clergy and the city guilds. At the Market Cross a Latin oration was delivered in his honour, to which he graciously replied in the same language. From the Cross he was escorted to the Cathedral, the bishop receiving him at the door. At the high altar he intoned the *Te Deum*, and gave the multitude the Apostolic benediction. Thence he was conducted to Kilkenny Castle, the magnificent seat of the Duke of Ormonde, where in the great gallery, which elicited even a Florentine's admiration, he was received in stately formality by the President of the Council, Lord Mountgarret. Another Latin oration on the nature of his mission was given by the Nuncio and responded to by the Bishop of Clogher, and so the reception ended.

The observations which the Pope's ambassador made upon the Irish people as he saw them are not without interest at the present time. He remarked that the native Irish were behind the rest of Europe in the knowledge of those things that tended to their *material improvement*. 'They were indifferent agriculturists, living from hand to mouth, caring more for the sword than the plough; good Catholics, though by nature barbarous, and placing their hopes of deliverance from English rule on foreign intervention. For this they were constantly straining their eyes towards France or Spain, and no matter where the ally came from, were ever ready to rise in revolt. One virtue, however, intense love of country, more or less redeemed these vices, for so they deserved to be called; "*but to establish anything like strict military discipline or organisation among themselves it must be owned they had no aptitude.*" "This," says the Rev. Mr. Meehan, "to some extent will account for the apathy of the Northern Catholics, while the undertakers were carrying on the gigantic eviction known as the Plantation of Ulster, for since Sir Cahir O'Dohart's rebellion till 1615 there was only one attempt to resist the intruders, an abortive raid on the city of Derry, for which, the meagre annals of that year tell us, six of the Earl of Tyrone's nearest kinsmen were put to death." '

Returning to Ulster, we may well imagine how disagreeable to General O'Neill was the long delay occasioned by those negotiations. He possibly foresaw their issue, for political events in England swayed the destiny of Ireland then as now. The poor vacillating, double-minded King, unstable in all his ways, was delivered to the Puritans by the Scotch army; and Christendom was horrified by the trial and execution of a king, one of the Lord's anointed. But before Cromwell crossed the Channel to smash the Kilkenny Confederation and everything Papal in Ireland, the Ulster chief gladdened the hearts of his countrymen by the glorious victory of Benburb, one of the most memorable in Irish history. In a naturally strong position, the Irish repulsed repeated charges of the Puritan horse. At length, as the sun began to descend, pouring its rays upon the face of the enemy, O'Neill led out his whole force—5,000 men against 8,000—and made a general attack. One terrible onset bore down all resistance. The Scotch were routed, and of them there were counted on the field 3,243, and of Catholics but 70 killed and 100 wounded. Lord Ards and 21 Scottish officers, 32 standards, 1,500 horses, with all the guns and tents, were captured. General Munroe fled to Lisburn, and thence to Carrickfergus, where he shut himself up until he could obtain reinforcements. O'Neill sent the captured colours to the Nuncio at Limerick, by whom they were solemnly placed in the choir of the cathedral, and afterwards, at the request of Pope Innocent, they were sent to Rome. The *Te Deum* was chanted in the Confederate capital, while penitential psalms were sung in the Protestant fortresses. O'Neill emblazoned the cross and keys of his banner with the Red Hand of Ulster; and Munroe wrote: 'The Lord of Hosts has rubbed shame on our faces till once we are humbled.'[1]

The stage of Irish politics now presented the most extraordinary complications, political, military, and religious. In the

---

[1] Mr. Froude, who misses no opportunity of reviling the O'Neills, is profoundly silent about the battle of Benburb! An avowed advocate of one side would hardly think it prudent to suppress facts in this fashion, however disagreeable to his clients the facts might be.

north was the 'Catholic army' exulting in its one brilliant victory; elsewhere commanders changed positions so rapidly, the several causes for which men had been fighting became so confused in the unaccountable scene-shifting, giving glimpses now of the King, now of the Commonwealth, and now of the Pope, that men hardly knew what they were fighting for, or what standard they should follow. In the mean time the Catholic Confederation was distracted by dissension, rent into factions, and exploded into fragments by those centrifugal forces of Irish division which no power has yet been able effectively to control. The Nuncio found, at all events, that the Pope's power was not able to do it, and he went back to Rome chagrined and disgusted that his blessings and his curses, which he dispensed with equal liberality, were utterly fruitless.

CHAPTER XIII.

RELIGION UNDER CROMWELL—THE SOLEMN LEAGUE AND COVENANT.

At length appeared upon the stage an actor who gave a terrible unity to the confused drama of Irish warfare and politics. Oliver Cromwell left London in July, 1649, 'in a coach drawn by six gallant Flanders mares;' and made a grand 'progress' to Bristol. There he embarked for Ireland, and landed at Ringsend, near Dublin, on the 14th of August. He entered the city in procession, accompanied by his son Henry, and by Blake, Jones, Ireton, Ludlow, Hardress, Waller, and others. The history of his military exploits, the massacre of the garrison of Drogheda and of all who had taken shelter in the church, a similar massacre in the town of Wexford, and the other cruel measures by which he struck terror into the hearts of the Irish enemy, and made his name synonymous with cruelty in the minds of the peasantry to the present day, are well known. It would, perhaps, have been better if they had been allowed to rest in oblivion. But Mr. Prendergast, a few years ago, called attention to them by his work on the 'Cromwellian Settlement'; and recently Mr. Froude in his 'English in Ireland,' and in his lectures in America, has caused the fame, or the infamy, of those deeds of horror to ring throughout the civilised world. Not only with the historians who make themselves the apostles of the anti-Christian principle that 'Might is Right,' and worship all tyrants, usurpers, and despots, no matter by what amount of perfidy, treachery, and murder they have risen to power, provided only they are successful, and rule with a rod of iron; but many Protestants also, who repudiate the atrocious dogma in question, Cromwell is a Christian hero, because he was so terribly in earnest in his love of truth and justice, and for this they are willing to condone his crimes against humanity. And it must be allowed that the exterminating persecution of Protestants on the Continent might well excuse in the Puritans of that age the conviction that no country could have peace or enjoy the blessings of Divine Providence while the upas tree of 'Popery' remained rooted in the soil. Mr. Froude labours to prove that the Puritan rulers of Ireland, whether Republicans or Royalists, punished Roman Catholics because 'the *Mass*' was the symbol of treason and rebellion. But that is a mistake. The Mass was to *them* not treason, but 'Idolatry;' and, in exterminating idolaters, they were simply discharging a solemn duty, which could not be neglected without bringing Divine judgments on themselves and their country.

We have seen how extreme the historian is to mark the iniquities of the Irish in the rebellion which Cromwell was now in Ireland to punish. There everything was intensified, exaggerated, and arranged for effect—to inspire horror and hatred. But when he comes to speak of the slaughter at Drogheda, it is only a 'so-called wholesale massacre.' It was reduced within narrow dimensions; and 'the wisdom of making a severe example was signally justified in its consequences.' Nay, he is so charmed with the work at Drogheda and its results, that he becomes sentimental and philanthropic over it, exclaiming 'Happier far would it have been for Ireland if, 40 years later, there had been a second Cromwell before Limerick!'

Cromwell is defended on two grounds. He was punishing the guilty Irish for the massacre of 1641, and he was bringing the war to a speedy issue by striking terror into the hearts of the natives. But as to the garrison, it was *English*, not Irish, and as innocent of the massacre as Cromwell himself. Mr. Froude had told us (p. 123) that 'several of the best regiments—*almost wholly English*—had been thrown into Drogheda, under Sir Arthur Ashton, late Governor of Reading.' These English regiments, with their gallant commander, were fighting for the King, to whom they had sworn allegiance. Was it noble work in Cromwell's Bible-reading Ironsides to spend two days and nights in butchering these English brethren? Yet the English historian maintains that this was the right thing to do. He denies, indeed, that the gallant butchers slaughtered the women and children as well as the men;

and he says, no eye-witness has proved it. Had he not heard of honest Anthony à Wood, whose brother Thomas was one of Cromwell's troopers at Drogheda? Mr. Edward Peacock has published a letter in the ' Athenæum,' in which he says:—' " Indiscriminate massacre " may perhaps be too strong an expression; but there is little room for doubt that women and children were put to death by the victors in their fury in a way which does not admit of the plea of accident.'

Thomas Wood, the eldest brother of Anthony à Wood, the Oxford antiquary, was a lieutenant in the regiment of Col. Henry Ingoldsby, and served in the Irish campaign. His report of what occurred is given by Anthony à Wood in his own memoirs. From the way in which it is recorded, it cannot be called the evidence of an eye-witness; but I imagine there can be no good reason found for rejecting it; for whatever Anthony's prejudices may have been, he was a strictly honest man, who would never have recorded his own inventions as facts for the sake of damaging his bitterest enemies. His words are these:—

'" In 1650 he [Thomas Wood] returned for a time to Oxon., to take up his arrears at Ch. Church, and to settle his other affaires; at which time, being often with his mother and brethren, he would tell them of the most terrible assaulting and storming of Tredagh, wherein he himself had been engaged. He told them that 3,000 at least, besides some women and children, were, after the assailants had taken part, and afterwards all the towne, put to the sword on the 11 and 12 of Sept. 1649; at which time Sr Arth Aston, the governour, had his braines beat out, and his body hack'd to pieces. He told them that when they were to make the way up to the lofts and galleries in the church, and up to the tower where the enemy had fled, each of the assailants would take up a child and use it as a buckler of defence, when they ascended the steps, to keep themselves from being shot or brain'd.

'" After they had kil'd all in the church they went into the *vaults underneath, where all the flower and choicest of the women and ladies had hid themselves.* One of these, a most handsome virgin, arrai'd in costly and gorgeous apparel, kneel'd downe to Tho. Wood with teares and prayers to save her life: and being strucken with a profound pitie, took her under his arme, went with her out of the church, with intentions to put her over the works to shift for herself; but a soldier, perceiving his intentions, ran his sword up her belly. Whereupon Mr. Wood, seeing her gasping, took away her money, jewells, &c., and flung her downe over the works." [1]

'In the year 1680 Anthony met Col. Ingoldsby at Oxford, and "did discourse with him concerning his brother Thomas." He does not tell us that any words passed between them concerning the Drogheda slaughter. We may be quite sure, however, that had the Colonel said anything to throw discredit on Thomas Wood's horrible narrative, it would have been duly recorded by the honest antiquary.' Of course, the other ladies, the flower and choicest, fared no better than the beautiful creature who had thus vainly pleaded for mercy; and what of the poor infants used as helmets!

If Cromwell were an Irishman—one of the O'Neills or O'Briens—what a thrilling narrative Mr. Froude would have given us of those two days' slaughter in cold blood! The little children held up as shields and bucklers over the heads of the heroes who were slaying their parents, and who had been induced to surrender their arms; the women and lovely young girls dragged out of the vaults and ripped open with swords; the blood of the victims flowing down the streets like a river; the blood gushing from 5,000 or 6,000 English Christian hearts; the piercing cries and shrieks of the victims, borne through the thick air to the General's camp, but calling forth no response of mercy from his iron heart. How such a monster of cruelty, *if Irish*, would have been denounced as 'not even a human savage, but a ferocious wild beast!'

What object could he have had except to make his troops drunk with blood, that henceforth they might fight as savages, not as soldiers? As to striking terror, the awful human sacrifice, worthy of Dahomey, was a failure; for the fearful work was repeated at Wexford still more wantonly and fiendishly, no time being given to the garrison for deliberation. Mr. Froude treats the horrid business very cavalierly, contemplates it with much

---

[1] 'Life of Ant. à Wood,' written by Himself, ed. 1848, p. 51.

gaiety of heart, and a sally of playful rhetoric. His hero is sitting down to a feast; he is cutting up the living body of Ireland, and he leaves his followers to enjoy the detestable banquet at their leisure. Here is the sympathetic historian's gastronomic illustration :—' Cromwell himself, after breaking the neck of the coalition, went back to England, but others were easily able to finish the meal which Cromwell had carved!' Ireland was used to that sort of vivisection, like the Abyssinian cows from whose living bodies the owners sliced off beefsteaks, stitching up the hide over the bare bones.

Exit Cromwell, off to England in a blaze of glory, ' with garments rolled in blood!' What a splendid finale! But it would have been spoiled if the historian had told all the truth, and therefore he did not tell it, for he never spoils a rhetorical effect for the sake of truth. The truth is, that Cromwell went from Wexford and laid siege to Clonmel, the garrison of which, despite the terror of two massacres, resisted with undaunted spirit, repelled his assaults repeatedly, inflicted heavy losses upon him, and ultimately surrendered on honourable terms. After this he returned to England, baffled, wearied, and vexed no doubt that his two bloody lessons had not produced their anticipated results.[1]

Mr. Froude frequently misleads his readers, quite unintentionally of course, by the fallacy of using the word ' Ireland ' in several different senses, perhaps in the same paragraph. Sometimes it means the land, sometimes the Irish nation, and sometimes the Anglo-Irish colony. The oddest misapplication of the word is where, after the chiefs, landed proprietors, bishops and priests, had been all got rid of, he speaks of the miserable remnant of the people as being so terrorised and debased, that to save themselves the more desperate of them brought in to their rulers the heads of their fathers, uncles, brothers, and cousins in sacks, claiming the Government reward for having cut them off, as if they were

---

[1] This occurred on May 10, 1650. Cromwell had been then nine months in Ireland. Whitelocke states that ' they found in Clonmel the stoutest enemy this army had ever met in Ireland ; and that there was never seen so hot a storm of so long continuance, and so gallantly defended, either in England or Ireland.' The Irish commander here was Hugh O'Neill, a kinsman of Owen Roe's. Was it for this reason that Mr. Froude was silent about the siege of Clonmel ?—See ' Cromwell's Letters and Speeches,' by Carlyle, vol. ii. p. 147.

wolves. The rulers asked no questions for conscience' sake. On this Mr. Froude remarks:—' It was a hateful method, but under the circumstances inevitable.' And in doing work like this, in order to clear the country effectually of its inhabitants, he says, Cromwell ' meant to rule *Ireland for Ireland's good,* and *Ireland* never prospered as *she* prospered in the years of the Protectorate.' What was *she?*

The policy of 'rooting out Popery' had been long acted upon. It was aimed at chiefly by destroying the crops and other provisions, so that the people might be starved into Protestantism. There had been fifteen years of this sort of war in Ulster when James I. ascended the throne, and it left the country to a large extent waste and desolate. It was believed that James would put an end to a war which, as Sir John Davis remarked, had been continued between the two nations for ' 400 and odd years.' Now at length, under a wise and good king, James I., the Lord Deputy announced that the remnant of the people should have ' estates ' in their holdings, and he told them that the King ' thus made a year of jubilee to the poor inhabitants, because every man was to return to his own house and be restored to his ancient possessions, and they all went home rejoicing.'

Poor people! they soon saw the folly of putting their trust in princes; and now after seven years' war the nation was again visited with famine. Three-fourths of the cattle had been destroyed, and the Commissioners for Ireland reported in 1651 that four parts in five of the best and most fertile land lay waste and uninhabited! They therefore gave orders to bring back by force the natives who had fled to the mountains, that they might till the land, promising them the crops if they did so. The soldiers tilled what they could around their posts. In the meantime corn had to be imported from Wales, and meat was so scarce that no person was permitted to kill a lamb without special licence from the authorities. In 1654 the Irish revenue from all sources was only 198,000*l.,* while the cost of the army was 500,000*l.* A sort of conditional amnesty was granted from necessity, pending the decision of Parliament; and on May 12, 1652, the Leinster army surrendered on terms signed at Kilkenny. The other armies followed during the summer. All persons ' except those guilty of the first blood' were received into protection on laying down their arms, and those who were not satisfied with the conclusions to which the English Parliament might come concerning the Irish nation might transport themselves with their men to serve any foreign state in amity with England. In any case, the commissioners were faithfully to mediate with the Parliament, that they might enjoy such a remnant of their lands as would make their lives comfortable at home, or enable them to emigrate.

Accordingly, in the session of 1652, it was formally announced that the rebellion in Ireland was subdued and ended. The country was now for the first time completely subjugated, and the conqueror proceeded to legislate for it. On August 12 was passed the famous Act of Settlement, under which four descriptions of persons were dealt with. All ecclesiastics and royalist proprietors were excluded from pardon of life or estate. All royalist commissioned officers were condemned to banishment and forfeiture of their estates, one-third being retained for the support of their wives and children. The third class was to forfeit one-third of their estates and receive an equivalent for the remaining two-thirds west of the Shannon; and all husbandmen and others of the inferior sort, not being worth more than 10*l.*, were to have a free pardon on condition of their transporting themselves to Connaught.

Mr. Froude calls this a 'great province.' It is great, no doubt, in superficial extent, but it has an immense proportion of mountain, water, and moor land lying along the Atlantic coast, and subject to an enormous quantity of rain. It was, indeed, to a very large extent, nothing but a dreary swamp. But the evicted nation of unfortunate Catholics did not get the whole province to themselves, for the best lands of it were in possession of Protestant settlers, and the new inhabitants, which were to be deported from the other provinces before May 1, under penalty of outlawry, were forbidden to come within two miles of the Shannon on one side, or within four miles of the sea on the other. A rigorous passport system, the evasion of which subjected the offender to death without trial, completed this settlement, the design of which was to shut out the remaining Catholic inhabitants from all communication with mankind. In 1641, when the rebellion began,

5,000,000 of acres were in Catholic hands; 300,000 were church and college lands, and 2,000,000 were in possession of the Protestant settlers who went over during the reigns of Elizabeth and James. Now, under the Protectorate, 5,000,000 acres were confiscated, and this enormous spoil went to the soldiers and adventurers who had served against the Irish, or who had contributed to the military chest since 1641, except 700,000 acres given in exchange to the banished in Clare and Connaught, and 1,200,000 to 'innocent papists.' Such was the complete uprooting of the original inhabitants from the homes of their ancestors, that during the survey orders were issued to bring back individuals from Connaught to point out the boundaries of parishes and town lands. There was no Irish Parliament now, the Protestant colony being represented in an English Parliament summoned in 1653—the assembly over which 'Praise-God-Barebones' presided. The Protector's deputy in Ireland was his son-in-law Fleetwood, his son Henry Cromwell being Commander-in-Chief of the army. To him, in 1658, the title of Lord Deputy was transferred, and thenceforth, till the Restoration, which he did not oppose, he united in his own person the supreme civil and military authority. He had associated with him, as council or commissioners, Ludlow, Corbett, Jones, and Weaver. There was, moreover, a High Court of Justice, which itinerated through the kingdom, and exercised an absolute authority over life and property. By this court Sir Phelim O'Neill, Lord Mayo, and Colonel O'Toole, were condemned and executed. Children of both sexes were captured by thousands, and sold as slaves to the tobacco-planters of Virginia and the West Indies. Sir William Petty, makes the number 6,000; but the number of all ages and sexes thus exported was estimated at 100,000 souls. Petty in his 'Political Anatomy,' records that the chiefest and most eminent of the nobility, and many of the gentry, had taken conditions from the King of Spain, and had transported 40,000 of the most active, spirited men, most acquainted with the dangers and discipline of war.

All traces of the Catholic religion, save ruined churches and cathedrals, disappeared from the landscape and from society. Catholic lawyers and schoolmasters were silenced. All ecclesiastics found lingering in the country were slain, like the priests of Baal. Three bishops and 300 of the inferior clergy thus perished, the bedridden old Bishop of Kilmore being the only native clergyman permitted to survive. Peasants detected at mass in mountain recesses or caves were smoked out and shot. In places where a miserable residue of the population was required to till the lands for its new owners, they were tolerated, as the Gibeonites had been by Joshua. Irish gentlemen who had obtained pardons were obliged to wear a distinctive badge on their dress, on pain of death. Persons of inferior rank were distinguished by a black mark on the right cheek; wanting this, their punishment was the branding iron or the gallows.

Yet the most popular English historian of the present day undertook to convince the Americans that the best use Cromwell and the great Englishmen of his time could have made of this people was to kill them and banish them, and to do it thoroughly, not sparing any by whom the vile race could be propagated. At the end of 1653, however, the Parliament made a division of the spoil among the conquerors and adventurers; and on September 26 an Act for the new planting of Ireland by English was passed. The Government reserved for itself the towns, church lands, and tithes—the Established Church having been utterly abolished. The four counties of Dublin, Kildare, Carlow, and Cork, were also reserved. The amount due to adventurers was 360,000*l*. This they divided into three portions, the allocation of the settlers being determined by lot. The lottery was held in Grocers' Hall, London. The arrears due to the officers and soldiers amounted to 1,550,000*l*., and for advances of provisions and other supplies to the army of the Commonwealth in Ireland there was due the sum of 1,750,000*l*. The claims of the officers and soldiers were satisfied by allotments of land. But before they could enter into possession, the natives must be cleared off. Accordingly, a proclamation was issued, at the Castle of Kilkenny, on October 11, 1652, and signed by the four Commissioners, to the effect that the Commissioners of Revenue within every precinct should cause the Act of Settlement to be published and proclaimed by beat of drum and sound of trumpet on some market-day, as a warning for the Catholics of the three provinces to pack up and be off with all convenient speed to Connaught. A letter from Dublin, dated

December 21, 1654, just at Christmas Eve, says:—' The transplantation has now far advanced, the men being gone to prepare their new habitations in Connaught. Their wives and children, and dependents, are packing away after them apace, and all to be gone by 1st March next.'

It has been found all over the world, in every age, that it is not a pleasant thing for a people to be driven from their homes, and compelled to seek new settlements in a sterile and inhospitable region. When we read of such forced migrations in foreign lands, we are not at all surprised that the victims should be discontented, or even greatly exasperated. Indeed, we should think it very unnatural if they were not; and, doubtless, if a similar process of expulsion were applied to the English people themselves in Kent, Surrey, Gloucestershire, or Cumberland, they would make a tremendous outcry about the violated rights of humanity, and very likely they would fight desperately against their oppressors; and, failing to beat them in open war, they might kill and rob them in a cowardly way if they got the opportunity; and, in fact, the Saxons did so, as we all know, when vanquished and despoiled by the French under William the Conqueror. Yet the writer above quoted makes this remark about the savage reluctance of the Irish to leave their homes:—' It is the *nature* of this people to be rebellious, and they have been so much the more disposed to it, having been highly exasperated to it by the transplanting work.'

The temper of the settlers against the natives may be further inferred from a petition to the Lord Deputy and Council, praying for the enforcement of the original order, requiring the removal of all the Irish nation into Connaught:—' The first purpose of the plantation, they said, is to prevent those of natural principles (that is of natural affections) becoming one with these Irish as well in affinity as in idolatry, as many thousands did who came over in Elizabeth's time, many of whom have had a deep hand in all the late murders and massacres.' This is an important fact. It appears that the English who had settled in Elizabeth's time had become not only Catholics, but so Irish in feeling that they joined in the massacre of their own countrymen. But the petition proceeds:—' And shall we join in affinity with a people of these abominations? Would not the LORD be angry with us until He consume us, having said, " The land which ye go to possess is an unclean land, because of the filthiness of the people who dwell therein. Ye shall not give your sons therefore to their daughters, nor take their daughters to your sons, as it is in Ezra ix. 11, 12, 14. *Nay ye shall surely root them out, lest they cause you to forsake the Lord your God.* Deut. vii." In this way they hoped that honest men might be induced to come and live among them, and if any one objected to this thorough mode of effecting the work of Irish regeneration, Colonel Norris doubted not but that God would enable the authorities to let out the rebellious blood, and cure the fit of sullenness in such advocates.'

Nothing could be more edifying to the godly men of that generation than the spirit in which the transplantation of *the nation* to Connaught was undertaken by the English Commissioners. They were overwhelmed with the sense of their unworthiness to be entrusted with a work so holy and of their natural weakness to encounter such tremendous difficulties. They said, pathetically :—' The child is now come to the birth, and much is desired and expected, but there is no strength to bring forth.' They, therefore, fasted and humbled themselves before the Lord, inviting the officers of the army to join them ' in lifting up prayers, with strong crying and tears, to Him to whom nothing is too strong, that His servants, whom He hath called forth this day to act in these great transactions, might be made faithful, and carried on by His own outstretched arm against all opposition and difficulty to do what was pleasing in His sight.'

There were, however, circumstances which lessened considerably the difficulties and dangers. There was no longer any question of fighting, no work for the sword; it was only a matter of rooting out and transporting helpless families. ' The chiefest and eminentest of the nobility, and many of the gentry, had taken conditions from the King of Spain,' and had transported 40,000 of the most active, spirited men, most acquainted with the dangers and discipline of war. The priests, too, were all gone. Then comes the statement of an awful fact, the very thought of which is enough to make one shudder at the present day. 'The remaining portion of the whole nation was scarce *one-sixth* of what they were at the beginning of the war, so great a devastion had God and man wrought upon that land; and *that handful of natives left were poor labourers, simple creatures,* whose sole design was to live and maintain their families.'

Those philosophic historians who complain of the want of thoroughness in the English policy towards Ireland, might be contented with the sparing of this remnant, one out of every six of the people—the utter refuse of the race—five-sixths, including all but the poor labourers and simple creatures, with their wives and children, gone. Of course it would have been easy enough for the soldiers to make an end of them, so that a single idolater should not have been able to save his soul alive. But then how was the land to be cultivated? And how were the familiar wolves to be kept from prowling about the homesteads of the settlers? There is one thought which does not seem to have troubled the consciences of the exterminators. The Papists were 'Idolaters,' their religion was 'damnable,' and, according to the Puritan belief, there was nothing for them in the next world but eternal perdition. Yet they were sent into it by thousands, as remorselessly as if they had no souls.

Some of the few aged gentlemen left in the country petitioned that their flight to Connaught might not be in winter, alleging that their wives and children were sick, or that their cattle were unfit to drive so far, or that they had some of their crops to get in. To them dispensations were granted. They were warned, however, that if they did not clear off in good time, the officers had resolved to fill the gaols with them, by which, they said, 'This bloody people will know that they (the officers) are not degenerated from English principles. Though they would be very tender of hanging any except leading men, yet they would make no scruple of sending them to the Indies. Accordingly, when March came, a clean sweep was made. All the remaining crops were seized and sold to the English. There was a general arrest of all transplantable persons. 'All over the three provinces, men and women were hauled out of their beds, in the dead hour of the night, to prison, till the gaols were choked.' In order to expedite the removal of the few nobility and gentry, a court-martial sat in St. Patrick's Cathedral, and ordered the lingering delinquents, who clung desperately to their old roof-trees, to be hanged, with a placard on the breast and back of each victim, inscribed ' *For not transplanting.*'

The land having been cleared, the next thing was to arrange matters between the settlers. On the 20th of August, 1655, the Lord Deputy, Fleetwood, addressed one of the officers on this subject, congratulating the disbanded soldiers, who had obtained allotments, on the great blessings which God had conferred upon them after all their suffering and hardships, praying that the blessing of the Lord might be on them all, and keep them in His fear, and that they might be ' kept from the sins and pollutions which God had so eminently witnessed against in those whose possessions they were to take up. By the blessing of God they might now sit down in the enjoyment of *the enemy's fields and houses, which they planted not, and built not.*'[1] Yet many refused to settle, selling their debentures to their officers. What could they do with those houses and farms? They had no horses, or ploughs, or cattle; they had no labourers to till the soil; and, worst of all, they had no women. ' Flogging was the punishment for amours with Irish girls, and marriage with the idolatrous race was forbidden under heavy penalties.' Here, at the very beginning, was a root of degeneracy planted. The Puritan soldiers, stern as they were, had a hankering after the daughters of Heth, and their honest truth-loving nature began to be perverted and corrupted in more ways than one; for they pretended that their Catholic wives had embraced Protestantism. Thence arose a testing cathechetical examination of the wife. If she did not stand the test, the husband was liable to be sent to Connaught with his fair seducer. The danger was so great, that all the women were compelled to transplant; for there were but few amongst the settlers who could sing, from his heart (with a Cromwellian patriot), that they,

> Rather than turne
> From English principles, would sooner burne ;
> And rather than marrie an Irish wife,
> Would batchellers remain for terme of life.

[1] With statements like this before him, Mr. Froude says the peasantry were allowed to remain in 'their natural homes.'

And it was, in fact, impossible to prevent the intermixture of races, or the rapid 'degeneracy' always attendant upon such intermixture with the Irish, whose power of fascination seemed to bear almost an exact proportion to their 'barbarism.' Only forty years had elapsed from the time of this transplantation, when an English writer accounted for a similar tendency after the Revolution, saying:—'We cannot so much wonder at this, when we consider how many there are of the children of Oliver's soldiers in Ireland who cannot speak one word of English. And [which is strange] the same may be said of some of the children of King William's soldiers, who came but t'other day into the country. This misfortune is owing to the marrying of Irish women, for want of English, who come not over in such great numbers as are requisite. 'Tis sure that no Englishman in Ireland knows what his children may be, as things are now. They cannot well live in the country without growing Irish; for none take such care as Sir Gerald Alexander, Justice of the Common Pleas for Ireland, who left his estate to his daughter, but made the gift void if she married any Irishman, including in that term any lord of Ireland, any archbishop, bishop, prelate, any baronet, knight, esquire, or gentleman of Irish extraction or descent, born and bred in Ireland, or having his relations and means of subsistence there.'[1]

The government of Oliver, vigorous as it was, and stern withal, could not keep out human nature with the sword or the gallows. The consequences were frauds, evasions, dispensations, and other devices, by which the English settlers contrived to avail themselves of the services of the natives, in spite of the strongest possible measures on the part of the Government. They dared everything, and shrunk from no consequences; *thorough* was their word. They found Dublin full of Catholics; and in the summer of 1651 Mr. John Hewson had the felicity of making the following report on the state of religion in the Irish metropolis:—'Mr. Winter, a godly man, came with the Commissioners, and they flocked to hear him with great desire. Besides, there is in Dublin, since January last, about 150 Papists forsaking their priests and the mass, and attend the public

[1] 'Cromwellian Settlement,' p. 130.

ordinances, I having appointed Mr. Chambers, a minister, to instruct them at his own house once a week. They all repaire to him with much affection, and desireth satisfaction; and though Dublin hath formerly swarmed with Papists, I know none there now but *one*, who is a chirurgeon, and a peaceable man. It is much hoped that the glad tidings of salvation will be acceptable in Ireland, and that this savage people may see the salvation of God.' This hope was not realized. 'Glad tidings' from Cromwell's ministers were not easily credited by the Irish 'savages.' Indeed, so long as the children of mixed marriages learned no language but Irish, and no religious instruction or education of any kind was allowed to be imparted to them in that tongue, the hopes of Protestantism, according to the ideas of the time, must rest in the plantation of the country with a 'wholly right seed.' This was to be found in the union of English men with English women, newly arrived from the land of the free. The more precious this seed was, the more care should there be in bringing the precious seed into the field. This was a delicate and difficult matter. There were plenty of Irish midwives, affectionate, no doubt, and possibly skilful, but they were idolaters and disloyal; and was it right to place English mothers and their infants at the mercy of such nurses? Certainly not; and so the Government in Council, after much deliberation, agreed 'to lay this matter before the Lord in prayer.' The result was a resolution to bring over a State Nurse from England, to take charge of all the accouchements in the city of Dublin. As may be easily supposed, Mrs. Jane Preswick, a lady in much repute for godliness, found, when she came to Dublin, that she had roused a nest of hornets. The midwives whom she superseded were so exasperated that they mobbed her in the streets. The consequence was a proclamation, directing that 'a person so eminently qualified for public good, and so well reported of for piety and knowledge in her art, should receive encouragement and protection.'

The Cromwellian plantation entailed three heavy burdens upon the colony. Of these a strong complaint was made in the united Parliament at Westminster, in 1657. Major Morgan, member for Wicklow, said: ' We have three beasts to destroy, that lay burdens upon us. The first is the wolf, on whom we lay 5*l*. per head, if a dog, and 10*l*. if a bitch; the second beast is a priest, on whose head we lay 10*l*.; if he be eminent, more. The third beast is a Tory, on whose head, if he be a public Tory, we lay 20*l*.; and 40*s*. on a private Tory. Your army cannot catch them: the Irish bring them in; brothers and cousins cut one another's throats.' That the wolves abounded we need not wonder, for they had a good time of it, feeding upon human bodies which they found lying about in the woods. Four years before the Irish member complained of the heavy taxation, the Dublin Council had issued a printed document containing the following preamble:—' Upon serious consideration of the great multitudes of poor swarming in all parts of this nation, occasioned by devastation of the country, and by the habits of licentiousness and idleness which the generality of the people have acquired in the time of this rebellion, insomuch that frequently some are found feeding on carrion and weeds, some starving in the highways, and many times poor children who have lost their parents, or have been deserted by them, are found exposed to, and some of them fed upon by beasts, ravening wolves, and others by birds of prey, &c.' Consequently the commanders of the various districts were directed to appoint days and times for hunting the wolf, and those that brought in the heads of those animals were paid out of the Treasury. Galway was the capital of the 'great province of Connaught' in which Mr. Froude told the Americans the transplanted had found comfortable locations. Yet from the 'precinct of Galway' in March 1655, the sum of 243*l*. 5*s*. 4*d*. was due for rewards paid for the heads of wolves. What is more surprising is, that a tract of land only nine miles north of Dublin was leased to a person who kept a pack of wolf-hounds, and part of his rent was paid in wolves' heads, the numbers of which were allowed to diminish from year to year, as the stock fell short. Other stipulations of a similar kind may be found in the book of printed declarations of the 'Commissioners for the Affairs of Ireland,' in the British Museum.

The second 'burdensome beast' is the one with which this history is most concerned. It was the *priest*. By the law of the land, the penalty for harbouring this 'beast' was death; and the reward for discovering him was 20*l*. When discovered, the priests were cast into prison, and shipped off at the first opportunity for Spain or the West Indies. But it was ordered (May 29, 1654), on reading a petition from them, that security should be taken of those who undertook to transport them, that they should, on the first opportunity, be shipped for some parts in amity with the Commonwealth,' provided the 5*l*. for each of the said priests, due to the persons that took them, pursuant to the tenor of a declaration dated January 6, 1653, be first paid or secured. William Shiel, priest, being 'old, lame, and weak, and not able to travel without crutches, was permitted to reside in Connaught, where the governour of Athlone thought fit, provided, however, he did not remove one mile beyond the appointed place without licence, nor use his priestly functions.' But no matter to what region beyond the seas those Irish priests were banished, they found means of returning to their country and to their scattered flocks, though at the imminent risk of sharing the fate of the wolves. And we find, at the close of the year 1655, the Irish Government complaining that the worst penalties did not daunt them, nor prevent their recourse to Ireland; so that a general arrest was ordered, under which, in April following, the prisons in every part of the country seem to have been filled. On May 3 the governors of the respective 'precincts' or districts were ordered to forward the priests, well guarded, from garrison to garrison, onward to Carrickfergus, to be there shipped to Barbadoes, having traversed the country on foot to this port in the county Antrim. There it seems that the horrors of approaching exile shook the faith of some of them, for we read that Colonel Cooper, who had charge of the prison, reported that many would, under their hands, renounce the Pope's supremacy, and frequent the Protestant meetings, and no other; and he was directed to dispense with the transportation if they could give good Protestant security for the sincerity of their professions.

It is a pity that the government of Henry Cromwell could not have embraced within its beneficent action the poor Roman Catholics and their clergy. Had the same measure of justice and protection been meted to them as to the Protestants, had permission been given to preach the gospel to them in their native

language, there was then an opportunity of sowing effectually the
seeds of that righteousness that exalteth a nation; but the cruel
antipathy of races was fostered by religious fanaticism, inflamed
by the lust of conquest, and the dread of retaliation prevented
any relaxation of the oppressive system till the restoration of
Charles II. Then the imprisoned Irish rushed across the Shannon
to see their old homes, and returned to the desolated cities full of
hope that the king for whom they had suffered so much would
reward their loyalty by giving them back their inheritances—' the
just satisfaction' he had solemnly promised them. The exiled
nobility and gentry and the priests hurried home from every land
in which they had found refuge; and again the native Irish,
rallying under the standard of the Catholic cause, soon became a
formidable power in the land. The Presbyterians, too, counted on
the gratitude of Charles for their devotion to his cause, notwithstanding the wrongs inflicted on them by Strafford and the bishops,
in the name of his father; but they were sadly disappointed.

When order was established, the Presbyterians returned from
Scotland in large numbers, followed by many new settlers from
that country. Now much favoured by the gentry and the public
authorities, they set about laying the foundations of the Presbyterian church in Ulster, in exact accordance with the Scottish
model; and from this period Dr. Reid states, 'the history of her
ministry, her congregations, and her ecclesiastical courts as they
now exist, can be traced in uninterrupted succession. The
Church in Ulster rapidly revived, and broke forth on the right
hand and on the left. The seed sown prior to the rebellion, though
long checked in its growth by the chilling severities of the prelates, now began to spring up with renovated vigour, and to
gladden the wilderness with its verdure and fertility.'

Now came the turn for the ascendancy of the Kirk. Prelacy
had had its day, and it was believed that its short-lived triumphs
were at an end for ever in Ireland, if not in England also.
Presbytery claimed a divine right not less absolute or less exclusive, and it inspired a spirit of domination not less resolute and
uncompromising. It had not its Star Chamber to enforce its
decrees; but, although it had but just escaped alive in Ulster
from the horrors of the 'Black Oath,' it came out with its

'Solemn League and Covenant,' an instrument of persecution almost equally effective for crushing Popery, Prelacy, and all sorts of Dissent. In 1644 Commissioners were sent to Ulster to administer this famous Solemn League and Covenant. They reached Carrickfergus in the end of March, and produced their commission at a meeting of the Presbytery, with a letter from the Scottish General Assembly. The oath was administered first to the regiments of the Scotch army, and it is stated that the whole country about came and willingly joined themselves in the Covenant, a very few excepted, 'who were either some old Conformist ministers or known profane, ungodly persons.' At Belfast, however, there was no liberty granted yet to offer the Covenant, and the Commissioners were, with difficulty, permitted to preach. 'As they went towards their lodgings through the streets,' says a contemporary record, 'there seemed to be a commotion among the people, some by their countenance and carriage declaring their indignation, and some their affection.' The Commissioners then proceeded to Raphoe, Letterkenny, and Enniskillen, where they were kindly received by Sir William Cole—ancestor of the Earl of Enniskillen—whose family took the Covenant. 'From this period,' says Dr. Reid, ' may be dated the commencement of the second Reformation with which this province has been favoured—a Reformation observable not only in the rapid increase of churches and of faithful and zealous ministers, but still more unequivocally manifested in the improving manners and habits of society, and in the growing attention of the people to religious duties and ordinances. It was reported to the Scottish Assembly that in the two counties of Down and Antrim above 16,000 persons of age and understanding had embraced the Covenant, besides the Scottish forces, yet there were only two ministers in all those bounds who actually adhered to the Presbyterian discipline in all things. The former clergy were distrusted for their conformity, because they had taken the Black Oath; hence application was made for Scottish ministers, on the ground that if great pains had not been taken by the few that had been sent, ' both the army and the inhabitants had removed themselves thence and left the land for a free habitation to the bloody and barbarous idolaters.' Supplies of ministers soon reached Ulster, and the Presbyterian historian relates, that 'no sooner had prelacy been deprived of the warlike support of the State, than the people, left to their own unrestricted choice, declared their preference for the Presbyterian form of government.' The ministers of the Kirk having the field very much to themselves, soon showed that they were but little in advance of the age they lived in, and persecution had failed to teach them the rudiments of toleration or respect for the rights of conscience. Accordingly, in 1645, the Presbytery, 'finding the Papists to grow numerous in the country, and considering their numbers might thereafter prove dangerous to the Protestant religion, and that, by the treaty between Scotland and England, no toleration was to be given to Papists; and also, pitying their souls in their ignorant and hardened condition, made an Act that they should be dealt with by the several Presbyteries, to convince them of their idolatry and errors, and bring them to own the truth; or otherwise to enter into process against them in order to *excommunication*; and they appointed some of their number to speak to the Major-General, that he use his authority for *forcing them out of this part*, and wholly out of the army, if they remained obstinate. This act of the Presbytery was publicly intimated in the several parish churches.'

Thus commenced the feud between the Scottish settlers and the 'bloody Popish idolaters,' which has lasted ever since, and which has been illustrated in a manner bloody enough in the summer of the year of grace 1872, when—after a civil war raging for nearly a week, in presence of immense military forces, in the streets of Belfast, the pre-eminently enlightened capital of Ulster—the lives of peaceable families on each side could be preserved only by their being forced to remove out of the quarters of each faction respectively and reciprocally. But it was not with the Roman Catholics only the Presbyterians were at war under the Commonwealth. They were also jealous of the Independents and the Baptists, who were favoured by Cromwell's Government, and had great influence in Ireland; Dr. Owen, Howe, and other eminent Independent ministers having preached with great acceptance in the parish churches in Dublin. When General Monk was commanding the British forces in

Ulster, he assisted the Presbyterians in carrying out their discipline; for with all their Divine Right, and the power of the Word of God, which they proclaimed to be mighty to the pulling down of strongholds, they were very ready to apply for the support of the arm of flesh, whilst striking the refractory with their spiritual weapons. Accordingly, under the General's auspices, they called before them a number of ministers, whom they deposed for various offences, amongst which are mentioned 'intruding in a neighbouring parish, railing against the professors of godliness, and baptizing promiscuously.' In 1649 the Presbytery of Belfast published a manifesto called ' A necessary representation of the present evils and imminent dangers to religion, laws, and liberties, arising from the late and present practice of the *Sectarian party* in England, and their abettors.' Among the charges made against the Sectarian party, as they were pleased to call the Nonconformists, were these:—' That they loved a rough garment to deceive; that they held a high hand, despised the Covenant, calling it a "bundle of particular and contrary interests, and a snare to the people;" and, most heinous of all, they endeavoured to establish by law a *universal toleration* of all religions, which would embrace even Paganism and Judaism in its arms.'

Eternal honour to the Sectaries!—the Independents and the Baptists, who were then in power—for this proposal to establish religious liberty by law, and on the most comprehensive basis. Their descendants in England at the present day may be well proud of such an ancestry. And it is a fact that ought to excite our wonder, that they are now engaged in agitating for the same principles which their ancestors proclaimed more than two centuries ago! Oh how different would have been the history of Ireland—what a saving of blood and treasure it would have been to England—how it would have strengthened the empire; how it would have added to the glory of Britain; how it would have secured the triumph of truth, freedom, and Biblical Protestantism in Ireland, if the policy advocated by the so-called ' Sectarian party,' and denounced by the Presbytery, had been the policy of England from that day to this! The English historian would have had a different story to tell of the rule of his countrymen in the sister island ; and there never would have been a question of the repeal of the union between the two countries.

However, the Presbytery of Belfast having reviewed the conduct of the Puritans, proceeded to express its horror of the execution of Charles I. in the following terms :—' Neither hath their fury stopped here; but, without rule or example, being but private men, they have proceeded to the trial of the King, against both the interest and protestations of the kingdom of Scotland— and the former public declarations of both kingdoms—with cruel hands they put him to death, an act so horrible as no history, divine or human, ever had a precedent of the like.' This was too much for the patience of Milton, the illustrious champion of civil and religious freedom, who was then Secretary to the Protector.

' What mean these men ? ' he indignantly asked. ' Is the Presbytery of Belfast, a small town in Ulster, of so large extent that their voices cannot serve to teach duties in the congregations which they oversee, without spreading and divulging to all parts, far beyond the diocese of Patrick or Columba, the written representation under the subtle pretence of feeding their own flock ; or do they think to oversee or undertake to give account to all to whom they send greeting. And surely in vain were bishops for these and other causes forbid to sit and vote in the House, if these men, out of the House, and without vote, shall claim to be permitted more license upon their Presbyterial stools to breed continual disturbance, by interposing in the Commonwealth. Of this representation we can esteem and judge no other than of a slanderous and seditious libel, sent abroad by a sort of incendiaries to delude and make better way under the cunning and plausible name of a Presbytery.' Milton proceeds with running observations on the Declaration, in which he speaks of its notorious falsities, its shameless hypocrisy, charging its authors— ' unhallowed priestlings '—with designing a rebellion against the Government. He reminded his readers that ' the Scottish inhabitants joined Ormonde and the Irish rebels in an open war against the Parliament.' He spoke of the rancour that leavened them as having somewhat ' quickened the common drawling of their pulpit elocution.' Answering the charge made against

Cromwell's Government, that it had not endeavoured to extirpate Prelacy and Popery according to the Covenant, the poet said :— 'No man well in his wits, endeavouring to root up weeds out of his ground, instead of using the spade will take up a mallet or a beetle; nor doth the Covenant in any way engage us to extirpate or prosecute the *men,* but the heresies and errors in them, which we tell these divines and the rest that understand not, belongs chiefly to their own functions in the diligent preaching and insisting on sound doctrine, in the confuting—not the railing down—encountering errors, both in public and private conference, and by the power of truth—not a persecution—subduing those authors of heretical opinions; and, lastly, in the spiritual execution of church discipline within their congregations.'[1]

This is the spirit in which the English in Ireland, during the 17th and 18th centuries, ought to have conducted the government of that country. If they had done so, they would not have been troubled with civil wars or invasions from Spain and France; nor would their statesmen have now to confess with shame and regret the errors and crimes which have made the whole of Christendom take part with the Church of Rome in Ireland, whose fold has been crowded by persecution. It is, however, curious to remark that the late Rev. Dr. Reid, though regarded as one of the liberal party in the Presbyterian Assembly, of which he was one of the most learned members, in referring to this manifesto by Milton, speaks as bitterly about it as if he had been the clerk of the Belfast Presbytery. He says it was 'a fair sample of the scurrility and overbearing violence and contempt of the ministerial office by which the usurping faction and their abettors were characterised.'[2] He adds, that during the vicissitudes of the civil war the Presbytery persevered in testifying against the power of the usurpers, and in favour of a limited monarchy. Commissioners were sent over from Scotland in 1650 to encourage them in their opposition to the Government, and in their adherence to the King, who was now solemnly pledged to support the Covenant. Providence, as if in anger, at length granted their prayer, but before that consummation which they

[1] Observations upon Articles of Peace with Irish Rebels, &c.
[2] 'History,' vol. ii. p. 178.

so devoutly wished and had afterwards so much reason to deplore, they had an opportunity of enjoying the blessings of civil government, conducted on the principles of Christian equity and religious freedom, by the men whom they had reprobated as a 'usurping faction.' With them at that time all other Christians were divided into three classes:—the Roman Catholics were 'Popish Idolaters,' the Episcopalians were 'Malignants,' and the Independents and Baptists were 'Sectaries.'

The brief reign of peace, order, and prosperity which Ireland enjoyed under the Protectorate was due in a great measure to the personal character of Henry Cromwell, who arrived in Dublin in March 1654. He found the government in a most unsatisfactory state, the Council doing very little except making orders to give away the public lands from which the natives had been swept off by sword, famine, and pestilence, or by deportation to Connaught. As might be expected, they appropriated the larger shares to each of themselves. Of course such a *régime* must have produced general discontent. But Henry announced that the great desire of his father's Government was 'that all might be upon an equal account, as to encouragement and countenance.' The next year he went over again as Major-General of the army in Ireland, and he was soon after invested with the government of the country. It was reserved for him to give the most convincing and satisfactory proof of the truth of the oft-quoted testimony of Sir John Davis, so little regarded in his own practice and in the conduct of his colleagues, that of all people the Irish were emphatically 'lovers of equal and impartial justice, though it be against themselves.' This novelty they found under the administration of Henry Cromwell. His policy had a marvellous effect in tranquillising the minds of all parties, and softening sectarian animosities. The various denominations rivalled one another in the warmth of their testimony to 'his equal justice to all and mercy to the poor.' Notwithstanding the seditious proceedings of the Presbyterians, they were protected by him in the exercise of their discipline, and the observance of public worship. They were even allowed to enjoy the State endowment 'without any ensnaring engagement,' though they refused to keep the days of public fasting and thanksgiving ordered by the Government. In 1658 he invited a number of the more eminent Independent and Presbyterian ministers to meet him in Dublin, in order to treat about the 'regulation and improvement of their maintenance, which had hitherto been carried on " in a mongrel way between salary and tithes."' The result was, that they adopted a plan by which each minister should have a salary of 100*l.* a year—a very liberal stipend considering the value of money in those times. The Independents were the ablest and most devoted champions of the Commonwealth, and they were naturally favourites of the Lord Protector. The Chancellor of Ireland was the head of that party in Dublin, and he was dissatisfied because it was not in the ascendant. But Henry Cromwell was determined to maintain the principle of religious equality, no matter what might be his personal predilections. 'I wish,' he wrote, 'I could truly say that the Independents were not dissatisfied. It may be some of them thought they should ride when they had thrown the Anabaptists out of the saddle. But I must neither respect persons, nor parties, nor rumours, so as to be thereby diverted from an equal distribution of respect and justice to all; though I hope I shall always take a good care of all (under what form soever) in whom I see the least appearance of godliness.'[1]

We should not be surprised to learn that under the system of equal justice the kingdom continued to enjoy unusual tranquillity, and that in no part of the empire did there exist a more cordial and general submission to the new Protector. The Presbyterians improved the opportunity to the utmost of extending and strengthening their Church in Ulster; but while they did so, they were so blinded by political prejudice, that they exerted themselves by every means in their power to bring about the Restoration. Had not Charles solemnly sworn to maintain the League and Covenant? Would he not, therefore, favour the Presbyterians and establish their Church in Ireland, to the perpetual exclusion of 'Papists, Malignants, and Sectaries'? The event they so much desired came to pass; but never was a loyal Church so disappointed.

[1] Reid, vol. ii. p. 317.

CHAPTER XIV.

THE RESTORATION OF PRELACY.

CHARLES II. was brought back in triumph to his throne. Immediately a Presbyterian Synod was held at Ballymena, when all the brethren in the North were present. Mr. Adare brought to every one of them a warrant for the *tithes* of their respective parishes, as far as was in the power of the Commissioners in Dublin. Two ministers were deputed to present an address of congratulation to the King in London, expecting, no doubt, that their loyalty would obtain for them the warmest welcome, and that his Majesty would hasten to redeem his pledge to enforce the Solemn League and Covenant in Ireland. But they were disheartened as they approached the metropolis by ominous rumours of a change in the royal mind. One powerful friend after another declined to introduce them to the court. Monk, now Duke of Albemarle, who had lent them his troops to help them to enforce their discipline, now 'disgusted their address, and would not concern himself in it as it was drawn up,' because it contained a denunciation of Prelacy and a laudation of the Covenant. Sorely against their conscience they were obliged to expunge those repulsive words. The King condescended to hear the address read when it was thus expurgated. 'But he looked with an awful, majestical countenance on them,' meaning, no doubt, to assume the most sublime expression of Divine Right as the head of the Church. As usual with him, he gave them good words and told them they had nothing to fear; but, as Strafford said with reference to Charles I., that he knew the mind of the king best, and had his real meaning hid in his own breast, so the Ministers of Charles II. knew what he meant to do, in whatever contrary sense his royal declarations might be understood.

This the Presbyterians soon found to their cost. Under the

Government which they had laboured to overthrow, their ministers had increased from half-a-dozen to seventy, regularly and permanently settled, and having under their charge eighty parishes or congregations, with a population not far from 100,000. But the flocks were soon scattered, and the shepherds compelled to flee. The bishops were immediately restored to their sees; and Bramhall and Leslie, their old enemies, came back to their posts, having a long account to settle with those who had been ruling in their places and denouncing them as 'Malignants.' Three of the Leslies, a lucky Scotch family, well represented still among the landed gentry of Ireland, then wore mitres in Ulster: John in Raphoe, Robert in Dromore, and Henry in Down and Connor. The latter was translated to Meath, and was succeeded by Jeremy Taylor, one of the most illustrious of the Irish bishops, who, during the Commonwealth, had been distinguished as the eloquent champion of religious freedom and the rights of conscience; but such is the weakness of human nature, such the effect of official position on the greatest minds, that when he came to his see at Lisburn he forgot the spirit and principles of his *Liberty of Prophesying*; and so he dealt with Presbyterians just as the Presbyterians had dealt with the Catholics. Presbytery was now scornfully repudiated by the nobility and gentry who had zealously patronised it a little while ago; by the Broghills, the Cootes, the Blaneys, the Caulfields, the Coles, the Rawdons, the Trevors, the Hills, and many others. It was no longer regarded by them as the religion of a gentleman, and their carriages were no longer seen driving up to the door of the meeting-house. Four Presbyterian ministers were sent as a deputation to Dublin to plead for freedom and fair play with the new authorities; but the Council being composed of bishops and their friends, they were received coldly, and by some rudely repulsed, reviled, and mocked. Jeremy Taylor summoned the incumbents he found in his diocese, and set before them a cruel dilemma, worthy of the casuistical mind of the author of *Ductor Dubitantium*. He told them that he perceived that 'they were in a hard taking; for if they did conform contrary to conscience, they would be but knaves, and if not, they could not be endured contrary to law.' He wished them, therefore, *deponere conscientiam erroneam.* As they were not able to do this to his satisfaction, he declared thirty-six of their churches vacant in one day. Their pastors were silenced and thrust out of their charges and their parsonages—in some cases with violence. Altogether, sixty-one Presbyterian ministers—nearly the whole number then in Ulster—were evicted by the prelates and deprived of their benefices, while the penalties for *recusancy* were in many districts inflicted on both ministers and people, by intolerant magistrates, with unwonted severity. For two or three years their condition was deplorable; and again the ministers began to think of emigrating to America, because of persecution and general poverty abounding in those parts; and, on account of their straits, they had little or no access to their ministry.[1]

Coote and Broghill still ruled in Dublin Castle as Lords Justices. The first Parliament that assembled there for twenty years (the Cromwellian *Union* being now repealed) contained an overwhelming majority of undertakers, adventurers, and Puritan representatives of boroughs, from which all the Catholic electors had been excluded. 'The *Protestant Interest*,' a phrase of immense potency in the subsequent history of Ireland, counted one hundred and ninety-eight members, against sixty-four Catholics in the Commons; and in the Lords seventy-two, against twenty-one Peers. A court was established in Dublin to try the claims of 'Nocent and Innocent proprietors.' The judges, who were Englishmen, declared, in their first session, that one hundred and sixty-eight were innocent and only nineteen guilty. The Protestant Interest was alarmed. Hence, through the influence of Ormonde, then Lord Lieutenant, the duration of the court was limited; and when it was compelled to close its doors only eight hundred out of three thousand cases had been decided. Fifteen years after the Restoration English settlers were in possession of 4,500,0000 acres, while the old owners retained 2,250,000 acres. By an Act passed in 1665 it was declared that no Papist who had not already been adjudged innocent should ever be entitled to claim any lands or settlements. While the panic lasted about

---

[1] See Reid, vol. ii. p. 425.

the danger of the Protestant Interest, the Catholics were subjected to cruel restrictions and privations. They were forbidden by proclamation to enter the Castle of Dublin, or any fortress ; to hold fairs or markets within the walls of fortified towns, or to carry arms in such places.

Lord Macaulay, who understood the case of Ireland better than most English historians, remarks 'that the Irish were the only people of Northern Europe who had remained true to the old religion,' which he ascribes to the fact that they were some centuries behind their neighbours in 'knowledge.' But other causes had co-operated. The Reformation had been a national as well as a moral revolt. It had been an insurrection of the laity against the clergy, but also of all the branches of the great German race against an alien domination. It is a most significant circumstance that no large society of which the tongue is not Teutonic has ever turned Protestant, and that wherever a language derived from that of ancient Rome is spoken, the religion of modern Rome prevails. The patriotism of the Irish had taken a peculiar direction. The object of their animosity was not Rome, but England; and they had special reason to abhor those English sovereigns who had been the chiefs of the great schism. During the vain struggle which two generations of Milesian princes had maintained against the Tudors, religious enthusiasm and national enthusiasm became inseparably blended in the minds of the vanquished race. The new feud of Protestant and Papist inflamed the old feud of Saxon and Celt. The English conquerors had meanwhile neglected all legitimate means of conversion. No care was taken to provide the vanquished nation with instructions capable of making themselves understood. No translation of the Bible was put forth in the Irish language. The Government contented itself with setting up a vast hierarchy of archbishops, bishops, and rectors, who did nothing; and who, for doing nothing, were paid out of the spoils of the Church loved and revered by the great body of the people. In other words, as he elsewhere strikingly expressed it, 'Ireland, cursed by the dominion of race over race, and of religion over religion, remained indeed a member of the empire, but a withered and distorted member, adding no strength to the body politic, and reproachfully pointed at by all who feared or envied the greatness of England.'

This evil destiny, however, seemed to be on the eve of being reversed when a Catholic ascended the throne of England, in the person of James II. It was believed throughout Catholic Christendom and, of course, fervently hoped by the Irish themselves, that James would effect a counter-Reformation. He would restore the national hierarchy to the proud position it had been dragged down from by the Cromwellians; he would give back to the Irish nobility their estates; and, to effect this glorious revolution, he relied upon the fidelity and valour of the Irish. His conduct soon favoured their most sanguine expectations. In Ireland the Protestant militia were disarmed; a Catholic army was formed, the corporations were thrown open to the natives. Catholic mayors and sheriffs, escorted by troops, went in state to their places of worship. The Protestant Chancellor was dismissed to make way for a Catholic. The plate of Trinity College was seized as public property. The Protestants, as well they might, were now thoroughly alarmed, and they fled to England in thousands. Many went to Holland, and joined the army of the Prince of Orange. Protestants who would not cross the Channel fled to Enniskillen and Derry, which closed its gates and prepared for its memorable siege; for there was a rumour of another massacre of the English and the repeal of the Act of Settlement, while dreadful stories were circulated of an intended invasion of England by wild Irish regiments under Tyrconnel.

In the meantime James, who had escaped to France, plucked up courage to go to Ireland, and to make a stand there in defence of his crown. His progress from Kinsale to Dublin was an ovation. Fifteen royal chaplains scattered blessings around him; Gaelic songs and dances amused him; he was flattered in Latin orations, and conducted to the capital under triumphant arches. The trades turned out to meet him with new banners; two national harpers played by the gate at which he entered; the clergy, in their robes, chanted as they went; and forty young girls dressed in white, tripped before him on the light fantastic toe, strewing flowers on the newly sanded streets. Tyrconnel, now a Duke, the Judges, the Mayor, and

Corporation in their robes, completed the procession, which moved beneath arches of evergreens and windows hung with tapestry and cloth of Arras. The Recorder delivered to his Majesty the keys of the city, and the Catholic Primate waited to conduct him to the royal chapel, where the *Te Deum* was sung. On that day the green flag floated from the main tower of the Castle, bearing the motto ' Now or never—now and for ever.'

Such is the picture drawn by the Irish historian, all brilliant and rose-coloured. Very different is the one photographed on the spot by the French ambassador Aviaux, who accompanied King James, as copied by Macaulay. The Frenchman was there to watch the Irish case on behalf of his master. The French policy was that Ireland must be severed from the English crown, purged of the English colonists, reunited to the Church of Rome, placed under the protection of the House of Bourbon, and made in everything but name *a French province*. In war, her resources would be absolutely at the command of her lord paramount. She would furnish his army with recruits; she would furnish his navy with fine harbours, commanding all the great western outlets of the English trade. The strong national and religious antipathy with which her aboriginal population regarded the inhabitants of the neighbouring island would be sufficient guarantee for their fidelity to that Government, which could alone protect her against the Saxon. The contemporary sketches of the progress of the King from Kinsale (where he landed) to Dublin are instructive. He arrived there March 12, 1689. By the Roman Catholic population he was received with intense joy. A day was spent there in putting the arms and ammunition out of reach of danger. Horses sufficient to carry a few travellers were, with some difficulty, procured; and on the 14th he proceeded to Cork.

While the King and his Council were employed in trying to procure carriages and horses to convey them to Dublin, Tyrconnel arrived, bringing news of the resistance at Londonderry, which would not, in his judgment, hold out many days. The first part of the journey was through wild highlands, where it was not strange that there should be few traces of art and industry. From Kilkenny to the gates of Dublin the path of the travellers lay over gently undulating ground, and a limestone district rich with natural verdure; but, instead of being covered with orchards, corn-fields, flocks, and herds, it was a desert. 'An *untilled* and *unpeopled* desert' are the words of Macaulay: strange words for him, as if tilled and peopled, it could not be a desert. Manufactured articles were hardly to be found, or, if found, could only be had at immense prices. The men who were bred in the courts of France and England were struck with the uncouth and ominous appearance of the people who crowded to welcome James along the road. It was lined with 'Rapparees,' armed with staves, stakes, and half-pikes. The highway presented the aspect of a street in which a fair is held. Pipers came forth to play before him, and the villagers danced wildly to the music. ' Long frieze *mantles*, resembling those that Spenser had, a century before, described as "meet beds for rebels and apt cloaks for thieves," were spread along the path which the cavalcade was to tread; and garlands, in which *cabbage-stalks* supplied the place of laurels, were offered to the royal hand. ' The women insisted on kissing his Majesty; but it would seem that they bore little resemblance to their posterity; for this was so distasteful to him, that he ordered his retinue to keep them at a distance. Most of the dwellings in Dublin at that time were built of timber, and the Castle had, in 1686, been almost uninhabitable. Clarendon knew no gentleman in Pall Mall who was not more conveniently and handsomely lodged than the Lord Lieutenant of Ireland; and in spite of constant glazing and tiling, the rain continually drenched the viceregal apartments—not a bad symbol of the viceregal government. The King was conducted to another building. Every exertion had been made to give an air of festivity and splendour to the districts which he was to traverse. ' The streets, which were generally deep in mud, were strewn with gravel; boughs and flowers were scattered over the path; tapestry and Arras hung from the windows of those who could afford to exhibit such finery. The poor supplied the place of rich stuffs with blankets and coverlids. In one place was stationed a troop of friars with a cross. Pipers and harpers played 'The King shall enjoy his own again.' The Lord Deputy carried the sword of state before his master. The judges, the heralds, the lord mayor and aldermen, appeared in all the pomp of office. A procession of twenty coaches belonging to public functionaries was mustered. Before the Castle gates the King was met by the host, under a canopy borne by four bishops. At the sight he fell on his knees, and passed some time in devotion. He then rose, and was conducted to the chapel of his palace—once the riding-house of Henry Cromwell. A *Te Deum* was performed in honour of his Majesty's arrival. The next morning he held a Privy Council, discharged Chief Justice Keating from further attendance, ordered Aviaux and Bishop Cartwright to be sworn in, and issued a proclamation convoking a Parliament to meet on May 7.

The followers of James, according to Henry Grattan, 'though papists, were not slaves; they wrung a constitution from him before they accompanied him to the field.' But a constitution wrung from such a man was not worth much. The House of Commons, which was elected, consisted almost exclusively of Roman Catholics. Tyrconnel had given lists of the names he wished to have chosen, with the writs, to the returning officers. Scarcely any but Roman Catholic electors dared to show their faces, and these were so few that in some counties they did not exceed ten or twelve. In the leading cities, such as Cork, Limerick, and Galway, the number qualified under the new charters did not exceed twenty-four. Of the 250 members who took their seats only *six* were Protestants. In the speech from the throne James invited the Parliament to take the Act of Settlement into consideration, in order to redress the grievances of the old proprietors. The debates are described as 'all rant and tumult.' Judge Daly, a Roman Catholic, an honest and able man, could not refrain from lamenting 'the indecency and folly' with which the members of his Church carried on the work of legislation. 'Those gentlemen,' he said, 'were not a Parliament; they were a mere rabble; they resembled nothing so much as the mob of fishermen and market-gardeners who, at Naples, yelled and threw up their caps in honour of Massaniello. It was painful to hear member after member talking wild nonsense about his own losses, when the lives of all, and the independence of their common country, were in peril.' These words were spoken in private, but some tale-bearer repeated them to the Commons. A violent storm broke forth; Daly was ordered to attend at the bar. But just when he was at the door, one of the members rushed in, shouting ' Good news! Londonderry is taken!' The whole House rose, all the hats were flung into the air, three loud huzzas were raised. Every heart was softened by the happy tidings. Nobody would hear of punishment at such a moment. The order for Daly's attendance was discharged amid cries of ' No submission! no submission! we pardon him!' In a few hours it was known that Londonderry held out as obstinately as ever; 'and this assembly,' says Lord Macaulay, 'without experience, without gravity, and without temper, was now to legislate on questions which would have tasked to the utmost the capacity of the greatest statesman. Among the first of the Acts passed was one purporting to grant ' entire liberty of conscience to all Christian sects.' Of this proceeding Mr. O'Connell was accustomed to boast; and the fact was, at the time, triumphantly proclaimed as an answer to James's Protestant enemies in England. But, unfortunately, the same wind which carried the tidings of toleration across the Channel carried also the evidence of insincerity and double-dealing. ' A single law worthy of Turgot or of Franklin seemed ludicrously out of place amidst a crowd of laws which would have disgraced Gardiner or Alva. An Act which prepared the way for these was one annulling the authority of the English Parliament in Ireland. This was quickly followed by confiscations and proscriptions on a gigantic scale. The personal estates of absentees above the age of seventeen were transferred to the King. By one sweeping Act the greater part of the tithes was made over to the Roman Catholic clergy, the existing incumbents being left without one farthing of compensation, to die of hunger. A Bill repealing the Act of Settlement, and transferring many thousands of square miles of territory, was brought in and carried ' by acclamation.'

Lord Macaulay suggests excuses for this conduct of the Irish Catholic Parliament:—' The stern domination of a hostile class had blighted the faculties of the Irish gentleman. If he had been able to retain his lands, he passed his time in shooting, fishing, carousing, and making love among his vassals. If his estate had been confiscated, he had wandered about from bawn to bawn, and cabin to cabin, levying small contributions, and living at the expense of other men. He had never sat in the House of Commons; he had never taken an active part at an election; he had never been a magistrate; scarcely ever had he been on a grand jury. He had, therefore, absolutely no experience of public affairs. It would be absurd to expect mercy, justice, or wisdom from a class of men first abased by many years of oppression and then maddened by the joy of a sudden deliverance and armed with irresistible power. The representatives of the Irish nation were, with few exceptions, rude and ignorant. They had lived in a state of constant irritation. With aristocratic sentiments, they had been in a servile position. With the highest pride of blood, they had been exposed to daily affronts such as might well have aroused the choler of the humblest plebeian. In sight of the fields and castles which they regarded as their own, they had been glad to be invited by a peasant to partake of his whey and his potatoes. Those violent emotions of hatred and cupidity which the situation of the native gentleman could scarcely fail to call forth, appeared to him under the specious guise of patriotism and piety; for his enemies were the enemies of his nation, and the same tyranny which had robbed him of his patrimony had robbed his Church of vast wealth, bestowed on her by the devotion of an earlier age. How was power likely to be used by an uneducated and inexperienced man, agitated by strong desires and resentments, which he mistook for sacred duties? And when 200 or 300 such men were brought together in one assembly, what was to be expected but that the passions which each had long nursed in silence would be at once matured into fearful vigour by the influence of sympathy?'

The King did all in his power to stem the torrent, but in vain. Among the few Protestant members of the House of Peers was Lord Granard, who exerted himself strenuously on the side of public faith and sound policy, for which James sent him a special message of thanks. One day he met Lord Granard riding towards the Parliament House. 'Where are you going, my lord?' asked the King. 'To enter my protest, sire,' answered Granard, 'against the repeal of the Act of Settlement.' 'You are right,' said the

King; 'but I am fallen into the hands of people who will ram that and much more down my throat.' Among the things which it seemed they rammed down his throat was the issue of base money, by which he conceived he could get rid of his financial difficulties by calling a farthing a shilling. Pots, pans, knockers of doors, pieces of old ordnance, were carried to the mint, coined, put into circulation, and declared to be a legal tender in all cases whatsoever. A mortgage for 1,000*l.* was cleared off by a bag of counters made out of old kettles. Legal redress was out of the question. If the base money was refused, the soldiers that kept guard at the shop door carried off the traders to the Provost Marshal, who cursed them, swore at them, locked them up in dark cells, and by threatening to hang them at their own doors soon overcame their resistance. This plundering tyranny made a deep impression, and one of the most damaging associations connected with '*Popery*' during the subsequent age of Protestant ascendancy was James's 'brass money.'

But the Commons did not remonstrate against the iniquity. On the contrary there was no power, however unconstitutional, which they were not willing to concede him so long as he used it to crush and plunder the Protestants. Nor did they respect any prerogative which stood in the way of their inclinations on this point, or which they apprehended might be used to protect the race that they abhorred. They were not satisfied until they had extorted the King's consent to 'a portentous law—a law without parallel in the history of civilised countries'—the Act of Attainder. A list was framed, containing between 2,000 and 3,000 names. At the top was half the peerage of Ireland; then came baronets, knights, clergymen, squires, merchants, yeomen, artisans, women, children; no investigation was made. Any member of Parliament who wished to rid himself of a creditor, a rival, a private enemy, gave in the name to the clerk at the table, and it was generally inserted without discussion. Days were fixed for the attainted parties to surrender; and if anyone failed to appear on the appointed day, though his doing so might be a physical impossibility, he was to be *hanged, drawn, and quartered without a trial,* and his property was to be confiscated. He might be bedridden, he might be in prison, in the West

Indies, in France; but it was all the same. If he did not appear he was to be put to death whenever he could be caught, and his estates forfeited. This was the case with Lord Mountjoy, who was at the time a prisoner in the Bastile. Not a man of the proscribed had been heard in his own defence. And lest the King should be inclined to pardon any of them, an Act was passed restraining the prerogative of mercy, so that any pardons granted after November 1689, of persons who had been sentenced to death without a trial, should be absolutely null and void. Sir Richard Nagle came in state to the bar of the Lords, and presented the bill, with a speech worthy of the occasion. ' Many of the persons here attainted,' said he, ' have been proved traitors by such evidence as satisfies us. As to the rest, we have followed common fame.'

After legislation like this, we cannot be surprised at the determination with which the Protestants fought in Derry, on the banks of the Boyne, at Aughrim, and Limerick. Manifestly there was no cruelty which these Protestants embodied in Acts of Parliament and carried out in their subsequent policy, which could not be justified by an appeal to the conduct of James's Parliament in Dublin, and the vindictive tyranny of the Catholic Government of that day.

CHAPTER XV.

THE REVOLUTION AND THE PENAL CODE.

MR. FROUDE has given full details of the penal legislation which followed the Revolution of 1689, while lamenting all this trouble entailed by the weakness of William III. in not imitating the exterminating policy of Cromwell. But surely the Penal Code might have satisfied any moderate and reasonable lover of persecution. A mild summary of it is given by Hallam, who says:—'The penal laws against papists have scarce a parallel in European history, unless it be that of the Protestants in France, after the revocation of the edict of Nantes, who yet were but a feeble minority of the whole people. *No papist was allowed to keep a school, or to teach any in private houses, except the children of the family.* Severe penalties were denounced against such as should go themselves, or send others, for education beyond seas in the Romish religion; and on probable information given to a magistrate, the burden of proving the contrary was thrown on the accused; the offence not to be tried by a jury, but by justices at the quarter sessions. Intermarriages between persons of different religions, and possessing any estates in Ireland, were forbidden; the children, in case of either parent being Protestant, might be taken from the other to be educated in that faith. No papist could be a guardian to any child; but the Court of Chancery might appoint some relation, or other person, to bring up the ward in the Protestant religion. The eldest son, being a Protestant, might turn his father's estate in fee-simple into a tenancy for life, and thus secure his own inheritance. But if the children were all papists, the father's lands were to be of the nature of gavelkind, and descend equally among them. Papists were disabled from purchasing lands, except for terms of not more than thirty-one years, at a rent not less than two-thirds of the full value. They were even to conform within six months after any title should accrue by descent, devise, or settlement, on pain of forfeiture to the next Protestant heir; a provision which seems intended to exclude them from real property altogether, and to render the other supererogatory. Arms, says the poet, remain to be plundered; but the Irish legislature knew that the plunder would be imperfect and insecure while the arms remained; no papist was permitted to retain them, and search might be made by any two justices. The bare celebration of Catholic rites was not subjected to any fresh penalties; but regular priests, bishops, and others claiming jurisdiction, and all who should come into the kingdom from foreign parts, were banished, on pain of transportation in case of neglecting to comply, and of high treason in case of returning from banishment. Lest these provisions should be evaded, priests were required to be registered; they were forbidden to leave their own parishes; and rewards were held out to informers, who should detect the violation of these statutes, to be levied on the Popish inhabitants of the country. To have exterminated the Catholics with the sword, or expelled them like the Moriscoes of Spain, would have been a little more repugnant to justice and humanity, but incomparably more politic.'[1]

Such was the grand scheme which the collective wisdom of two parliaments devised for the evangelisation of a kingdom, after the light of Christianity had been shining on the nations for sixteen hundred years. There is not a base propensity in our fallen nature to which it did not minister temptation; not a virtue in the human heart which it did not strive to undermine; not a noble passion which it did not aim to pervert. It loosened the tenderest ties of life, and poisoned the vital springs of society. It rooted up confidence, and planted suspicion in the family, in the neighbourhood, everywhere. It made mammon, perfidy, and ingratitude household gods, which children were taught to worship; and it brought to the altars of Protestantism feigned consciences and rotten hearts. Where it won a convert, it ruined a soul; for if natural religion be destroyed, what foundation have we left for Christianity?

Mr. Froude has devoted a considerable portion of his volume

[1] 'Const. Hist.' ch. xviii.

on Ireland to a picturesque description of the moral and social state of the country under the operation of this code, by way of illustrating ' *Irish ideas*,' and the characteristics of Irish human nature. I may observe on this, in the first place, that it is not fair to judge of any people in a state of subjection, of compulsory impoverishment, compulsory ignorance, and consequent degradation. When the English went to destroy the crops in some parts of the country, they were astonished at the abundance of corn, the good cultivation, and the settled appearance of the landscape, which, in some districts, they said would favourably compare with the best parts of England at that time. But what must have been the appearance of those districts when the corn had been destroyed by the English armies, and the houses burnt? And let us remember how often this process of destruction was repeated. From the Invasion till the Reformation, or rather till the complete conquest of the country by Cromwell, the two nations which peopled it were in a state of constant warfare. There was on both sides a struggle for existence—society was disorganised, and there was little time or inclination for the study of literature or the work of education. Great social degeneracy was inevitable. We may judge of the temper of those times, when there was yet no distinction of Protestant and Catholic, from the advice coolly given to the Government of Henry VIII. by Robert Cowley, afterwards Master of the Rolls in Dublin.

'The very living of the native Irish,' said he, 'doth clearly consist in two things [*corn and cattle*]. Take these away, and they are past for ever to recover, or yet annoy any subject in Ireland. Take first from them their *corns*, and as much as cannot be husbanded, *burn* and *destroy* the same, so as the Irishry cannot live thereupon. Then to have their cattle and beasts, which will be most hardiest to come by, as they shall be in woods; and yet by reason that the several armies, as I devised, should proceed at once in continuance of *one year*—the same cattle shall be dead, destroyed, stolen, eaten!'

Here are '*English ideas*' with a vengeance, delivered by a judge. Of course the Irish must have been very stupid not to have received them with gratitude! And this reminds me of a fallacy which pervades the historian's treatment of the Irish.

He suggests comparisons with England, not as it existed then, but as it exists now. It would be quite easy, from the best English writers of the eighteenth century, to fill volumes with records of barbarities to match the worst things he has brought against the unfortunate race on whose character he has fastened, like a woman who clothes her step-daughter in rags, starves her almost to death, beats her black and blue, drives her into mischief, and then calls her neighbours to behold the contrast between this persecuted child and her own well-clad, well-fed, highly-cultured pet daughter, declaring that the other is a graceless reprobate, that she can get no good out of her, and that it is all in the incurable depravity of her nature.

The Irish had excuse enough for *smuggling* in the eighteenth century, because their legitimate trade had been deliberately destroyed, from the most odiously, the most vulgarly selfish motives. But in the ruling country—the civilised country, the land of monopolies—smuggling prevailed at the same time, and with all its demoralising consequences. Mr. Buckle might have reminded Mr. Froude of this, if he had not read Harriet Martineau's 'History of England.' 'Smuggling was very common around the English coasts, and the smugglers,' says Mr. Buckle, 'accustomed to the commission of every crime, contaminated the surrounding population, introducing vices formerly unknown, caused the ruin of entire families, spread, wherever they went, drunkenness, theft, and dissoluteness, which were the natural habits of so vagrant a life.'[1]

Want of truth is supposed to be a characteristic of the Irish peasantry, a characteristic which is said to belong to every subjugated and oppressed people—duplicity and falsehood being the only available defence of the weak against the impulsive fury of the strong, producing abject servility, one of the worst effects of tyranny. It is supposed that ruling nations are exempt from this vice, and especially England, the most truthful of them all. But what says Mr. Buckle, who has enquired into the subject? He says, 'All are agreed in this, that the *perjury* habitually practised in England, and of which Government is the immediate creator, is so general that it has become a source

[1] 'History of Civilisation,' vol. i. p. 256. See Martineau's 'History,' vol. i. p. 341.

of national corruption, has diminished the value of human testimony, and shaken the confidence which men naturally place in their fellow men.' Oxford and Cambridge are the eyes of England. Through them her cultured men—'the lords of human kind'—see the true, the beautiful, and the good. And what does Sir William Hamilton, the great philosopher, say of the Universities? He says, 'But if the *perjury of England stands pre-eminent in the world*, the perjury of the English Universities, and of *Oxford* in particular, stands pre-eminent in England.'[1]

Again, Englishmen love freedom, and they boast of a constitution the envy and admiration of the world. Well, so late as the year 1799 a law was passed by the English Parliament against *public lecturing*, circulating libraries, and reading rooms, without a special license from the Government. No man, without such license, was permitted to lend or sell a newspaper, a pamphlet or a book of any kind, even to a person residing in the same house.

At the close of the last century the Slave Trade was in full vigour in England. It was carried on openly by the most religious and respectable men in Liverpool. They prayed that God might speed the vessel freighted with human beings for sale, and they were careful to say 'D.V.,' or 'God willing,' in connection with the proceedings of their diabolical traffic. George III., who wished that every family in England should have a copy of the Bible, was their patron saint. When the law was invoked against the traders, he strained his prerogative in favour of the slave-dealing violators of it in the West Indies; and at one of his levées he turned his back insultingly upon Mr. Wilberforce, disgusted with his Anti-Slavery advocacy. In one year—1786—England had 130 ships engaged in the abominable traffic, and in that same year they carried off 42,000 innocent human beings into slavery. The trade was not finally abolished till 1807. Englishmen have carried it on since in many countries, and the world never heard more dreadful accounts of wrong and outrage of this kind than those which have reached us lately from the South Sea Islands, where human

[1] 'Discussions on Philosophy,' &c. p. 528. Buckle, vol. i. p. 260.

beings, allured by fiends dressed in the garb of Christian missionaries, have been seized and carried off, or, if they resisted, shot in the water like otters or rats. What volumes of disgusting 'English ideas' might be collected from our police courts, about wife murders and other heinous brutalities!

But if a man wrote such a book with such a title, would he give a true representation of the English nation? There is, in fact, an Irish Catholic gentleman, an able writer, Mr. T. D. Sullivan, of the Dublin *Nation*, now compiling 'The Story of England,' on Mr. Froude's race-blackening principle. His brother, Mr. A. M. Sullivan, some years ago wrote 'The Story of Ireland,' on the opposite plan, that is, relating all that was bright and good, and suppressing all that was dark and evil in the history of the Celtic race. When the black story of England, and the bright story of Ireland are placed side by side, the devoted nationalists may say, 'Look on this picture and on this!'

> On our side virtue and Erin ;
> On hers are the Saxon and guilt.

But of such performances we may fairly say,—the work composed by the illuminating process is a romance, and the work composed by the blackening process is national defamation, than which there is no sort of writing more pernicious, or more unworthy of a man of cultivated mind. Yet the disparagement of other nations and races is a prevailing fault with English authors and travellers.

Mr. Froude has made it a point on every occasion to exalt Cromwell at the expense of William III. He misses no opportunity of disparaging the illustrious victor at the battle of the Boyne, for no reason that can be divined, except that he was Macaulay's hero, and that he wished to deal justly and honourably by the Catholics of Ireland. Cromwell saw all the truth about the Irish at a glance, and if *his* ideas had been carried out, there would have been four Ulsters instead of one, and no Papist alive in any of them. But William did not understand the Irish problem. He was 'studiously lenient' with all the Irish. 'He felt no desire to break down by violence a people whom, *in his inexperience*, he deemed it possible to win by indulgent terms.' 'He imagined, as many an amiable person has imagined before and since, that the native Irish had been handled *irrationally and cruelly*' (silly man to believe such a thing) 'and needed only kindness to become faithful subjects. Neither should the Irish race be dealt with hardly—if William could help it—nor the Irish religion.' (pp. 164–5.)

The Limerick Treaty secured the rights of the Catholics to a certain extent. But the Irish Government designedly left out one of its most important clauses. William being an honourable man, desired to have it restored, and to preserve the faith of treaties inviolate. He was over-ruled by the English Parliament, and was obliged to succumb. Mr. Froude despises the Prince of Orange for this weakness, saying that his liberality 'was but a repetition of an experiment which had been tried many times, but had miserably failed.' (p. 207.) 'Had the Catholic bishops been compelled in earnest to betake themselves elsewhere, and had the importation of priests from abroad been seriously and sternly prohibited, the sacerdotal system must have died a natural death, and the Creed have perished along with it.' (p. 213.) All this only proves that William was a large-minded statesman, a friend of religious liberty and the rights of conscience, in an age of stupid intolerance, while Cromwell, with all his strength of character, was an ignorant and narrow-minded fanatic, who had but one method of dealing with political and religious problems, the savage method of cutting every knot with the sword, and uprooting every tree that would not bear fruit to his liking.

Dean Swift thus wrote to his friend Pope in 1735:—'This kingdom is now absolutely starving by the means of every oppression that can be inflicted on mankind. "Shall I not visit for these things, saith the Lord." You advise me right not to trouble myself about the world, but oppression tortures me. Corrupt as England is, it is a habitation of saints in comparison with Ireland. We are slaves, knaves, and fools, and all, but bishops and people in employment, beggars. The people of Lapland or the Hottentots are not so miserable a people as we.'

All this oppression was inflicted ostensibly for the sake of 'the Protestant Interest,' which it was the policy of the oppressors to identify with the 'English Interest,' in order that the power of this country might sustain them in their wrong-doing. Primate Boulter, who was the chief ruler in Ireland at that time, while admitting the utter failure of the Established Church, seems to have laboured earnestly to make the best of a bad system. Finding that all the institutions founded for the conversion of the natives had proved abortive, and that the funds and estates granted for the purpose were perverted to private uses by the clergy and gentry, he resolved to adopt some new measures for the cure of disaffection. Accordingly, in 1731, a petition was presented to George II., signed by all the archbishops and bishops, and thirty other dignitaries, as well as many of the nobility and gentry of highest rank and station, praying for an 'Incorporated Society,' for the education of 'popish and other natives.' In a letter which Boulter had addressed to an English prelate in 1730, we have a striking picture of the state of things produced by the system of coercion and oppression embodied in the penal code :—' The great numbers of Papists in this country, the obstinacy with which they adhere to their own religion, occasions our trying what may be done with their children to bring them over to our Church. . . . I can assure you that the Papists here are so numerous that it highly concerns us in point of interest as well as out of concern for the salvation of these poor creatures, who are our fellow subjects, to try all possible means to bring them and theirs over to the knowledge of the true religion, and one of the likeliest methods we can think of is instructing and converting the young generation: for, instead of converting those that are adult, *we are daily losing many of our meaner people, who go off to Popery.*'

When we reflect how strongly the interests of these meaner people must have bound them to the Church of their landlords and employers, at a time when Popery was not only a bar to all advancement in life, shutting out its disciples even from the right of earning their bread in any guild or trade, but was almost synonymous with treason—the fact of their secession from the ranks of Protestantism proves that there must have been the grossest dereliction of duty on the part of the Church. In fact, the Protestant families scattered in remote districts, and even small

English colonies planted in the south and west, were so utterly neglected by bishops and clergy, even during the early part of the present century, that they must either have lived and died as heathens, or else availed themselves of the services of the priests for uniting them in marriage, baptizing their children, and burying their dead. However, in 1733, a charter was obtained for the establishment of schools, which were supported by large Parliamentary grants, as well as private endowments. In order to ensure the Protestantism of the pupils, the schools were made *boarding* establishments, and when the children were taken in, thenceforth no relation, priest, or stranger was suffered to speak in private to any of them.

For some years the working of the system did not attract much attention. There was no free press then to take note of abuses, and no public opinion to condemn them if exposed. But somehow rumours got abroad which excited suspicion, and the celebrated philanthropist Howard was induced to visit them in 1784, and again in 1787. In his examination subsequently before a Parliamentary Committee he stated, that he found the Charter school children generally 'ill fed, ill clad, and ill taught; sickly, pale, miserable objects—a disgrace to all society.' In 1817–18–19 the Rev. Messrs. Thackeray and Lee inspected those schools. They found the children living in hunger, filth, and ignorance, learning and religion being totally neglected. They were compelled to almost slave labour at farms, looms, &c., for the benefit of their masters. Even in the exceptional cases, where the children were allowed sufficient food and clothing, they pined under the blighting influence of the system, and their sullen and dogged appearance betrayed some dreadful violation of the laws of nature. Mr. Lee, comparing these State schools, exclusively managed by clergymen, with the voluntary schools in the neighbourhood, says:—'I was invariably struck with the vast superiority, in health, in appearance, in vivacity and intelligence, of the half-naked and, one would almost suppose, half-starved children who live in their parents' cabins, over those who are well maintained and so carefully instructed in the Charter schools. In the Charter schools all social and family affections are dried up. Children once received into them are, as it were, the children, the sisters, the brothers, relations of nobody. They have no vacations, they know not the feelings of *home;* and hence it is, primarily, whatever concomitant causes there may be, that they are so frequently stunted in body, mind, and heart!'

In accordance with this testimony was the Report of the Commission of 1824, the Commissioners having inspected these schools personally. In the immediate neighbourhood of these church seminaries they found 'pay schools' in cabins and stables crowded with pupils, both Protestant and Roman Catholic, the parents refusing to send their children to the Government schools, where they could be taught free. There were clerical catechists who were required to make a monthly return to the Secretary in Dublin of the state and progress of their respective schools. On this condition they took their situations and received their salaries. But a report was rarely sent, nor did either the diocesan or the authorities in Dublin take any pains to correct or punish this flagrant neglect of duty. The local clergy were equally negligent, and when they did interfere it was not to protect the enslaved children, but to screen their cruel task-masters. The Commissioners observe, ' that no offence a Charter school child can commit seems to be less pardonable than daring to utter a complaint.' Notwithstanding, however, the difficulty of punishing delinquent masters, which was never done without legal proof, so enormous were the abuses of the system that between 1800 and 1825 no less than thirty-two masters had been dismissed for misconduct from a total of only thirty schools, and seventeen more resigned to avoid the same fate.

According to the notions of some persons, who mistake the means for the end, and the letter for the spirit, these schools were ' *Scriptural,*' the education was chiefly ' *religious.*' There was the Church Catechism, with an exposition of it; and there was the Bible, thumbed and torn as a hated task-book.

A system of such dishonesty, cruelty, rapacity, and impiety, was surely calculated to bring Scriptural education, so-called, into very bad odour. But this is what the Irish Church had to show as the result of her labours during one hundred years of absolute sway; and this is the spirit in which she did her work so late as seventy years ago, before voluntary agencies began to come into operation. She was amply paid in tithes and lands, and power and privileges, for the religious instruction of the people. Yet in the course of nineteen years these demoralising Charter schools cost the country no less than 1,612,138*l.*, of which 1,027,715*l.* consisted of Parliamentary grants. The total number apprenticed from the beginning till 1824 was only 12,745. Of these but a small number received the fee of 5*l.* each, allotted to those who served out their apprenticeship and married Protestants. A large proportion turned out badly; and 7,905 of these spoiled children cost the public just one million sterling.

So much for the educational work of the Irish Church. When we look to her spiritual condition we do not find matters much more satisfactory. But if she failed to accomplish her mission, the failure was not the result of any deficiency in the funds placed at her disposal. From 1791 to 1803 the Board of First Fruits granted the sum of 500*l.* in eighty-eight cases for the building of churches, making a total of 44,000*l.* During the same period the Board granted 100*l.* each for 116 glebe houses, making a total of 11,600*l.*; and from a Parliamentary return, ordered in 1826, it appears that within the present century the following sums had been voted by the Imperial Parliament up to that date :—

Gifts for building churches	£224,946
Loans ,, ...	286,572
Total	£511,518

for building churches in twenty-five years. During the same period gifts were made for glebes, 61,484*l.*; gifts for building glebe houses, 144,734*l.* Loans were granted for the same purpose amounting to 222,291*l.*, making a total for glebe lands and glebe houses of 428,509*l.* Thus, between the years 1791 and 1826, the Establishment obtained for churches and glebes the sum of 940,047*l.*[1]

The Church ought certainly to have been well-housed, yet there was unfortunately a very little to show for this vast expenditure of public money, for the accommodation of a small section of the community, which included nine-tenths of the owners of

---

[1] 'Liber Munorum Publicorum Hiberniæ,' vol. ii. pp. 208, 226.

property in the country. In those times everything was jobbed in Ireland. The churches which cost so much were about the ugliest buildings that could be imagined, and the most uncomfortable for the scanty congregations by which they were occupied. A small, barn-like structure, supported at one end by a broad, stunted tower, which served as a belfry, presented the only style of ecclesiastical edifice which the architects of those days seemed capable of understanding. These unsightly buildings generally cost double what they should have cost; and in a very few years they were in a state of dilapidation, requiring an additional outlay for repairs. Even the fine old cathedrals, appropriated at the time of the Reformation, not excepting St. Patrick's in Dublin, were allowed to go to ruin, the chancel being generally used for public worship, while the most beautiful ornaments were hid behind piles of rubbish, and marble pillars were bedaubed with whitewash.

These external appearances were but too sadly emblematic of the spiritual condition of the Church. Where Divine service was performed at all, it was conducted in a careless and a slovenly manner. Everything about it was cold, formal, and lifeless. The 'duty' was done because it *must* be done, but in such a hurried, careless way, as to show that it was most irksome to those appointed to minister in sacred things. The clergy, for the most part, belonged to the families of the aristocracy and the landed gentry, the younger sons who had no taste for the army or the navy going into 'the Church,' as the ministry was called, for the sake of a 'living,' and for the chance of its 'prizes.' They lived very much like the rest of the gentry, shooting, hunting, gambling, drinking, swearing, &c. The prizes were certainly magnificent. A large number of Irish bishops, beginning life with nothing but their profession, became the founders of noble families; and clerical blood, to a large extent, runs in the veins of the Irish aristocracy of the present day. From a calculation I made by examining the wills of twenty Irish bishops who died since 1822, it appears that they left personal property amounting to 861,868*l.*, giving for each bishop an average of 43,093*l.* This, of course, does not include the large amounts that may have been invested in landed property, or given as dowries to daughters, or spent in the purchase of commissions for sons; nor does it include the church patronage, by which the prelates were enabled to provide so well for their relatives.

Let us now glance at the condition in which the Roman Catholic Church emerged from the era of persecution, and see how she appeared to the world after experiencing the liberality of the Irish Parliament from 1782 to 1800, and of the Imperial Parliament, which had promised emancipation as an essential condition or a necessary consequence of the Act of Union. Two clergymen of the Established Church, the Rev. Messrs. Whitelaw and Walsh, in their 'History of Dublin,' published in 1818, notice the existence of Roman Catholic schools supported by Catholics in that city, as a striking feature 'in the toleration of the present day.' The historians state that while the penal laws were in force the Roman Catholic clergy were obliged to administer spiritual consolation to their flocks rather according to temporary convenience than to any systematic plan. No places of worship were permitted, and the clergyman moved his altar, books, and everything necessary for the celebration of his religious rites, from house to house, among such of his flock as were enabled, in this way, to support an itinerant domestic chaplain; while for the poorer sort some waste house or stable in a remote or retired situation was selected, and here the service was silently and secretly performed, unobserved by the public eye. . . . The crowds of poor people who flocked to receive the consolations of their religion, were too great for the crazy edifices to contain or support them, and serious accidents, attended by the loss of sundry lives, occasioned by the falling down of these places of resort, called for the interference of a humane Government. In the year 1745, Lord Chesterfield, then Viceroy, permitted the congregations to assemble in more safe and public places. The old edifices consecrated to public worship were re-opened, and new ones gradually built in the city. In the year when George IV. visited Ireland, just half a century ago, another Protestant clergyman, the Rev. G. N. Wright, described the state of the Roman Catholic Church in the Irish metropolis. There were then only three chapels deserving of notice. One of these was the 'Metropolitan Chapel,' a grand structure for the time, commenced in 1816, on a plot of ground formerly occupied by the mansion of Lord Annesly, just opposite Tyrone House, the town residence of the Marquis of Waterford, now the headquarters of the Board of National Education. It was built by subscription; but, grand as it was, the Catholics of that day did not presume to call it by any more pretentious name than 'chapel.' When they got more courage and confidence they called it a cathedral. But now they do not think it worthy of that name, and it is styled the 'pro-cathedral church,' doing duty provisionally until Cardinal Cullen finds a commanding site for a cathedral worthy the aspirations of a Church now working hard for ascendency in the country.

Indeed, the progress of Romanism in that country during the last half century has been so marvellous as to account for almost any pitch of soaring ambition on the part of the Hierarchy. When George III. died, there were in Dublin only ten parochial chapels, most of them of the humblest character and in the most obscure positions; and there were at the same time seven humble 'friaries,' as monasteries were then called, and ten nunneries. Now there are thirty-two churches, most of them fine, costly buildings, in Dublin and its vicinity, the total number of priests, regular and secular, being 412, and the number of nuns, 1,150. I do not speak here of the numerous colleges, schools, hospitals, refuges, orphanages, asylums, reformatories, fraternities, and other religious and charitable organisations with which the diocese abounds—all the result of voluntary zeal. The Protestant Episcopal Church has also made immense progress during the last half century, as we shall see hereafter, but, in comparing the two rival Churches, it is but fair to bear in mind how weak at the starting, and how heavily weighted, the Church of Rome was in the race of improvement. On the Protestant side were the attraction and patronage of the Court, the support of the heads of all the administrative departments, the State dignitaries, the judges, the bar, the magistracy, the corporation, and a continuous stream of extra public endowments which, from the Union to 1844, produced the following amounts, in addition to the ordinary revenues:—

		£
For building churches	. . . . .	525,371
„ glebe houses	. . . . .	336,889
„ Protestant charity schools	. . . .	1,105,588
„ the Society for Discountenancing Vice, &c.	.	101,991

A person travelling through Ireland in the present day would find it difficult to conceive the state of things with which earnest Roman Catholics had to contend half a century ago, when, in many places, the ' mass-houses ' were thatched cabins. Priests and people were alike demoralised and degraded. Very striking are the pictures illustrating this fact presented by Mr. Fitzpatrick in his ' Life of Bishop Doyle.' The united dioceses, Kildare and Leighlin, over which that prelate ruled, embrace two of the best counties in Ireland, Kildare and Carlow, and from their spiritual state we may infer the degree of debasement through which the Church had sunk in wilder districts. It appears that it had been the custom to appoint very aged men to the episcopal office, and that, owing to their infirmities and consequent inactivity, great laxity of discipline prevailed. Many of the parish priests were engaged in farming; others attended races, which were then very common; and not a few followed the hunt, to which the Irish gentry were then passionately addicted. The black coats and long clerical boots of the parsons and priests presented a curious contrast to the gay scarlet coats and white tops of their lay companions. 'As for the priests,' says Mr. Fitzpatrick, ' they ejaculated " Tally-ho ! " as often as " *Dominus vobiscum*."' The spirit of persecution having passed away to a great extent from social life, and there being no earnestness in religious matters anywhere, the priest and the parson became very good friends. They hunted together, dined together, drank together, played cards together, and they were about equally negligent and slovenly in their performance of their clerical duties. But in the Church of Rome there arose a reformer who showed how much one man can accomplish in his day and generation.

Dr. Doyle, so well known as a public writer under his signature of ' J.K.L.,' did more than all the bishops of his Church to achieve the work of emancipation. But he was a man of energetic action, as well as a powerful writer and speaker. He was endowed with one of those moral natures which can never rest when surrounded by abuses and disorders which they have the power to correct; one to which meanness, feebleness, and deformity are intolerable, when there is a possibility of replacing them by dignity, power, beauty, and utility. He was, therefore, the originator of that course of ecclesiastical renovation, material and spiritual, which has since his day produced such wonderful results; and his 'monument in stone,' the cathedral at Carlow, presented a model and an example which roused emulation in his brethren, and showed what could be accomplished under the greatest difficulties by the faith and courage of energetic minds. In 1841 Mr. Thackeray visited Carlow, and wrote thus in his Irish Sketch Book:—' The Catholics point to the structure with considerable pride. It was the first, I believe, of the many handsome cathedrals for their worship which have been built of late years in this country by the noble contributions of the poor man's penny, and by the untiring energies and sacrifices of the clergy. Bishop Doyle, the founder of the church, has the place of honour within it; nor, perhaps, did any Christian pastor ever merit the affection of his flock more than that great and high-minded man. He was the best champion the Catholic Church and cause ever had in Ireland—in learning and admirable kindness and virtue, the best example to the clergy in religion; and if the country is now filled with schools where the humblest peasant in it can have the benefit of a liberal and wholesome education, it owes this great boon mainly to his noble exertions and to the spirit which they awakened.'

Doctor Doyle, who was a very young bishop, began at once to root up the abuses which prevailed among the clergy. He felt that the words addressed to the prophet were meant emphatically for him:—' Behold I have this day set thee to root up and pull down, and to destroy, and to build and to plant.' If, after rebuking a priest for carelessness and dirt, he again found the vestments or altar cloths soiled or shabby, he tore them into ribands; and the Mass Book, if not clean, was also torn up and flung away. Objectionable vestments were sometimes cast into the fire of the sacristy. On one occasion, when repeated remonstrances had been disregarded by an old wealthy priest, who had got his torn chasuble stitched up by his housekeeper, the bishop, who appeared in the chapel unexpectedly, came out on the altar and addressed the congregation, saying:—' I regret there cannot be mass to-day; I have repeatedly impressed on your pastor the necessity and duty of providing himself with vestments befitting the dignity of the Holy Sacrifice. He has neglected to do so.' He then publicly destroyed the threadbare and dirty vestments, which had been kept in a turf basket.

The utter neglect of duty on the part of the priesthood, forty years ago, was strikingly exhibited in the case of Portarlington, one of the best towns in the county of Kildare, and then containing a population of 9,000 Roman Catholics. Yet for nearly twenty years there had been no confirmation in that parish. When visited by Dr. Doyle, it is said there were many present to be confirmed over sixty years of age. 'Good God,' he exclaimed, 'can these persons need confirmation?' On a subsequent occasion he returned to confirm the young people. The multitude was so great that the chapel could not contain them, and Lord Portarlington threw open Emo Park for their accommodation. Mr. Fitzpatrick says that this scene may be regarded as 'a random sample of what widely took place elsewhere.' The bishop himself, writing long afterwards to a brother about his labours at this time, said :—' James, you know what I suffered in mind. My brain was bursting with the myriad dictates of duty which crowded into it.' The most powerful means he used for the revival of religion among his priests was the 'spiritual retreat.' The Rev. Mr. Delaney describes the scene of one which he witnessed in 1820, when, at the invitation of this youthful bishop, one thousand priests and nearly all the prelates in Ireland assembled at Carlow. He conducted the retreat unaided, and preached three times every day for a week. These sermons, says Mr. Delaney, were of an extraordinarily impressive character; we have never heard anything equal to them before or since. I saw the venerable Archbishop Troy weep like a child, and raise his hands in thanksgiving.' 'More than forty years have elapsed,' observes another priest, 'but my recollection of all that Dr. Doyle said or did on that occasion is fresh and vivid. He laboured like a giant, and with the zeal of an apostle. There he stood, like some commanding archangel, raising and depressing a thousand hearts that hung fondly on his words. I never can forget that tall majestic figure pointing the way to heaven with an arm that seemed made to wield thunderbolts.'

Fifty-one years ago George IV. visited Ireland. He was

the first English sovereign that had set foot on Irish soil for 130 years; indeed, the first that had ever done so with a peaceful object. Sir Francis Burdett once wrote a letter of a single sentence to his friend Lord Cloncurry, as follows :—' Dear Lord Cloncurry, I should like to know what you think would allay Irish agitation. Yours truly, F. B.' The question might be put now with perhaps as little hope of obtaining a satisfactory answer, after half a century of concession and conciliation.

It was fully expected, however, that the Royal visit would inaugurate an era of peace, union, and prosperity. No exertions were spared to secure that most desirable result. The old exclusive Corporation of Dublin, the very stronghold of Protestant ascendency and Orangeism, was all liberality on this occasion. The Lord Mayor, afterwards Sir Bradley King, gave directions to prevent the dressing and re-painting in orange tints the statue of William III., as was the custom for the anniversary of the battle of the Boyne. The Earl of Fingal and the leading Catholics were invited to co-operate in the reception of his Majesty, being assured that this proposal was 'for the purpose of lasting concord and harmony.' On the other hand, the Catholics welcomed this offer 'as an auspicious omen of the future happiness of Ireland.' Mr. O'Connell, who had then become the most influential of the popular leaders, exerted himself to the utmost to bring about a consummation so devoutly to be wished. Accordingly a preliminary banquet took place at Morrison's Hotel, when 400 of the most distinguished Protestants and Catholics sat down at the same table, the tickets being two guineas each. The Lord Mayor presided, the vice-chair being occupied by Lord Fingal, representing the Catholic peers. Fifteen hogsheads of porter were given to the people to drink the King's health. All the speeches breathed fraternity and union. Mr. O'Connell said that in sorrow and bitterness, but with the best intention, he had for the last fifteen years ineffectually laboured for his unhappy country. One bright day had now realised all his fond expectations. Next to the gratification of the present scene was the expected arrival of his Majesty, who came of his own free will, the sound of his footsteps proclaiming unanimity and peace. On this occasion the Protestant was ready to meet the Catholic and the Catholic the Protestant; and surely from a prince who declared that the Crown was only kept for the benefit of the people everything was to be expected.

The King arrived on Sunday, the 12th of August, landing at Howth, in so joyous a mood that he shook hands with everybody all round on the pier. He was received wherever he presented himself with demonstrations of loyalty for which the word 'enthusiastic' would be far too weak. The people of all classes, from the highest to the lowest, seemed delirious with loyalty, while the King responded in a manner almost equally fervid and demonstrative. On Monday, the 20th, he held a levée at Dublin Castle, when upwards of 2,000 gentlemen went to do him homage. Among these were the Irish Roman Catholic bishops. It was the first time since the Revolution that the prelates of the Roman Catholic Church had been allowed the privilege of standing before the throne of their sovereign. They appeared as a deputation, which consisted of the Primate, Dr. Curtis; Dr. Troy, Archbishop of Dublin; his coadjutor, Dr. Murray; Dr. O'Kelly, Archbishop of Tuam; Drs. Plunket, Marum, Doyle, Macguarin, Archdeacon, and Murphy. An address, presented by the Primate, was read by Dr. Murray. The King read a reply, after which all the prelates in turn kissed hands, having been received in the most gracious manner. In their address they glanced at the past history of Ireland when its sovereigns only approached its shores in hostile array. 'For us,' they said, 'has been reserved the happier lot of welcoming for the first time a sovereign who comes to his people with the olive branch of peace in his hand and with healing on his wing, to receive the willing and undivided allegiance of every individual within the wide range of his extended rule, the homage of the confidence and zealous attachment of all his subjects of every class and description. For ourselves and for the clergy of our communion, the spiritual pastors of four-fifths of the population of this portion of your Majesty's dominions, we acknowledge the weighty debt of gratitude by which we are bound to your Majesty's august house.' Having observed that they had never failed in their duty at the worst of times, they added: 'How many and how important are the additional inducements which must now stimulate our humble endeavours in the discharge of the same bounden duty when protected as we are by the legislation of our country.'

This address was presented before the passing of Catholic Emancipation, which had been promised as part and parcel of the Act of Union, a promise which the Imperial Parliament had failed for twenty years to fulfil, owing to the bigotry of George III., to whose august house they declared themselves to be so grateful. Since that time the Church of Rome in Ireland has received a series of the most important concessions, culminating in the abolition of the Church Establishment and the settlement of the Land Question upon principles of equity. Yet the attitude of the Papal Hierarchy towards the English Government was never so hostile, nor its tone so arrogant, even in the worst days of Tory oppression. How then shall we answer Sir Francis Burdett's question: 'What would allay Irish agitation?' What is the *fons malorum* which has so long baffled the efforts of British statesmen to dry it up? A hundred contradictory answers would ring in our ears from each side of the Channel.

CHAPTER XVI.

EVANGELICAL MISSIONS.

During the great revival movement in the British Churches in the early part of this century special attention was directed to Ireland as a field for missionary operations. Christian philanthropists pitied the natives as the victims of misgovernment and landlord oppression on the one hand, and of priestcraft and superstition on the other. Earnest Protestants felt humiliated at the disgraceful failure of the Reformation after an experiment of 300 years. The French Revolution had exerted a mighty influence on the masses everywhere, and the Irish in particular sympathised with a power which had promised, and more than once attempted, to break the English yoke under which they had so long groaned. Lord Chancellor Redesdale, an Englishman, lamented the fact that the temper of the peasantry had completely changed, and that a Jacobinical spirit prevailed amongst them extensively; and that spirit found a no less congenial predisposition even among the Presbyterians of Ulster. This state of things seems to have produced a powerful effect on the minds of the more thoughtful of the Irish peers, and upon many of the landed proprietors. Accordingly, when the strain and excitement of the French War had ceased, and the rapid fall of prices, combined with a vastly increased population upon their estates, threatened a dangerous crisis, it became a serious question how the Roman Catholics were to be dealt with in order to make them peaceable Christians and loyal subjects. It is no wonder, indeed, that reflecting men should be alarmed at the reckless lawlessness that prevailed in the south, notwithstanding the sternest methods of repression. When the late Chief Justice Lefroy, then Serjeant Lefroy, was called upon to take the place of one of the judges at the Special Commission under the

Insurrection Act at Limerick and Cork in 1822 (not a year after the King's visit), no less than thirty-five men were condemned to death at Cork, some of them being ordered for *immediate* execution, and others for *speedy* execution. With respect to the remainder, the penalty was suspended, with a hope held out that their lives would be spared if the country became tranquillised, and the peasantry would surrender their arms ; but if no signs of returning peace appeared they must die. In spite of this warning, at the Spring Assizes, which took place a few weeks later, the gaols were again full of persons committed for capital offences. At Limerick, Serjeant Lefroy presided at the adjourned assizes, and in writing to his wife, that pious, Bible-reading judge recorded, without apparent emotion, that on this, his first, appearance on the Bench he had consigned *nine* men to the gallows, four others having received the same doom from the lips of Baron Pennefather. Mr. Lefroy consoled himself with the reflection that, ' in answer to his constant prayers, he had been enabled to discharge his duty faithfully, firmly, and yet *mercifully*, and that he felt a strength of body and mind which it would be actual infidelity not to ascribe to Him from whom cometh down every good gift.'[1]

Mr. Lefroy was a thoroughly good man, a model in all the relations of private life, and an excellent judge; but his Toryism was so inveterate that he could see no cause for popular discontent in exorbitant rents, excessive taxes, want of employment, and extensive destitution caused by turning tillage land into pasture. His firm belief was that nothing was needed, and that nothing would avail, to produce peace and loyalty—to secure life and property—but the scriptural education of Roman Catholic youth, disregarding the authority of their priests ; and he proved his sincerity by proposing the formation of a society ' to teach the Scriptures to the people in their native language,' and by subscribing 1,000*l.* for the purpose.

A considerable number of the resident nobility were animated by similar feelings. Among the most prominent of these were Lord Roden, Lord Farnham, Lord Lorton, Lord de Vesci, Lord Powerscourt, and Lord Mount Cashel. Some of these, as well as a number of wealthy Commoners, engaged personally in the

[1] ' Memoir,' by his Son, p. 81.

work of religious instruction, assembling their tenants and dependents in their own houses, for the purpose of praying with them, and reading and expounding the Scriptures to them. The Earl of Mount Cashel, in a letter to the late Rev. Dr. Cooke, said, 'I am happy to tell you that long before I had the pleasure of hearing from you I had established morning and evening prayers in this house. All my servants, whether Protestants or Romanists, attend. In the morning I read a chapter to them out of the Old and New Testaments, and explain some of the most striking passages. This has done much good, and has evidently made an impression on the minds of many Roman Catholic hearers. The priest is, of course, displeased, and has denied them the Sacrament; but they remain steady.'

This was in the County Cork, where agrarian outrages abounded at the time. But such landlords as Lord Mount Cashel, belonging to old families to which the peasantry were attached for generations, could do almost anything with them, before the agitation of the Catholic Association and the retaliatory measures of the priesthood had inspired them with a sense of their rights, and persuaded them that their freedom, their nationality, and their prosperity were bound up with the authority of their Church.

However that may be, the religious feeling of the Irish nobility and gentry was excited and strengthened by the visits of zealous men from England and the Continent, whose hearts were glowing with missionary ardour. One of the most influential of these was Dr. Malan, of Geneva, who seems to have produced a powerful effect on all those with whom he came in contact. In England and Scotland the leading ministers of all denominations, especially the Congregationalists, felt the liveliest interest in Ireland as a missionary field. In London the Rev. Matthew Wilkes, Rowland Hill, Dr. Fletcher, Dr. Pye Smith, Dr. Bennett, Dr. Andrew Reed, Dr. Leifchild, Dr. Morrison, and other leading ministers, lent all their influence to the cause of Evangelism in long-neglected Ireland. In the principal provincial centres it was the same. John Angel James, at Birmingham, Dr. M'cAll, at Manchester, Dr. Raffles, at Liverpool, Mr. Jay, at Bath, were always ready to help in the great work by commending it to their people, and opening their pulpits to its advocates. In Scotland, the Rev. Greville Ewing, of Glasgow, the Rev. Dr. Russell, of Dundee, Dr. Chalmers, Dr. Wardlaw, and many others, evinced a most generous sympathy on behalf of Ireland, and were liberally sustained by their congregations. The Messrs. Haldane, two brothers, possessed of considerable property, sold their estates, and devoted the proceeds to missionary purposes, at the same time consecrating their time and talents to the preaching of the Gospel. One of the first things they did was to get young men of ability trained and sent over to Ireland as missionaries.

In order to combine the efforts of those who wished to prosecute the work, and to give them extended and permanent effect, the *Irish Evangelical Society* was founded in London in 1814. An influential committee of ministers and laymen was appointed, and the late Rev. Dr. Tidman acted for many years as its honorary secretary. Its constitution was 'Catholic,'—meant to include Independents, Presbyterians, and Baptists, although practically it was in the hands of the Congregationalists, and most of the missionaries it sent forth belonged to that denomination. Chapels were gradually opened in the principal cities and towns—in Dublin, Cork, Limerick, Belfast, Londonderry, Armagh, Newry, Sligo, &c. The 'agents' of the Evangelical Society, as they were then called, besides conducting public worship and managing Sunday-schools at their respective headquarters, itinerated through the surrounding districts, preaching the Gospel in school-houses, barns, and sometimes in the drawing-rooms of the gentry, wherever an opening offered. English and Scotch ministers volunteered for this service at first; but a sort of Training College was established in an old mansion house in Manor Street, Dublin, for the purpose of raising up a native agency by the education of young Irishmen who felt called to this work.

In this itinerant work the example had been set by the Methodists. The brothers Wesley in their visits to that country kindled the fire which has burned more and more widely ever since; and in the course of years almost every town in the kingdom had its Wesleyan chapel. The Methodist preacher, mounted on his missionary horse, might be seen every month, as regularly as the day came, wending his solitary way by mountains, glens, and bogs, to the farmer's house, where the ' prophet's chamber' was prepared for him, and where he preached the Gospel, and expounded the Word of God with wonted fervour to the delighted hearers, who had been gathered from the surrounding district. Chief among these Wesleyan missionaries was Gideon Ousely, who devoted himself to the Roman Catholics, preaching on horseback, in fairs and markets, and at the chapel gates, his head protected from cold by a close-fitting black cap. He was sometimes roughly treated, and he lost an eye from a blow of a stone. His 'Life' presents a vivid picture of those times.

These Nonconformist home-missionaries thus, traversing the country in all directions, produced a great effect on the Protestant people, who had been so grievously neglected by the parochial clergy, many of them complaining, even in towns, that, though they had large families and attended church, they had not received a pastoral visit for ten or twenty years. The preaching of the Evangelical missionaries they found to be delightfully refreshing and stimulating on account of their fluency and ardour, their familiarity with the Scriptures, the earnestness of their appeals to the conscience, their constant exaltation of CHRIST as the only Saviour and Mediator, and of the Bible as the only and all-sufficient rule of faith. The cheering animation of religious services thus conducted, the fervent singing of hymns in which most of the congregation joined, the varied, comprehensive, and impressive prayers, skilfully adapted to local circumstances and personal experience, and the eloquent, practical, extemporaneous sermon, abounding in Scriptural illustrations, all these, contrasted with the Church service, made the people feel more and more dissatisfied with the Established clergy and their cold, formal, drawling, if not hurried and irreverent, reading of the Bible and the Liturgy, as well as with the moral essays which they called sermons. To the bishops, therefore, and to all serious Churchmen, who believed the Irish Establishment to be the bulwark of Protestantism and the mainstay of the Constitution, it became more and more apparent, from year to year, that, unless there was a revival of real Evangelical religion in the Church, she must perish ignominiously. Although, from habit and through social influence and political feeling, many families attended the church in the forenoon, they crowded the 'conventicles' on Sunday evenings, because, as they said, they wanted to hear the 'Gospel,' which their own pastor did not preach; their souls hungered and thirsted for the Word of Life, which he did not dispense. 'What, then, was he good for?'

The metropolis was at this time favoured by the ministry of several able men of different denominations. One of the first of the Englishmen who devoted themselves to the missionary work in Ireland was the Rev. William Cooper, who had belonged to Lady Huntingdon's Connection. He was a remarkably energetic, courageous man, a powerful controversialist, who delighted in exposing and denouncing Popery and priestcraft in no measured terms. For many years he preached in Plunket Street Meeting House, and although the building was in one of the lowest parts of the city, surrounded by a dense Roman Catholic population, neither his vehemence as a controversialist nor his sarcastic attacks upon the priesthood, caused him to be mobbed or seriously molested. His son, the Rev. William H. Cooper, a man of more polish and culture, a fluent public speaker and a good scholar, became the 'Resident Tutor' of the Manor Street College in connection with the Irish Evangelical Society. With him were afterwards associated the Rev. Dr. Urwick and the Rev. Dr. Stuart as Theological Tutors. Mr. Urwick, remarkable for his diminutive figure, his large head, and his powerful voice, as well as for his theological attainments, and the gravity and dignity of his bearing, laboured for a number of years at Sligo, a town with a considerable Protestant population, in the west of Ireland, which, owing largely to the exertions of an English layman, Mr. Albert Best, Agent of the London Hibernian Society, had become a centre of missionary operations for Connaught. Mr. Urwick won great celebrity by a discussion which he and two scripture-readers had with three priests at a place called Easkey. The peculiarity of this affair was, that the discussion was held in the parish chapel, the speakers on each side addressing from the altar the crowded and excited congregations which assembled there from day to day. Dr. Urwick was soon after invited to be the pastor of York Street, Dublin, whither he came with the important prestige of a successful champion of Protestantism, and where he remained till his death, after a long and useful career, greatly respected by all denominations.

The Rev. David Stuart, minister of Union Chapel, Abbey Street, belonged to the Secession Church in Ulster. Being a good Hebrew scholar, an excellent Biblical critic, and an effective speaker, his expository lectures attracted much attention at this time; and as many as half a score Church clergymen were sometimes counted among his hearers. Another Presbyterian minister, the Rev. Dr. Carlile, one of the ministers of the Scotch Church, Mary's Abbey, took an active and very influential part in the religious movements of that period. He was a hesitating, ungraceful speaker, but full of thought and useful matter; methodical and business-like in his habits, with a sound judgment and a practical turn of mind. These qualities, combined with his impartial position as a Scotchman, recommended him to the Government as the fittest man to be a 'Resident or paid Commissioner' on the National Board of Education, in which capacity he worked harmoniously with Archbishop Murray; and to Dr. Carlile was entrusted the very delicate task of compiling the Scriptural Lessons which were used for many years in the National Schools.

These four men—Urwick, Cooper, Stuart, and Carlile—by their commanding talents, their multifarious labours, their public spirit and temperate zeal, working together with cordiality, raised very high in popular esteem the cause of Evangelical Dissent, while powerfully stimulating, by their example and influence, the Evangelical clergy in the Church. A similar effect was produced in the provincial towns by the gifted young men sent forth from the Manor Street College. They were not so thoroughly educated as they should have been, in most cases being prematurely thrust forth into the vineyard because the labourers were so few; but some of them distinguished themselves greatly as preachers and as controversialists, rendering important service to the cause of truth and freedom also by their writings.

The 'Bethesda' was for many years the only Episcopal place

of worship in Dublin in which ' the Gospel was preached.' But although it was the most fashionably attended church, crowded with a congregation that included the highest and noblest in the land, yet it was for years regarded as a ' Conventicle,' and no amount of influence could, for a long time, induce the Archbishop to grant a licence to its minister, the Rev. Mr. Mathias. This excellent man may be regarded as the father of the Evangelical party in the Irish Church. He was eminently successful as a preacher; his style of pulpit eloquence being distinguished by directness, simplicity, and pathos. He was the first Hon. Secretary of the Hibernian Bible Society; an indefatigable worker on religious committees, always lending his influence to promote union among Evangelical Protestants acting together on the ' Catholic principle,' merging denominational peculiarities for the sake of the common cause. Gradually Mr. Mathias found himself surrounded by a number of ministers holding the same principles, full of energy and ardour, some of them masters of a thrilling and impetuous eloquence which drew crowds to hear them whenever and wherever they preached.

The most influential among these ministers was Dr. Singer, the late Bishop of Meath. He was Regius Professor of Divinity in the Dublin University, and for many years Chaplain of the Magdalen Asylum, Leeson Street, where he had for his assistant the late Cæsar Otway. Dr. Singer exerted immense influence on the rising ministry as a Fellow and Tutor of Trinity College, and as a Professor. He took the liveliest interest in Divinity students, holding meetings with them in his rooms, and labouring in every way to give them just ideas of the duties and responsibilities of the Christian ministry, and to fit them for their proper discharge. Very many of the Evangelical clergy who became most distinguished in different parts of the country, looked up gratefully to Dr. Singer as the Gamaliel at whose feet they had sat. His earnestness in religion was accompanied not only by sound learning, but by many graceful accomplishments, a genial, attractive manner, and a tolerant spirit, which made him at one time the most popular man in the Irish Church. There was general rejoicing, therefore, when, in 1852, he was appointed to the See of Meath, although he did not, in that position, acquit himself so as to satisfy fully the expectations of his friends. He, and the Rev. Cæsar Otway, established a periodical called the 'Christian Examiner,' which for many years rendered valuable service to the Evangelical cause. Mr. Otway was a brilliant writer, very graphic in his descriptions of scenery, a humorous sketcher of character, with a zeal for Protestantism always tempered by kindness and benevolence.

In this band of Evangelical champions of Protestantism who always put the Bible before the Church, one of the most prominent and effective was the Rev. Robert Daly, late Bishop of Waterford, who was at that time Rector of Powerscourt. He was intensely Protestant in his spirit—an Ultra-Protestant we might almost say—from first to last. One of his latest charges, as an octogenarian bishop, was a vigorous and stern denunciation of Ritualism and its partisans, as traitors in the camp and papists in disguise. When Rector of Powerscourt, he distinguished himself as an impressive preacher, an able controversialist, and an indefatigable propagandist; always backed by the great social influence of Lord and Lady Powerscourt, whose magnificent mansion was open to ministers of different denominations engaged in the work of Evangelism.

A letter from the Rev. Charles Simeon, of Cambridge, who went to Dublin in April 1822 as a deputation from the Jews' Society, gives an interesting account of the state of religious feeling there at that time:—' No sooner were we arrived,' he says, ' than Irish hospitality evinced itself in an extraordinary degree. You who know the precise line in which I walk at Cambridge, will be astonished, as I myself was, to find earls and viscounts, deans and dignitaries, judges, &c., calling upon me, and bishops desirous to see me. Invitations to dinner were numerous from different quarters. One had been sent even to London and Cambridge to engage us to dinner on the Bible day.' He preached in St. George's Church to a congregation of 1,200. The Jews' Society took the lead; it was the most fashionable, and was carried on with surprising spirit. Dr. Trench, the last Archbishop of Tuam, presided at the public meeting. The Irish bishops had got frightened at the ' Calvinism ' introduced by the English as deputations to the anniversaries of the societies.

Mr. Simeon was induced by his Dublin friends to believe that, having preached at Cambridge for so many years, and published sixteen volumes, his presence in Dublin might have the effect of convincing their lordships that what they called Calvinism was not such a dangerous thing after all. But great was his astonishment on learning that the Archbishop (grandfather to the Bishop of Peterborough) would not allow him to enter a pulpit in his province unless he produced his 'letters of orders!' Forewarned by their friends, he and the Rev. Mr. Marsh came armed with their credentials, and when they produced them the churchwardens were summoned to the vestry to record and attest the exhibition of them. The excuse alleged by Archbishop Magee was, that he understood some foreign divines were coming over, who might expect to get into his pulpits, without having received the Holy Ghost from the hands of a bishop.

For about fifteen years previous to the passing of Catholic Emancipation, a most vigorous crusade was carried on against the Church of Rome, chiefly through the agency of voluntary societies of various kinds. The chief of these was the Hibernian Bible Society, established in 1813. The Hibernian Church Missionary Society, the Sunday School Society, the London Hibernian Society, and the Religious Tract Society were formed about the same time. All those societies held their anniversary meetings in Dublin, in the month of April, whence they were called 'the April Meetings,' or 'the Rotunda Meetings,' from the name of the building in which they were generally held, at the head of Sackville Street, as they are at the present day. But, for a young man who attends the April meetings now, it would be very difficult to conceive the excitement they produced and the attraction they put forth forty or fifty years ago. The spirit of revival seemed to pervade the very atmosphere; every eloquent speaker was a champion, a hero, who was looked upon with admiration as he passed along the streets. For hours, day after day, as society after society came upon the stage, to tell the story of the year and record its triumphs, a select audience from all parts of the kingdom, of which a majority were ladies, sat listening with rapt attention, or thrilled into wild excitement by the impassioned appeals of their favourite orators. Some of these were certainly among the most eloquent men that ever appeared upon a religious or political platform. Their speeches were fully reported in the Protestant newspapers, which were circulated by thousands throughout the country. Each of the societies had its auxiliaries in the provincial towns, and there, too, the most popular champions appeared to plead the cause. The staple of the oratory was almost invariably an attack upon the Church of Rome, dwelling chiefly upon its despotism and cruelty, the horrors of the Inquisition, and the dangers to the Constitution and the Throne, as well as to all Protestant churches and institutions, which would be involved in the concession of Emancipation. All the evils ever produced in Christendom by the scarlet 'Mother of Abominations' were collected and poured forth in torrents upon the head of the Irish priesthood. To those meetings the Roman Catholics of the neighbourhood were 'affectionately invited,' and their priests were challenged to come forth and defend their system if they dared. In several cases the challenges were accepted. The most popular of these orators was the Rev. Richard Pope. His eloquence was at once argumentative and impetuous, with a rapid flow of ideas, impelled by intense feeling, with a contagious power which seized on the sympathies of all his hearers, and seemed to carry their convictions whither he pleased. Next to him in popularity came the Rev. John Gregg, the present Bishop of Cork. He was equally fluent in the Irish and English tongues; a man of intense ardour, whose oratorical *forte* consisted in piling up climaxes and thus giving accumulative force to his arguments and appeals. He first distinguished himself while a curate in the country, then as assistant to Mr. Mathias in the 'Bethesda,' Dublin. There, his popularity became so great that Trinity Church, a large building, was erected for him near the Custom House, and there he continued to labour for thirty years, during which it was constantly crowded, attended by many of the most influential and intellectual men in Dublin, who found in his abrupt, rough manner, racy humour, and comic illustrations a source of relaxation, while instructed by his able exposition of Scripture and impressed by his pungent appeals to the conscience. Generally he did nothing but preach, the reading of the service having been performed by an assistant.

During the earliest period of this movement, there was in the south of Ireland a Dissenting minister who bore away the palm of dialectic eloquence from all competitors: this was the Rev. John Burnett, of Cork, where he had, as pastor of the Congregational Church, held high the banner of truth and freedom for fifteen years. Mr. Burnett is, no doubt, still remembered as minister of Camberwell, and as one of the most effective speakers in Exeter Hall. He never took notes, and scarcely seemed to heed what was going on around him; but so wonderful was his memory that nothing escaped him—no argument, no point, no expression—in the course of a long debate. Always calm and self-possessed, his speaking was pre-eminently logical, while he had a brilliant fancy, an easy flow of the best and most appropriate language, and an unfailing fund of wit and humour. The priests always found in him their most formidable antagonist, but animated by a spirit of liberality, the absence of which in the Church clergy so generally marred the effect of their appeals to the Catholic mind. Mr. Burnett had several discussions with priests; but the most famous of those pitched battles was the discussion between the Rev. Mr. Pope and Father Tom Maguire, which was held in the Rotunda, Dublin, and lasted several days. This was the greatest and most exciting event in the whole controversial war. It broke down Pope's health, and made Maguire's fortune as a controversial lecturer.

Later in the progress of this religious war, when the power of the Catholic Association became more alarming, and the concession of Emancipation more imminent, several of the most distinguished Fellows of the Dublin University came forth upon the platform, and exhibited oratorical powers of an extraordinary kind, wielding the most polished weapons of rhetoric with an intensity of passion that made them exceedingly effective. Among these were the Rev. Dr. Boyton, whom death removed in the prime of life; the Rev. Dr. Mortimer O'Sullivan, whom the best judges have pronounced the most powerful speaker they had ever heard; and the Rev. Dr. Martin, Rector of Killeshandra. These clerical agitators found a new platform in the 'Brunswick Clubs,' which were established shortly before Wellington and Peel surrendered to O'Connell and the Catholic Association. With Dr. O'Sullivan was associated the Rev. Robert M'Ghee, for many years minister of Harold's Cross Church, Dublin. These two men were the most prominent and distinguished champions of Protestantism in Ireland for many years. They published a number of books in which they brought history to bear against the Papacy with the most damaging effect. Like Cassandra, they were prophets whose predictions were unheeded; but one of them, the late Mr. M'Ghee, survived to see them fully accomplished, so far, at least, as the arrogant pretensions and daring aggressions of the Ultramontane party are concerned; that party being now identical with the Papacy, and wielding the dogma of Infallibility as the crowning achievement of their policy.

In all the earlier discussions, and lectures, and platform speeches by Evangelical clergymen, the ground taken was distinctly *Protestant*, in the Dissenting sense of that term. Church authority was either ignored or repudiated, and the famous maxim of Chillingworth was constantly repeated—' The Bible, and the Bible alone, is the religion of Protestants.' This anti-Church tendency naturally alarmed the bishops, and they were still more disturbed by the voluntary efforts made to meet the spiritual destitution of the many parishes, north and south, in which the 'Gospel' was not preached. The Evangelical clergy were no less concerned than the bishops for the interest of the Church, but they saw that, to a large extent, especially in Ulster, Nonconformist preachers were supplying her lack of service, and detaching her neglected children from her communion. Therefore they formed the *Established Church Home Mission*, directed by a committee in Dublin, which sent forth clergymen to preach in churches where they could get admission to them, and in school-houses, court-houses, or even in Dissenting chapels, where they were excluded as intruders by the Church incumbents. The people—Protestants of all denominations—and Roman Catholics, too, in many cases, flocked to hear them. The Church laity were delighted, and a great revival of religion was anticipated as the result of their labours. But the work was soon stopped by the Ecclesiastical authorities. A prosecution was set on foot by a rector in the northern province against a clergyman who had invaded his parish. The issue of such a prosecution in the Ecclesiastical Court could not be doubtful, and the costs, which were overwhelming, at once extinguished the 'Established Church Home Mission.'

But though the late Lord Primate must be held responsible for those proceedings, no one can doubt that that prelate was influenced by a sincere regard for the Church in putting down the irregularities in question. Lord John George Beresford may be said to have proved himself one of the most exemplary, pious, and princely of all the prelates that ever adorned the Irish Church. When he was only twenty-eight years of age he was appointed Dean of Clogher. At thirty-two he was consecrated Bishop of Cork and Ross. Two years later he was translated to Raphoe, a wealthy see in Ulster, which he held for twelve years. Then he was again translated to Clogher, a wealthier see, which he held for one year. He was next made Archbishop of Dublin, where he had been only two years when the greatest prize in the Irish Establishment fell to his lot. His early appointment to the Episcopal bench, and his repeated translations from one see to another as a better than the last became vacant, is to be accounted for by the fact that he was brother to the Marquis of Waterford, the Beresfords having been for a long time the most powerful family in Ireland, and the one most enriched by the Church, which seemed to be its patrimony. A Beresford was the last Archbishop of Tuam but one; a Beresford was the Bishop of Kilmore; and a Beresford, a first cousin, succeeded the late Primate in Armagh, and is now acquitting himself with admirable wisdom at the head of the Disestablished Church. The Most Rev. Lord George Beresford died in 1862, having been a bishop for the long period of fifty-seven years, during forty of which he was Lord Primate. The amount of Church revenue which he received during that period was estimated at about three-quarters of a million sterling. But he dispensed it liberally; he was one of the most benevolent of prelates, a munificent benefactor of the religious, charitable, and educational institutions connected with his diocese; he largely aided poor curates, and maintained some altogether at his own cost. He subscribed a large sum for the restoration of his cathedral, encouraged church building, and did all in his power to render more attractive and edifying the conducting of public worship throughout his united dioceses. Yet when, towards the close of his life—the object of the highest veneration with the Established clergy throughout the whole country—he felt conscientiously bound to advise them, in certain circumstances, to avail themselves of the funds of the National Board for the education of the poor—he became all at once the object of fanatical attacks, and a tempest of clerical vituperation began to beat upon his devoted head. And if a prelate so pious, so revered, so munificent, so loyal during his long career to the cause of Protestant ascendancy, of which his house had been the stay for generations, was thus treated for a conscientious difference of opinion, what chance of toleration was there for the humble advocates of free and united education, who might feel it their duty to plead for the children of poor Protestants debarred from the advantages of the sound secular instruction supplied by the State?

It appears, however, that the parochial system completely broke down in Ireland, especially in Dublin and Belfast, in consequence of the rapid growth of population and its inadequacy to meet the increasing wants of the religious community in the *quality* as well as the extent of the ministrations. The best part of the population moved out to suburban districts, and the right men could not be got into the pulpits by the old system of patronage. Consequently we find that in Dublin more than half the Episcopal population attend non-parochial churches, called Free Proprietary or District Churches. These were erected (though under an Act of Parliament) on the voluntary principle, chiefly by the laity, in order that they might have their spiritual wants supplied by ministers whom they considered more Evangelical, more spiritually-minded, more earnest and active than the parochial clergy. These Free Church congregations are for the greater part the most select, respectable, and fashionable, consisting generally of those who are able to pay their way, and prefer paying liberally for pews which they can call their own. The earliest of these, as I have said, was the Bethesda; then came Trinity Church, then St. Matthias', Harold's Cross, and several others in the suburbs; while large chapels were attached to a number of asylums and orphan houses, frequented by the most wealthy of the Episcopal community, who managed to secure the services, as chaplains, of ministers whose talents were best calculated to fill the pews. It is a remarkable fact, too, that of late years, when Evangelism had pervaded the Church, a number of the ministers of those semi-voluntary churches in the metropolis have been elevated to the Episcopal bench. Robert Daly's promotion to the see of Waterford might be ascribed to the fact that he was the brother of a peer; but it was a most popular appointment; and it was only on the ground of publicly acknowledged merit that Dr. Singer was made Bishop of Meath, Dr. Gregg Bishop of Cork, and Mr. Verschoyle Bishop of Kilmore, although the last gentleman was supposed to owe his mitre to his change of opinion on national education, after having been for many years the honorary secretary of the 'Church Education Society.' Again, the Rev. Maurice Day, the excellent minister of St. Matthias, Dublin, who has been unanimously chosen by the Disestablished Church to succeed Bishop Daly in Waterford, would most probably have received the same appointment from the Government which had made him Dean of Limerick.

CHAPTER XVII.

CATHOLIC AGITATION.

THE Catholic Association was established in 1824 by Mr. Daniel O'Connell and a few friends; and it very soon assumed a formidable power, having branches or ramifications of some kind in every parish in Ireland. It presented an admirable example of method or organisation, to be the work of Celtic hands. It found a place and a task for almost every member of the Roman Catholic body. The peer, the lawyer, the merchant, the country gentleman, the farmer, the peasant, and, above all, the priests worked together to one end. They got up petitions, formed deputations, conducted electioneering business, watched over the administration of justice, got up public meetings, prepared resolutions and documents touching every matter that could in the remotest degree promote the interests of Catholicity by glorifying its achievements and repelling attacks upon it. At the weekly meetings every Monday, in the Corn Exchange, Dublin, the work of each week was reported, correspondence was read, and the proceeds of the 'Catholic Rent' were announced. It did not matter much how these meetings were attended, for the speeches and letters were reported fully in the *Weekly Register* and *Freeman's Journal,* and these papers were sent free to every parish in Ireland, where they were read to admiring crowds by a schoolmaster or the leading local politician. 'Above all,' says Mr. Wyse, the historian of the Association, 'the voice of O'Connell, like some mighty minster-bell, was heard through Ireland, the empire, and the world. . . . The entire country formed but one association. It was regarded by the Government as a great centre of sedition, whence flowed through the press a perennial stream of turbulent matter into every parish in the kingdom. After mass the congregations were everywhere harangued from the altars by priests and other members of the Association. The Irish Attorney-General, afterwards Lord Plunket, described it in the House of Commons thus:—'Self-elected, self-controlled, acknowledging no superior, tolerating no equal, interfering at all stages with the administration of justice, denouncing individuals publicly before trial, re-judging and condemning those whom it has absolved, menacing the independent press with punishment, corrupting the part it could not intimidate, and for these and other purposes levying contributions on the whole people of Ireland.' 'Is this,' he asked, 'an association which, from its mere form and attributes independent of any religious opinion, the Legislature can tolerate? He could not conceive a more deadly instrument of tyranny than that Association. Magistrates were intimidated, feeling that there was no alternative but to yield, or be overwhelmed by the tide of fierce popular passions.'

It found defenders, however, in two English statesmen of the greatest eminence, Henry Brougham and Sir James Mackintosh. But a bill for its suppression was passed by a large majority, and in the Lords the numbers were nearly four to one in favour of the measure. Yet it had no sooner become law than O'Connell boasted that he would 'drive a coach and six through the Act,' and he immediately formed another association, which answered his purpose equally well. Indeed, the speeches at its first meetings were of a still more defiant and belligerent character; some of the orators prayed that Almighty God would increase the dissensions of the Government, and rejoiced in the prospect of a cloud bursting on England from the north.

An immense quantity of oil was thrown upon the blazing agitation by a violent speech made in the House of Lords by the Duke of York, then head of the Orange Society. As heir-apparent to the throne, after protesting strongly against all concessions to the Irish Roman Catholics, he said: 'I have uttered my honest and conscientious sentiments, founded upon principles I have imbibed from my earliest youth, to the justice of which I have subscribed, after a careful consideration, in maturer years; and these are the principles to which I will adhere and which I will maintain, and that up to the latest moment of my existence, *whatever may be my situation of life, so help me God!*'

The agitation became so tremendously democratic that it alarmed the Roman Catholic peers. Lord Redesdale, the Chancellor, writing to Lord Eldon, said: 'I learn that Lord Fingal and other Catholics of English blood, are alarmed at the present state of things; and they may well be alarmed. If a revolution were to happen in Ireland, it would be in the end an *Irish* revolution; and no Catholic of English blood would fare better than a Protestant of English blood. So said Lord Castlehaven 170 years ago, and so said a Roman Catholic confidentially to me above twenty years ago. The question is not simply Protestant and Catholic, but *English* and *Irish*; and the great motive of action will be hatred to the *Sassenach*, inflamed by the priests.' Mr. Canning at that time complained of the exactions and ingratitude of the leading agitators. 'Much as I wish to serve the Catholic cause,' he said, ' I have seen that the service of the Catholic leaders is no easy service. They are hard taskmasters, and the advocate who would satisfy them must deliver himself up to them bound hand and foot.'

However, the agitation proceeded, and won its crowning victory in the *Clare election*. O'Connell, a Catholic—disqualified by law—stood against Mr. Vesey Fitzgerald, a good landlord, and one of the most popular members of the Government. Every priest was an election agent in that contest. The Catholic electors to a man broke away from the control of their landlords; and so frantic was their religious excitement, that, as Mr. Sheil said at the time—'the feeling by which they were actuated would make them not only vote against their landlord, but make them scale the batteries of a fortress and mount the breach.' Sir Robert Peel in his 'Memoirs,' referring to the Clare election, said: ' It afforded a decisive proof, not only that the instrument on which the Protestant proprietor had mainly relied for the maintenance of his political influence (*i.e.* the franchise) had completely failed him, but that through the combined exertions of the agitator and the priest, or I should rather say through the contagious sympathies of a common cause among all classes of the Roman Catholic population, the instrument of defence and supremacy had been converted into a weapon fatal to the authority of the landlord.'

This decisive election took place in 1828. From the prorogation of Parliament that year the state of Ireland became more and more alarming. The peasantry in Tipperary and Limerick began to assemble in military array. The Orangemen of Ulster at the same time were furbishing their arms, and the 'Brunswick Clubs' established a rent of their own as the sinews of war. Ulster was divided into two camps, in which the forces were about equally divided—the Protestants, full of the proud confidence of a dominant race, and regarding the military pretensions of their antagonists as scornfully as the Turks would regard similar pretensions on the part of the Greeks. They had crushed the 'Papists' in 1798, and they felt quite satisfied that, if it came to fighting, which they by no means deprecated, they should be able to crush them again. In this way matters had come to such a crisis that Peel and Wellington saw no possibility of avoiding civil war but by granting emancipation. This was accordingly done in the next session of Parliament. They yielded, against their own convictions, to an overwhelming necessity. It would have been better had they retired, and left the concession to be made by statesmen who all along had advocated the Catholic claims. But perhaps they alone could have overcome the repugnance of George IV., who, notwithstanding his effusions of love to his Catholic subjects in Dublin twenty-eight years before, consented to sign the Act, but with the greatest possible reluctance, exclaiming, 'What can I do! I have nothing to fall back upon!' and complaining that he had been harshly and cruelly treated by his ministers, like a man who had been asked with a pistol pointed to his breast; or as if obliged, if he did not give it, to leap down from a five-pair-of-stairs window! Again, he exclaimed, 'I am a miserable wretch! my situation is dreadful! I go to Hanover, I will return no more; let them get a Catholic king in Clarence,' &c. At length, however, at Windsor on April 13, he pronounced over the Bill the words, '*Le Roi le veut.*'

But emancipation, which opened the doors of Parliament to the Catholic nobility and gentry, did little or nothing for the

people, who were still burdened and harassed by the exactions
of an 'alien Church.' In the 'Personal Recollections' of Lord
Cloncurry, that able statesman gave a sketch of English policy
in Ireland, and of Irish agitation—which is unfortunately too
much in accordance with the facts in each case—from the Union
up to the year 1829, when emancipation was *extorted*. 'The
type of British colonial government was the order of the day.
The Protestants were upheld as a superior caste, and paid in
power and official emoluments for their services in the army of
occupation. During the second Viceroyalty of Lord Anglesea, the
effort was made by him to evoke the energies of the whole nation
for its regeneration. That effort was defeated by the conjoint
influence of the cowardice of the English Cabinet, the petulance
of Lord Stanley, and the unreasonable violence and selfishness of
the lately emancipated popular leaders. Upon Lord Anglesea's
recall, the modern Whig model of statesmanship was set up and
followed. Popular grievances were allowed to remain unre-
dressed; the discontent and violence engendered by those
grievances were used from time to time for party purposes; the
people were hung and bayonetted when their aroused passions
exceeded the due measure of faction's requirement: and the
State patronage was employed to stimulate and reward a staff
of demagogues, by whom the masses were alternately excited to
madness and betrayed, according to the necessities of the English
factions. . . . The minister expectant, or trembling for his place,
spoke loudly of justice, or of compensation, of fraternity and freedom; to these key-notes the place-hunting demagogue pitched
his brawling. His talk was of pike-making, and sword-flesh-
ing, and monster-marching. The simple people were goaded
into madness, the end whereof was,—for them, suspension of the
Habeas Corpus Act, the hulks, and the gallows; for their stimu-
lators, silk gowns, commissionerships, and seats on the Bench.
Under this treatment the public mind became debauched: the
lower classes, forced to bear the charges of agitation as well
as to suffer its penalties, lost all faith in their social future.
To hold out hopes of the establishment of civil and religious
equality, of the attainment of complete freedom of industry or
even of local self-government, no longer sufficed to arouse the

passions of the mob, or to bring money into the exchequer of the demagogues. It therefore followed that the staple talk of the popular meetings came to be made out of the appeals to the basest passions of the multitude; old feuds between Irishmen were revived, a new appetite for vengeance was whetted—nay, even the bonds of society were loosened by intimations, not obscure, that a triumph of the people would be associated with an abatement of the sacredness of property.'

The peasantry had, as already said, very soon learned that whatever emancipation had done or might do for barristers and others qualified to hold public appointments from which the Roman Catholics had been previously excluded, it had done nothing to remove or mitigate their practical grievances. They found that the rack-rents of their holdings were not reduced, that the tax-collector did not abate his demand, and, above all, that the detested Tithe Proctor paid his customary visits, and, in default of payment, seized upon the cow, whose milk nourished the children; upon the pig, that paid the rent; upon the tenth sheaf of corn, the tenth stone of potatoes, and, in default of these, upon the pot in which the food of the family was cooked, or the blankets which protected them from the winter's cold at night. While exasperated by exactions of this kind, they were addressed from week to week in the most inflammatory language on the 'Monster Grievance of the Church Establishment.' Agitators asked their auditors to place themselves in the position of a half-famished cottier, surrounded by a wretched family clamorous for food; and to judge what his feelings must be when he saw the tenth part of the produce of his potato garden exposed at harvest time to public 'cant'; or if, as was most common—he had given a promissory note for the payment of a certain sum of money for tithes—heard the heart-rending cries of his offspring clinging round him and lamenting for the milk, of which they were deprived when the cow was driven off to be sold. No wonder that imprecations and threats were mingled with their sighs and tears. No wonder that, at night, houses were seen in flames, as if the country were suffering from the ravages of war. When the oppressed people read Henry Grattan's description of the 'Tithe Proctor,' that he was 'a species of wolf left by the shepherd to take care of the flock in his absence,' no wonder that they arose in their wrath and killed the wolf. One of those Proctors had at the same sessions proceeded against 1,100 persons for tithes, nearly all small farmers or peasants, the expense of each process being about eight shillings.

This system of clerical support would, indeed, be intolerable anywhere, even if the State clergy were the pastors of the majority. But as the proportion between the Protestants and Catholics was, in many parts of the country, as one to ten, and in some as one to twenty, the injustice necessarily involved in levying the impost was aggravated a hundred-fold. It was impossible to conceive anything in the shape of a tax more irritating and humiliating, or which violated more wantonly men's natural sense of justice. If the Tithe Proctor's system had been purposely devised to drive a nation into insurrection, it might be regarded as a masterpiece of Machiavelian policy. Besides, it tended directly to the impoverishment of the country, retarding agricultural improvement, and limiting production. If a man kept all his land in pasture, as most of the Protestant gentry did, he escaped the impost; but the moment he tilled it, as the small Catholic farmer must, he was subjected to a tax of 10 per cent. on the gross produce. The valuation being made by the Tithe Proctor—whose interest it was to defraud both the tenant and the parson, and whom the large farmers found means of corrupting—the main burden of Church support fell upon the small occupiers; and so heavily did it press, that they were known in many cases not to mow their meadows to avoid paying tithe for the hay. There was, besides, a tax called 'Church Cess,' levied by Protestants in vestry upon Roman Catholics for cleaning the church, ringing the bell, washing the minister's surplice, and purchasing bread and wine for the Communion. Against this tax there arose such fierce opposition that a sort of civil war raged in every parish in Ireland on Easter Monday, when the Roman Catholics assembled to denounce it, and to tell the chairman that he was not their pastor, but a tyrant, a persecutor, and a robber.

In 1831 the organised resistance to the collection of Tithes became so general and so terrible that they were not paid except where a composition had been made, and agreements had been adopted. The terrified Proctors gave up their dangerous occupation after some of their number had been victimized in the most barbarous manner. Some of the clergy preferred destitution to the exaction of their incomes under such circumstances; but others, more courageous, felt bound to persist, for the sake of the Church, in the enforcement of their rights. Strange scenes were then presented over extensive districts in many of the best counties. Not only bailiffs and policemen, but the military also, in strong detachments, were seen driving away cattle, sheep, pigs, and geese, to be sold by public auction; the 'Pounds' (uncovered enclosures), crowded with all sorts of animals, cold and starved, uttering doleful sounds; auctions without bidders, in the midst of groaning and jeering multitudes; the slaughtering of policemen with fiendish rage and yells of triumph; the mingling of fierce, vindictive passions with the warmest natural affections; and exultation in murder as if it were a glorious deed of war. The clergy and their families, shut up in their glebe-houses, trembled for their lives; and, but for the relief extended to them by sympathising friends, were liable to perish with hunger, to avert which many a precious library was sent to Dublin for sale.

During this desperate struggle between the people and the Government, bloody tragedies were enacted, and many lives were sacrificed. At Newtown Barry, in the county of Wexford, the mob attempted to rescue some cattle seized for tithes, when the yeomanry fired upon them, killing twelve persons. This was the result of a placard, posted through the town, announcing as follows:—" There will be an end of Church plunder; your pot, blanket, and pig will not hereafter be sold by auction to support men in luxury, idleness, and ease, while most of you are starving. Attend an auction of your neighbours' cattle." At Carrickshock there was another slaughter. A number of writs against defaulters were issued by the Court of Exchequer, and the process-servers were guarded by a strong body of the constabulary. They hastened to the place secretly and at night, hoping to be protected by the darkness. But they saw signal bonfires blazing along the surrounding hills, and heard shrill whistles on every side. They pushed boldly on, however, until they were confronted suddenly by an immense body of peasantry armed with scythes and pitchforks. A terrible hand-to-hand struggle then ensued, and in the course of a few moments eighteen of the constabulary, including the commanding officer, lay dead upon the field. The remainder fled, marking the course of their retreat with the blood which trickled from their wounds. At Castlepollard, in Westmeath, an attempt at rescue was made, when the police fired, and half a score persons were killed.

Among these tragedies the one which produced the most thrilling effect, and inflicted most damage on the Church, occurred at Gurtroe, near Rathcormac, in the county of Cork. Archdeacon Ryder brought a military force to recover the tithes of a farm belonging to a widow named Ryan; and he attended in person to see the enforcement of his legal rights. The crowd of countrymen resisted; the military were ordered to fire; eight persons were killed and thirteen wounded; and among the dead was found the bleeding body of a fine young man, the widow's son.

It was absolutely necessary that some strong measures should be adopted to put an end to a state of things threatening the utter disruption of society. In the first place, something should be promptly done to meet the wants of the destitute clergy and their families. Accordingly Lord Stanley, then Chief Secretary, in May 1832, brought in a Bill authorising the Lord Lieutenant to advance 60,000*l.* as a fund for the payment of the uncollected tithes of the previous year. This Bill became law on June 1st. But Lord Stanley was determined that the Roman Catholics should be made to '*respect the law,*' and that the tithes must be exacted from them at whatever cost. The Irish Government, therefore, undertook to be itself Collector-General of this odious and blood-stained impost, employing for the purpose the large military force then stationed in Ireland. The Roman Catholics, so far from being intimidated, broke forth into a state of frantic excitement, and met the threat of military force with defiance. Then commenced a sort of insurrection throughout the south of Ireland. Bonfires blazed upon the hills, rallying sounds of horns were heard along the valleys, and the mustering tread of thousands upon the roads, hurrying to the scene of a seizure or an auction. It was a bloody campaign. There was considerable loss of life, while the Church and the Government became more hateful to the people than ever. Stanley being the commander-in-chief on one side, and O'Connell on the other, the contest was embittered by their personal antipathies. The Government put forth all its energies, but its discomfiture was most signal. The amount of arrears due for 1831 was 104,285*l.*; but the total amount which the Government was able to levy was 12,000*l.*, and the expense of recovering this fraction of the debt was no less than 15,000*l*. This mode of making the people 'respect the law,' was therefore found to be too costly as well as too mortifying; so the proceedings were abandoned.

It was then found that after paying the clergy the arrears of 1831 and 1832, and the amount that would be due in 1833, about *one million sterling* would be required. This sum was provided by issuing Exchequer Bills, the reimbursement to be effected by a land tax. With these temporary arrangements to meet the exigency of the case, an Act was passed to render Tithe composition compulsory and permanent.

But the country was not yet pacified, and at the opening of the session for 1833, the Royal Speech recommended that Parliament should take into their consideration measures for the final settlement of the Church Question in Ireland. In the course of the debates, a new chief secretary, Mr. Lyttleton, deplored the failure of legislative efforts to make the tithe system work well. The statute book, he said, had been loaded with enactments for the purpose of giving the owners of tithes effectual means to enforce the law—many of the most severe description, extending even to capital punishment—but they had all proved utterly useless. During the following year, the results of the special Census of the Irish population, with the object of ascertaining the religious persuasions of the people, placed the Church Establishment in a worse light than ever. It was found that a total population of 7,954,760 was divided among the several denominations as follows:—

		Proportion per cent.
Roman Catholics	6,436,060	80·9
Established Church	853,160	10·7
Presbyterians	643,658	8·4
Other Dissenters	21,882	0·2

Enlightened by these statistics, the Government of Lord Grey introduced the Irish Church Temporalities Bill, which was brought into the House of Commons by Lord Althorpe. He avowed his conviction that any *surplus* funds resulting from the State management of ecclesiastical revenues should be devoted to State purposes. A motion to that effect was brought forward by Mr. Ward, who said that since 1819 it had been necessary to maintain in Ireland an army of 22,000 men, at the cost of one million sterling per annum, exclusive of a police force which cost 300,000*l.* a year. All this enormous expense and trouble in governing the country, he ascribed to the existence of a religious establishment hostile to the majority of the people. The motion, which was seconded by Mr. Grote, brought about an immediate crisis in the Cabinet. The majority were for accepting it, whereupon the late Lord Derby, Sir James Graham, Lord Ripon, and the Duke of Richmond resigned their offices, because they would not agree to any appropriation of Church revenues to other than the purposes of the Episcopal communion. The following day was the King's birthday, and the Irish prelates, headed by the Archbishop of Armagh, presented an address to his Majesty complaining of the attacks on their Church, deprecating the threatened innovations, and imploring his protection. King William, who was greatly moved by their appeals, broke through the customary restraint, and said—' I now remember you have a right to require of me to be resolute in defence of the Church.' He assured them that their rights should be preserved unimpaired; that if any amendment was required (of which he greatly doubted), he hoped it would be left to the bishops to effect it, without the interference of other parties. He had now completed his sixty-ninth year, and he must prepare to leave the world with a conscience clear in regard to the maintenance of the Church. Tears ran down the King's cheeks while, in conclusion, he said—' I have spoken more strongly than usual because of the unhappy circumstances that have forced themselves upon the observation of all. The threats of those who are the enemies of the Church, make it the more necessary for those who feel their duty to the Church, to speak out. The words which you hear spoken by me indeed come from my mouth, but they flow from my heart.'

The Church Temporalities Bill, however, ultimately passed both Houses of Parliament, and received the Royal Assent, but without the celebrated 'Appropriation Clause' for the employment of surplus revenue for other purposes, such as the education and relief of the poor, which the Lords rejected. The Ecclesiastical Commissioners appointed to carry it out were, the Lord Primate, the Archbishop of Dublin, the Lord Chancellor, the Chief Justice of Ireland, and four of the Bishops, with a subsequent addition of three laymen. The following are the principal features of this measure (3 and 4 Wm. IV. c. 37):— 'Church Cess' was immediately abolished, giving pecuniary relief to the extent of 18,000*l.* per annum. There was to be a reduction of the number of bishops and archbishops prospectively, from four of the former to *two*, and eighteen of the latter to *ten*; the revenues of the suppressed sees to be appropriated to general church purposes, and to those exclusively. Cashel and Tuam ceased to be *Arch*bishoprics, and the island was divided into two ecclesiastical provinces by a line drawn from the north of Dublin County to the south of Galway Bay. The funds obtained by the sale of bishops' lands, &c., were applied to the erection and repairs of churches, to providing for church expenses which had hitherto been defrayed out of vestry rates, and to other ecclesiastical purposes. The total amount of tithe-rent charge payable to ecclesiastical persons—bishops, deans, chapters, incumbents of benefices, and to the Ecclesiastical Commissioners, was 401,114*l.* The rental of Ireland was estimated by the valuers under the Poor Law Act, at about 12,000,000*l.*, this rental being about a third of the estimated produce of the land.

Another feature of this settlement of the Church question, then fondly believed to be final, was one which had the most tranquillising effect upon the Roman Catholic population. The payment of the tithes was cast exclusively upon the landlords, that is, it was with the landlord alone, and not with the tenant, that the incumbent had to do, 25 per cent. being allowed as compensation for the trouble of collection. This trouble was very small, as the tithe must be brought in with the rent; and in many cases it was bound up with the rent in such a way as to lose its ecclesiastical character and its irritating influence as a

Catholic grievance, so far, at least, as the tenants were concerned.

This arrangement lasted thirty-five years, during which it worked admirably for the Church. It was a period marked by great internal improvement and great progress. In every part of the country new churches were erected in a new and beautiful style of architecture, the building being largely aided by the funds, and superintended by the architect of the Ecclesiastical Commissioners.

It was now still, however, an imperative duty incumbent on British statesmen to deprive the Ultramontane and National parties of the most dangerous weapons which English policy in past times had put into their hands. These weapons they found in the Church Establishment, the greatest monument of that policy that had survived the ameliorating influences of liberal legislation. It was based upon conquest; it was a monument of national subjugation. It appropriated to a small fraction of the population, and that the wealthiest, the ecclesiastical revenues set apart for the religious worship and instruction of the whole nation. It was identified with the hateful system of exclusion and oppression, called 'Protestant Ascendancy,' and, as the embodiment of its spirit, inheriting and attracting all the sectarian antipathy and jealousy to which such an invidious position exposes a religious community. It enjoyed all the privileges and immunities of a legally dominant Church, boasting of the Sovereign as its head, wearing the livery of the State, exclusively performing certain civil functions, claiming precedence on all public occasions, flaunting its offensive distinctions in the faces of other Churches, talking in a tone of arrogance of its rights, and assuming an attitude of defiance towards the State to which it was indebted for all these means of public annoyance and disturbance.

Its advocates had of late years taken new ground in the controversy with Rome. A very able man, Dr. Lee, became Regius Professor of Divinity in Trinity College. His principles were most decidedly and uncompromisingly High Church. He allowed to Nonconformists, Presbyterians, Congregationalists, Wesleyans no authorised *locus standi* in the country. Their ministers were mere schismatic laymen, pretenders, intruders within the domains of the only lawful Church in the country. The Church of Rome was also an intruder; a right orthodox and excellent Church in the countries abroad where she was established, but in Ireland a schismatic, intrusive body, which had no legitimate authority. The Anglican Church was the Church of St. Patrick, retaining the Apostolic Succession, which he had brought from Rome, but inheriting with it independent jurisdiction, and rendered by its State connection the only lawful Christian teacher in the island. With these pretensions were associated the doctrines which are usually comprehended under the term Ritualism.

When Archbishop Trench was appointed to the see of Dublin, on the death of Dr. Whately, he completely reversed the policy of his Broad Church predecessor. He immediately sought out Dr. Lee, and finding him to be a theologian after his own heart, took him into his confidence, made him his chaplain, and appointed him to preach visitation sermons in which anti-Protestant doctrines and the highest 'Church principles' were very plainly enunciated. The Archbishop is a model prelate in all Christian virtues, and his character is universally revered; but there is no doubt that his appointment has proved a heavy blow and great discouragement to the Evangelical party in the Church; and it is owing mainly to his influence, most conscientiously exerted, that the work of Liturgical Revision, even in the hands of the disestablished, emancipated, and self-governing Church, has hitherto proved abortive.

CHAPTER XVIII.

THE TWO CHURCHES MILITANT IN CONNAUGHT.

THE last Protestant Archbishop of Tuam, from the time of his appointment in 1819, identified himself with the Evangelical Missionary Movement, which began about that time. He presided regularly at one or more of the anniversary meetings in the Rotunda, Dublin; and when all the other bishops had retired from the societies, because they fostered 'Calvinism' or 'Methodism,' which with them, as Mr. Simeon remarked, was but another name for vital religion, Archbishop Trench remained at his post, observing that as the bishops did not give their reasons, and he could see none, he declined to follow their example. In his own diocese he devoted all his energies and resources to the work of proselytising the Roman Catholic population, which, according to his theory of an establishment, were an integral part of his flock. His benevolence, however, was so great that he was for a long time exceedingly popular, and the 'Irish Church Mission to Roman Catholics' was attended with great apparent success.

The career of this prelate would form a most interesting chapter in the history of the Irish Church. Being the brother of Lord Clancarty, he was promoted at an early age to the see of Waterford. From that important city he was translated to Elphin, then considered one of the richest bishoprics in Ireland. The place had a wretched population, without a market and without business of any kind, and no one to care for the poor. The new bishop became very active as a country gentleman and a magistrate, reforming abuses in gaols, and protecting the poor from oppression, while largely ministering to their temporal wants. In 1819 the Prince Regent, on account of his 'singular piety and integrity,' made him Archbishop of Tuam, vacant by the death of Dr. Beresford. His benevolence had already made him so popular that when he entered the town bonfires were blazing in the streets, and his carriage could scarcely move through the crowds of people—nearly all Roman Catholics—who cheered and blessed him. This Catholic applause of a heretic bishop was not confined to the laity. The Rev. Mr. Gill, a Galway priest, spoke of him in the following terms: 'I call on them to co-operate with the wise appropriation already begun in favour of the distressed, by his Grace of Tuam, with that piety and zeal, with that ardent and indefatigable industry, that ever characterised his efforts and breathed on his actions an unearthly lustre.'

Then, referring to British liberality during the famine of 1822, this priest, with all the fervid and florid eloquence of his race, exclaimed: 'Oh we shall fondly entwine the loved shamrock of our valley with the fostering rose; they shall grow lovingly together. Their fragrance shall mingle like the incense of love. The dew-drops that will glisten on their leaves shall be like the tears of some celestial sympathy. We shall plant them in the sunniest beds of our gardens, as a grateful memorial of this generous people. Religious and political differences no longer remembered, our misfortunes have at length providentially accomplished what our brighter hours could never effect. No longer eying each other with distrust, the Irishman shall strain his English neighbour to his heart. Both may not kneel at the same shrine, yet both shall worship at the same burning altar of charity.'

The Rev. Dr. Ffrench, Catholic Warden of Galway, addressed the Protestant Archbishop in a similar strain of eulogy. What more could a Galway priest say to his own metropolitan than this:—'More glorious by your actions than even by your exalted station, you proceeded in the exercise of your sacred ministry, and with a singular devotion you interposed between the victims of contagion and the grave. You have fulfilled your holy task; and having reached the highest point of genuine glory, you now return to your home hailed by the benedictions of a grateful, affectionate, and applauding people.'

This was the language of the Distress Committee for the town and county of Galway, in September 1822. During this famine application was made to the absentee landlords, who drew from the county rents amounting to 83,000*l.* a year; and the total amount of their contributions, according to Bishop Jebb, was 83*l.*! While those absentees thus shamefully neglected the duties of property, when their tenants were suffering under a terrible calamity, it pleased Providence, said Bishop Jebb in the House of Lords, to raise up a diffusive instrument for good, and that instrument a Churchman. If the London Distress Committee, if the honourable and worthy chairman, were asked who at that period stood foremost in every act of beneficence and labour of love, they would with one voice pronounce the Archbishop of Tuam; from morning to night, from extremity to extremity of his province, at once the mainspring, the regulator, the minute-hand, of the whole charitable system. As distress deepened and spread abroad, he multiplied himself with a sort of moral ubiquity.'

The Metropolitan of Connaught had certainly ample means for the exercise of his benevolence. Ardagh, as well as Killala and Achonry, were held by him, *in commendam,* till the passing of the Church Temporalities Act. The archbishopric was indeed a sort of principality; and as a prince of the Church Dr. Trench ruled it for a period of about forty years. He might with such revenues have enjoyed life splendidly in London or on the Continent, like some of his brethren, especially at a time when the public were not so exacting as they are now, and when the clergy were apt to regard the incomes derived from the Church as much their own property as any private estate. Though Archbishop Trench held this opinion, he did not act upon it, but seemed evidently conscious that he was a trustee, bound to reside, to labour and to spend, in the midst of the population in which he was placed. The benefit of his local expenditure was so highly appreciated that when he thought of removing from Tuam to the palace at Killala, a public meeting was convened by the Sovereign as chairman, and by two hundred of the principal inhabitants, nearly all Roman Catholics, imploring him not to leave their town. When he gave his final answer to the Ecclesiastical Commissioners, on the 11th of June, 1834, stating that he felt it his duty to continue his residence at Tuam for the rest of his life, the population of that town broke out into manifestations of tumultuous joy. Large bonfires blazed in the streets, and the houses were brilliantly illuminated.

There was a recurrence of very severe destitution in the diocese in the year 1831. In the county of Mayo, of a population of 293,000 souls, no less than 226,532, or more than two-thirds of the whole people, had been placed on the charity list. The sufferers were, of course, nearly all Roman Catholics, so that out of an allotation of 203 tons of meal, made by the Central Committee at Galway, a single ton was set apart, with this entry: 'To the poor Protestants, one ton.' The effect, however, of this wide-spread distribution of relief was, as usual, grossly demoralising. Many of the recipients were in fact in affluent circumstances. At the head of the list was a farmer who had a large stock of cattle and plenty of oatmeal for sale, while he had deposited some hundreds of pounds for safe keeping with the churchwardens. Places which were not at all destitute received large grants. The cry was, 'As the provision is going, why should not this parish and that parish get its share.' In a word, as the Archbishop said, '*Starvation has become a trade,*' and provisions were sent in abundance where no calamity had occurred. There was not one tenant on a large estate who was not returned destitute. 'My means would not last a day if I had not most conscientiously and justly drawn the line where I did.' His Grace received altogether for distribution on this occasion the sum of 5,667*l*., of which he returned 2,839*l*. as not being required.

The feudal spirit still remained in full force beyond the Shannon, and many of the resident landlords had imbibed the missionary zeal of their archbishop, and warmly co-operated with him in the propagation of Evangelism. His own brother was one of the greatest and most influential of the old aristocratic houses of the province—a fact which in such a rank-worshipping community must have given his Grace an immense *prestige*, that a prelate sprung from the people—such as Elrington, Mant, or Magee—could not hope to acquire. The clergy, too, of the united dioceses were most zealous in prosecuting the missionary work. Some of them learned to preach in the Irish language; they were aided by a host of Scripture-readers, and by schoolmasters, supported by funds contributed in England. If these missionary efforts had been felt by the people to be purely spiritual in their object, they would no doubt have been much more effectual; but they were identified with the maintenance of a political system which excluded from the Legislature all persons holding the creed of the mass of the population. For two or three years preceding Catholic emancipation, the Protestant clergy were most active in agitating against that measure, and in their efforts to prove that Roman Catholics could not be bound by the most solemn oaths when the interests of their Church were concerned. As already remarked, the meetings of the Hibernian Bible Society, held throughout the country, were converted into a sort of political propagandism. It was the same with all other Protestant societies which appealed to the public for support. In October 1824 the Archbishop was announced to take the chair, at Loughrea, county Galway, when the leading Roman Catholic inhabitants received this circular: 'You are kindly invited to attend the annual meeting of the county Galway branch of the Hibernian Bible Society.' The Archbishop and his friends found the Courthouse crowded to excess with Roman Catholics, including a number of priests. It was quite evident that they had packed the house, and meant to carry everything their own way. So when the report was read, and the chairman rose to propose its adoption, he was interrupted by Father Daly, of Galway, who claimed to be heard, on the ground that he was included in the invitation. It was in vain the priests were told that an arrangement for discussion could be afterwards made; they insisted on speaking, then and there, and were about to appoint another chairman. But the Archbishop—a man of rare personal courage and firmness—said: 'I shall not leave this chair, Mr. Daly, until the business of this day is gone through, *unless I am forced out of it.*' This emphatic declaration disconcerted the leaders; but the mob, whose starving kinsmen his bounty so often had fed, now made frantic by religious bigotry, exclaimed, 'Turn him out! turn him out!' The late Dr. Urwick, one of the deputation, describing the scene, wrote: 'If demoniac rage was ever depicted in human countenances, it was in the mass before us then. Circumstanced as we were, pent up amid such sights and sounds, with no way of escape, it would have been little disgrace if even a stout heart had quailed. We had, however, one who showed no fear. His Grace lost not his self-possession for an instant, though undoubtedly, had violence been done, he would have been the first victim.' The new chairman then attempted to speak, sustained by the clamours of the multitude; but the Archbishop persistently refused to hear him, and the conflict lasted about two hours, till it was whispered that the military were coming. It was not until the Protestants sounded a retreat that he withdrew from his post as chairman, having no other alternative. Then the triumphant party held a meeting of their own, in which they resolved, that they regarded 'with disgust and indignation the arbitrary conduct of the Archbishop,' whom they further charged with countenancing the introduction of the military, 'to intimidate, or perhaps to massacre, the Roman Catholic clergy and laity.' All moderate Catholics were shocked at this outrage; and the leading Liberal organ of the day, the 'Dublin Evening Post,' indignantly remonstrated, saying: 'We can never mention the name of Dr. Trench but with feelings of admiration and respect. We can never forget the conduct of this exemplary prelate in the year of famine, and we are satisfied that the poor of the arch-diocese will remember it with gratitude. While others, who, with a species of bitter irony, are called the natural protectors of the people, were uttering fine sentiments on the banks of the Thames or of the Seine, he was visiting every part of his extensive and starving see, distributing food, and raiment, and medicine, comforting the afflicted, and saving hundreds from the jaws of death.'

In August 1827 the Archbishop presided at a Church missionary meeting in the town of Galway. Mr. O'Connell was there at the time, engaged at the assizes, and handbills were circulated intimating that he would attend the meeting. The place was consequently crowded. He entered during the proceedings; and as soon as the gentleman who was speaking sat down, he presented himself to the notice of the Chairman, who told him that he could not hear any one who was not a member of the society. But, assuming the bantering, bullying manner with which he was accustomed to win the cheers of the mob, he persisted in speaking. Referring to one of the speakers, who was a Presbyterian minister, he said: 'Mr. Freeland found one doctrine in the Bible and his Grace another. Let them settle their differences between themselves before they come to convert us. Let them toss up for it! There is a story of two cats who were constantly quarrelling. They were locked up in a room one night, and in the morning they were found to have eaten one another up except their tails. Let your lordship and that gentleman—looking at Mr. F.—be shut up together like these cats. . . . The Roman Catholics converted 4,000 in China. Two bishops and some priests had been martyred for their religion. Why did not your lordship tell that to the meeting? I will convict his lordship before a jury, because he did not tell the meeting of the murder of the Catholic bishops and priests.'

A lay gentleman who was present thus describes the scene. 'It was indeed a most triumphant day for the cause of God and missions. The contrast must have been as striking to others as to myself, even to the numerous band of priests as well as to the respectable and intelligent members of the Roman Catholic Church, who formed the great majority of our crowded and attentive assembly. Yes, there was a strong pictorial contrast of lights and shadows—there was the calm, unruffled forbearance of our Archbishop in the chair, unmoved by any ebullition of undue feeling under coarse ribaldry and personal insult, all evidently given vent to for the purpose of raising the often-expressed shout and laugh, and clapping of hands, and waving of handkerchiefs. There was also the calm, the dignified, the holy reply of the Warden Daly, breathing love and pity, as he unravelled the statements, corrected the erroneous assertions, of the assailants, and vindicated the truth of God our Saviour, and the sublime Christian object of our society in sending forth the Gospel of life and salvation to the ends of the earth. And there was in the dark background the man who called forth all this, trembling and ashamed as he felt the withering effect of Christian eloquence and Christian charity. Indeed, so powerful was the effect, that Mr. O'Connell arose immediately after the Warden had concluded and complimented him in the handsomest manner, saying

'Warden Daly was a scholar, a gentleman, and a Christian, and would to God all were like him!'

'The new Reformation' shone like a glorious dream in the imagination of English as well as Irish Churchmen at that period, and Tuam was regarded as the scene of its most singular triumphs. It is true that the movement which received that name began in the county of Cavan, under the auspices of Lord Farnham. Among his tenantry and those of the neighbouring gentry who sympathised with him, and caught the holy contagion of missionary zeal, which was to supersede Catholic emancipation by consuming Catholicism, and melting off the spiritual chains of the people, there were many who read their recantations in Cavan and King's Court. But in that neighbourhood the light that flashed so vividly for a time soon faded; and after the passing of emancipation the zeal of many Protestants waxed cold, and the battle against Popery was relinquished. In Connaught, however, it was not so, and the sanguine spirit of the Archbishop hoped on and persevered in spite of the political reaction. He did not—like others—admonish his clergy with the cold and selfish counsels of worldly prudence to abstain from provoking the bigotry of surrounding multitudes, whose religion still consisted very much of a belief in the efficacy of holy wells, holy trees, holy stones, of charms and 'gospels'—'amulets prepared by the monks, scapulary jubilees, pilgrimages, &c.' Galway was then described as the very head-quarters of Irish superstition, and there a decided impression had been made. It was time, indeed, that something serious should have been attempted by the Established Church in that part of the country, if it was to have anything at all to show in the shape of work done in return for its income and in fulfilment of its mission.

The Rev. M. H. Seymour, now Dean of Tuam, has stated that Archbishop Trench's visit to hold a confirmation in the parish of Killenummery was the first episcopal visit for such a purpose at that place for ninety years, in consequence of which a number of old women came forward to be confirmed. Archbishop Beresford had found it impossible to penetrate into Connemara, and a church which had been built at Ballinahinch had never been consecrated or used; it became a ruin, and not one stone remained upon another. Unless the poor abandoned Protestants scattered through that western region had chosen to live like heathens, they must have asked the priest to marry them, to baptize their children, and to bury their dead. They did so, and in this way the Church in the course of ages lost more families than she has been able to regain with all her Connaught missions. It is, therefore, much to the credit of the last Archbishop of Tuam that he made such extraordinary exertions to recover the ground that had been lost by the neglect of his predecessors. He left no likely means unemployed for this purpose. He encouraged the planting of Scriptural schools in every direction, and their masters became a sort of local missionaries, arguing in season and out of season against ' the errors of Popery.' He invited the ablest preachers and the best controversialists in Dublin and elsewhere to traverse the province and preach up the new Reformation. Aware of the great importance of the Irish language in conveying instruction to the natives—of which the Rev. John Gregg, the present Bishop of Cork, gave him a striking illustration in his own person—the Archbishop caused an advertisement to be published, announcing that he had come to the determination not to receive into holy orders, after January 1, 1832, any person for the ministry of that province not capable of addressing the people in their native tongue. But after two years no such candidates presented themselves, and this project therefore failed. A similar result attended another for the revival of the Irish language, as if that ancient tongue were destined to perish in the land where it had been most deeply rooted and best cultivated. But with the English came civilisation, new ideas, mental improvement, commercial knowledge, worldly advancement. The Archbishop, however, wished to establish a college at Tuam, where the Irish language would be taught to candidates for the ministry who had graduated in the University, and in which they might be specially prepared for the missionary work among the peasantry, most of whom did not understand English. He sent a prospectus of the institution to his brethren on the Bench, soliciting their co-operation. But only one or two of them deigned to notice it, even in the coldest manner, and the scheme fell to the ground. A project for establishing a Protestant colony on the waste lands of Connemara he also regarded with favour; and within a few years of his death the venerable prelate travelled all the way to the island of Achill to visit the missionary colony founded by the Rev. Edward Mangle. His carriage having broken down, he pursued his journey on an outside car. He died in the sixty-ninth year of his age, on March 26, 1839—the last Protestant Archbishop of Tuam—having occupied the see for the long period of forty years.

It may be safely said that, humanly speaking, no fitter agent could have been employed to extend the reformation in Connaught; nor could more suitable instruments have been selected than those which this truly good prelate kept sending into the field with sleepless care for nearly half a century. It was not his fault that he was regarded as part-and-parcel of Protestant ascendancy—of the political and ecclesiastical system imposed by conquest, against which the national instinct militated, and against which, therefore, the popular passions could be easily excited into wild fanaticism. While under its influence they could be easily made to believe that 'the Bible was the book of the devil—the poison of souls, the key of perdition'—and that Archbishop Trench —one of the most truly Christian and apostolic prelates that ever held a crozier in Connaught—was an enemy of his country, and deserved to have his name cast out as evil and to be trodden under the feet of men.

The missionary work in Connaught was carried on vigorously by the new bishop, Lord Plunket. For many years his nephew and chaplain, Mr. Conyngham Plunket, now the Rev. Lord Plunket, was the most active agent in carrying on this work. At a Church congress some years ago he stated that the number of converts made during the era of successful missionary labour which came to a crisis on the eve of emancipation was 2,357. Passing over the collapse which followed, he traced Church progress from 1834 downwards, showing that 306 new churches had been built and 171 enlarged by the year 1861, while the number of non-residents among the clergy had decreased from 368 to 150. The region of West Connaught presented the greatest results of the Church Missionary movement. This is a tract of country bordering upon the Atlantic, and comprising the districts of Achill, Erris, and Connemara, extending for 100 miles in length and 20 or 30 in breadth. Some thirty years ago this whole district contained but thirteen Protestant congregations, seven churches, and eleven clergymen. In 1861 there were fifty-seven congregations, twenty-seven churches, and thirty-five clergymen. In the reign of Queen Anne Sir Arthur Shaen introduced a Protestant colony in the northern part of West Connaught. There were also Protestant colonists settled southward, near Galway. Some remnants of them could be traced about sixty years ago; but as no minister of their own ever went near them, they were obliged to go to mass. The Rev. Dr. Hulme, of Liverpool, points attention to a curious ethnological fact bearing upon the social condition of Ireland. He says: 'It is peculiarly difficult to recover either those who have been perverted, or their descendants; yet the missionary fruits are twofold, embracing the Roman Catholic population and the descendants of lapsed Protestants. The former are pure Celts, mild, docile, and gentle in their dispositions; far different from the Romanised Normans imported from England, who make up the dangerous classes of the worst counties, and constituting England's great difficulty. No doubt the Connaught Celts—or the remnant of an older race which the Celts conquered and held in bondage, all mixed up and crushed by subsequent conquests in one degraded mass—have been remarkably gentle, tame, even abjectly submissive and servile to the gentry, in comparison with Tipperary and other counties planted by English settlers. But recent events, and above all the last Galway election, demonstrate that even in Connaught the Celtic nature has not lost its capacity of being roused by certain stimulants into wild turbulence and reckless ferocity, in which case the strongest bonds of ecclesiastical discipline have no more force to restrain its impetuosity than the withs that Samson broke 'as a thread of tow is broken when it toucheth the fire.'

The aggressive nature of the mission produced results to be lamented, but which were inevitable. These have been well pointed out by an 'Irish Peer.' He says: 'The priests on their side have not been idle during the attacks upon their religion;

and by enlisting the antipathies of race and creed and tradition against the Protestants, they have more than repulsed the assault. Where there was indifference before they have aroused hatred, which would in itself suffice to baffle the well-meant efforts of proselytism; and they have endeared Romanism to their flocks, not less as antagonistic to the Saxon creed than as connected with the history of the Celt. This policy, if not quite in the spirit of the Gospel, was still as natural as it was skilful.'

It is true that, so far as the Church was concerned, that part of Ireland was a spiritual wilderness until Archbishop Trench attempted to reclaim it. But his exertions provoked a powerful reaction; and on review of the whole, 'an Irish Peer' remarked: 'There are still a few worthy persons who after years of disappointment maintain their hopes and reiterate assurances which the experience of nearly forty years has contradicted. The man must be blind indeed to the signs of the times, blind to the external objects visible to all who have eyes, blind to what passes in our streets and fields, and equally blind to the lessons of a Press entirely devoted to the priests, who thinks that their influence is waning. If Roman Catholic chapels and cathedrals, emulating those of the Continent in costly architecture; if convents, monasteries, colleges, all built within the last twenty years; be any evidence of declining zeal, then Romanism may be declining. Nor need we confine ourselves to these indirect but significant proofs of zeal in a poor country; for no one resident in Ireland can be ignorant of the greatly increased sway of the Roman Catholic priesthood over their flocks. The chapels are everywhere better attended upon holidays, and the lower orders, at all events, are far more strict in their confessions, fasts, and other religious observances, than they used to be. Would that our poor Protestants in their own creed had emulated them!'

CHAPTER XIX.

PROGRESS OF ROMANISM.

ARCHBISHOP MCHALE has been for nearly fifty years the leader of the Catholics of Connaught, with more power over the masses around him, for evil or for good, than any leader ever enjoyed in that province. The last Galway election is a good stand-point from which to review his long career.

According to the arrangement of the Roman Catholic Church, which strictly preserves the old ecclesiastical land-marks, the province of Tuam consists of seven sees—Tuam, Clonfert, Achonry, Elphin, Kilmacduagh and Kilfenora, Killala, and Galway. Archbishop McHale, whose name has been almost constantly before the Irish public for half a century, is the Metropolitan, having his cathedral at Tuam. Born in 1791 at Tubbernaveen, county Mayo, he is a Connaught man and a Celt. Being a clever lad with a religious turn, he was destined for the priesthood, and entered Maynooth College at an early age. There having soon distinguished himself by his learning and abilities, he was appointed Professor of Dogmatic Theology when he was only about twenty-three years old. In 1825 he became Coadjutor Bishop of Killala, with right of succession, and was consecrated with the title of '*Maronia.*' He was then widely known as the author of a series of letters on the Established Church and Catholic grievances, under the signature of '*Hieropholis.*' A second series of the same kind was published later, under his own name. He is also author of a work on *The Evidences and Doctrines of the Catholic Church*; and not many years ago he translated Moore's Melodies into the Irish language. In 1834 he became Archbishop of Tuam; and in that position he has continued ever since to be a tower of strength to the Irish Catholic cause, being by far the ablest champion of that cause in the hierarchy since the death of Dr. Doyle. He has always been intensely national in his sentiments, and indefatigable in his exertions to check the advance of Protestantism. During the whole period when questions connected with the Church Establishment were agitated, he wrote letters very frequently in the newspapers, which were generally addressed to the Prime Minister of the day, or some other prominent statesman. Unlike Bishop Doyle, his style was pompous and inflated. He always affected a lofty scorn of the prelates of the Established Church as mere State-functionaries, thrust into the province to trouble his repose and steal stray members of the flock of which he had the lawful charge. His magniloquent epistles on political and ecclesiastical matters were eagerly read by the Roman Catholics, who admired them as the grandest displays of eloquence. O'Connell flattered him to the top of his bent, calling him 'The great Archbishop of the West,' 'The Apostolic Prelate of St. Jarlath's,' 'The Lion of Tuam,' and 'The Lion of Judah.' The 'Lion,' therefore, felt himself bound to roar as loudly as possible in support of the 'Liberator,' not only while he had been labouring for Catholic emancipation, but also when subsequently engaged in the agitation for the Repeal of the Union. When emancipation had been conceded, O'Connell's most gifted colleague, the late Richard Lalor Shiel, a man of genius and a brilliant orator, believed with that concession agitation should end; and when he went to a meeting of the Catholic Association to propose its dissolution, he stated that he was authorised to cast twenty-two mitres into the scale on the side of peace and social harmony. But some of the mitres were soon taken out of the scale; and Dr. McHale seems to have fancied that his own was a helmet, while grasping his crosier as if it had been a sword. There is something wonderful in the hierarchial system of Rome, which can thus raise the son of a peasant to such a *status*, and can thus animate him by a spirit that enables and emboldens him to maintain a bearing of superiority towards prelatic rivals of aristocratic blood, of princely revenues, and the highest social *prestige*, being himself dependent for his support upon the voluntary contributions of a poor and degraded people! Archbishop McHale lived for many years in the same town with Archbishop Trench, who was at one time, as we have seen, exceedingly popular with Roman Catholics because they were often fed by his bounty. His successor, Bishop Plunket, carried on the controversial war most vigorously; and it raged so fiercely that a number of outrages were, from time to time, perpetrated. Two of Dr. McHale's priests were very prominent in those conflicts—Father Conway and Father Lavelle. Lord Plunket resorted to evictions in some cases, in order to get rid of turbulent neighbours, and there was a great deal of bad blood. The agitation had ceased, however, for some years before that nobleman's death. He and his powerful rival, the Archbishop, dwelt together in their poor old town as peaceful neighbours, though without much social intercourse.[1]

It is in 'Protestant Ulster,' however, that the progress of Romanism, during the period under review, has been most surprising. This progress has been very much identified with the Primacy of Archbishop CROLLY, who was appointed coadjutor of the Bishop of Down in 1825. Soon after he was examined by an Education Commission, when he gave decided testimony in favour of the 'united system of education, as tending to extinguish party animosities, and as generating kindly feelings.' Previously the four Catholic Archbishops—Curtis, Murray, Laffan, and Kelly—advocated a system of united education, declaring that there could be no possible objection to Catholics receiving a scientific education from Protestants. In fact, in 1841, Gregory XVI. declared that Catholics might attend schools the masters of which were not Catholics, 'provided every exertion

[1] A curious story is told to account for this fact, and I have reason to believe it true. Three elderly gentlemen, on a certain day, dropped in, one after another, at the Turkish Baths, Lincoln Place, in Dublin. Sitting or reclining in the hot room, without anything in the way of costume to indicate their rank or station, they got into conversation. One of these was Lord Plunket, Bishop of Tuam; in the second he very soon recognised his old enemy Archbishop McHale, and in the third, his brother prelate, the Archbishop of Dublin. When Dr. Whately found in what companionship he was he laughed heartily, and stretching his gigantic limbs upon the couch, he began to give vent to his wit and humour so rapidly that the others forgot their quarrels, as well as gravity, and enjoyed the fun exceedingly. He chaffed them about their past contentions, turned their polemical battles into ridicule, reminded them of apostolic precepts about charity, brotherly love, good Samaritanism, and so forth; and it is stated that the two Tuam prelates parted as friends, and never quarrelled again.

was used to have no instruction given in religion, morality, or sacred history.' With those precautions he thought the Irish bishops would easily understand that the religion and virtue of the children were sufficiently provided for, the religious instruction being imparted by Roman Catholics.[1]

In 1835, Dr. Crolly became Archbishop of Armagh, carrying with him all the energy and zeal which had distinguished him in his native diocese. He immediately set to work, and erected on a hill beside the town a large and beautiful diocesan seminary, for which he advanced 600*l.* out of his own pocket. On Patrick's Day, 1840, he laid the foundation of a new cathedral which took twenty years in the building,—an edifice which, as his nephew truly says, 'might vie in majesty of design and beauty of workmanship with those hallowed fanes which uprose from the fervid devotion of the middle ages, and which even now in their solitary ruins, reproach the apathy and indifference of our utilitarian generation.'

The memory of Primate Crolly will not be the less respected by the friends of religious freedom because it has been virulently assailed by writers of the ultramontane party on account of his liberality on the education question, and his friendly intercourse with Protestants. It was with the view of reversing his conciliatory policy and drawing a hard separating line between Romanists and Protestants, that the election of his successor by the parish priests, according to the custom and laws of the Irish Church, was set aside by the Pope, who, by his own absolute authority, appointed Dr. Cullen to this see. Dr. Cullen, though a native of Ireland, had been long estranged from the country, having resided for twenty years in Rome, where he learned to regard all Christians but those of his own Church as beyond the pale of salvation, and to detest freedom of conscience, and all other freedom, as a thing to be extinguished as speedily as possible, but quietly, cautiously, and prudently. At Rome it was perceived with alarm that 'the herb that cures Irish dissension,' was at last beginning to grow with the Shamrock, and it was determined to crush it in the bud. Although Armagh is the first of the Irish

[1] 'Life of the Most Rev. Dr. Crolly.' By the Rev. George Crolly, Professor of Theology, Maynooth, p. 59.

sees, and its Archbishop is styled 'Primate of all Ireland,' the occupant of it is not so influential as the Archbishop of Dublin, because it is too remote from the centre of national authority. It was, therefore, determined on the death of Archbishop Murray, to remove Dr. Cullen to the metropolis, and to place him at the head of the Hierarchy by investing him with the authority of Papal Legate. Dr. Murray was a most estimable prelate, true to his Church, but not ready to sacrifice to its supremacy the interests of his country. He believed that those interests would be promoted greatly, and that his people, long degraded, would be enlightened and elevated by the sound system of education which he assisted in directing, working with Archbishop Whately and the other Protestant Commissioners, for many years, without a word of difference. But the enlightenment and elevation of the people were the very things which the policy of Rome aimed to prevent. In its view, the Irish people were nothing—the Irish nation was nothing, except as mere appendages to the Church—as sources of revenue, and as instruments of power, to be wielded against the heretical government of England, and to be made, it possible, the means of its subversion.

Dr. Cullen was succeeded at Armagh by Dr. Dixon, a moderate divine, whom the parish priests were allowed to choose, the see being now reduced to a secondary position, and the authority of the Primate being superseded. He died soon, and was succeeded by Dr. Kieran, a clergyman of the diocese whom his brethren had returned to the Pope as '*dignissimus.*' The ceremony of consecration took place in his own beautiful church at Dundalk, on Feb. 3rd, 1867. Cardinal Cullen, assisted by a number of prelates, officiated; several of the Catholic nobility and gentry were present, and among the rest Sir George Bowyer, then M.P. for Dundalk. The newspapers stated that the honourable gentleman walked in the procession of bishops and priests in the uniform of a Deputy-Lieutenant, with the Cross of St. Gregory, and the decorations of a Knight of Malta; and continued in attendance on the Cardinal during the day.

If Protestant gentlemen were so silly as to appear at the consecration of a bishop of the Established Church, which has so often been called the 'Church Militant,' they would be laughed at. The reasons why some lay-members of the Roman Catholic Church, more remarkable for zeal than discretion, were so fond of parading in this ridiculous fashion, were the absurd restrictions as to costume, &c., imposed by the Emancipation Act. Civic functionaries and Government officials should have the same liberty to carry their uniforms and insignia into Roman Catholic places of worship as into Protestant places of worship. There could be no more invidious distinction than the 'Catholic Relief Act' recognised and enforced when it made conspicuous to the eye of the multitude the religious differences of Her Majesty's subjects by privileges, colours, and costume, accorded to one class and denied to another; the favoured class being a small minority. We cannot be surprised then that when those distinctions were abolished, the Catholic Lord Mayor of Dublin, followed by his co-religionists in the Corporation, went to their Metropolitan Church in grand procession, in their robes, his lordship flaunting the symbols of his office, and displaying his massive gold chain near the altar, that the multitude might see how completely the tables had been turned upon the Protestants, and how the evil spirit of ecclesiastical domination was passing out of one body into another.

From a return made by the priests of the diocese of Armagh it appears that between 1800 and 1864 the cost of churches within its bounds had been 203,857l., of convents 43,334l., and of seminaries and schools 10,000l.—total, 257,191l. The parochial schools, which were not taken into account in the above return, were numerous; and though most of them received grants of salary from the National Board, they had been almost wholly built at the expense of the Catholic people of the diocese. If we go over the dioceses of Dromore, Down, and Connor, of Derry, Raphoe, and Clogher, we shall find similar proofs of effort and progress among the Roman Catholics. In Ulster, from being a disinherited, impoverished, and oppressed minority, they have grown to be the majority of the population. This is the case even in 'the Maiden City,' celebrated for its siege—the Irish Thermopylæ of civil and religious liberty—within whose sacred walls—still religiously preserved in all their strength, with 'Roaring Meg' occupying the place of honour on the bastions—no 'Papist' was allowed to lodge, one hundred years ago. A short time since a large military force was necessary to prevent the Protestants and Roman Catholics from fighting over again on this historic ground the battles which resulted in Protestant ascendancy.

In 1834 the population of the diocese of Derry consisted of 50,350 members of the Established Church, 118,339 Presbyterians, 1,738 other Protestant Dissenters, and 196,614 Roman Catholics. It thus appeared that, as compared with the members of the Established Church in this Protestant diocese, the Presbyterians were more than two to one; and the Roman Catholics nearly four to one! The population of Raphoe at the same time comprised 33,507 members of the Church, 28,914 Presbyterians, and 145,385 Roman Catholics; so that the latter were nearly three times as numerous as the Protestants of all denominations! By the census of 1861 the total population of Raphoe was 169,204, of which 75 per cent. were Roman Catholics. In Derry the number of Roman Catholic priests is 97, officiating in 74 churches and chapels, and three nunneries.

Thus we see that whatever may be the fate of the Irish Episcopal Church in the enjoyment of her freedom and independence, and with an amount of property at her disposal which might well excite the envy of the most prosperous and wealthy Nonconformist denominations, there is no doubt that she will have to meet with the most formidable competition. The Church of Rome is exceedingly strong in her organisation and resources. The income for the support of her institutions which she derives from the bequests of her dying members is enormous; and her financial system is so perfect and so well worked—from the pence of the poor at the church-doors to the steadily exacted contributions of the affluent—that it maintains over the whole body a graduated pressure which never relaxes. We cannot contemplate without astonishment the results produced by the system during the last twenty years. There are now 32 churches and chapels in Dublin and its vicinity. In the diocese the total number of secular clergy is 287, and of regulars 125, the number of nuns being 1,150. Besides 'the Catholic University,' with its ample staff of professors, there are six colleges, 21 superior schools, 12 monastic schools, 40 convent schools, and 200 lay schools, without including those under the National Board. Maynooth, with its magnificent endowments, contains 500 or 600 students, all designed for the priesthood; and there are 250 young men being trained for foreign missions at All Hallows', Drumcondra. The Roman Catholic charities of the city are numerous, including large hospitals, one of which—the Mater Misericordiæ—has been called the 'Palace of the Sick Poor,' from the extent and grandeur of the building. There are orphanages, widows' houses, and other refuges for women; penitentiaries, reformatories; institutions for the blind, the deaf and dumb; industrial schools, Christian doctrine fraternities, and mutual benefit societies almost innumerable. Nearly all these have sprung into existence during the last quarter of a century. Their lay managers are kept in hand so well by Cardinal Cullen, that a word from him to his private secretary can set them all in motion at the same moment, in such a manner as to direct and control the whole mass of the Roman Catholic population for any political object in which the Church is for the moment interested.[1]

Almost equal progress has been made throughout the provinces. In the diocese of Ferns, for example, where the proportion of Catholics to Protestants is more than nine to one, very large sums have been expended on religious edifices. The new churches and chapels of the principal towns are stated, in the 'Irish Catholic Directory,' to have cost 112,800*l*.; while the parochial houses, or manses, have cost 20,000*l*. The sum-total for the half-century is set down as 180,000*l*. to 200,000*l*. In this diocese the proportion of Catholic children in the National Schools during the education contest was 147 to one. In the neighbouring dioceses of Kildare and Leighlin, since Bishop Doyle's time, 200,000*l*. has been spent on 100 chapels, 35,000*l*. on 14 convents, and 30,000*l*. on two colleges. A similar story is to be told of the dioceses of Cashel, Cork, and Kerry, the statistics of which it would be tedious to enumerate. The Bishop of the latter, Dr. Moriarty, resides at Killarney, where a magnifi-

[1] See Canon Pope's remarkable work on the 'Vatican Council,' &c.

cent cathedral has been erected, close to the demesne of Lord Kenmare, a zealous Catholic.

Some of the oldest Protestant families in the country have been won over to the Church of Rome in Ireland; and however deplorable those secessions may be, they must be admitted to have been the result of honest convictions, and their moral influence is therefore the greater. Among gains of this kind by far the greatest is the Earl of Granard, who has added to his extensive estates in the County Longford the magnificent property of Johnstown, Wexford, inherited by Lady Granard, who also became a convert to Catholicism. Little could her father have imagined that a cardinal and a host of Catholic bishops and priests would be entertained at a banquet, in the beautiful castle which he had erected, by his son-in-law. Lord Granard adds tenfold to the influence and *prestige* of his property by the attractiveness of his personal character and his popularity as a landlord.

A very singular meeting was held in Exeter Hall on June 20th, 1835, in which the Rev. Dr. Cooke was one of the chief actors, the other two were the Rev. Dr. Mortimer O'Sullivan and the Rev. Robert McGhee. It was held in consequence of allegations that were made on the subject of 'Dens' Theology,' adopted by the Irish bishops as a class-book in Maynooth, and as a casuistical guide to the priests in the Confessional. In an address to the Protestants of Great Britain and Ireland, signed by three deans, Dr. Singer of Trinity College, the Rev. Robert Daly, Dr. Cooke and others, it was stated that they had recently discovered, by authentic and unquestionable documents, which they had reason to believe had never met the public eye, that 'the standards adopted, and the principles inculcated by the Roman Catholic Hierarchy of Ireland, were of the same intolerant and persecuting nature that were well known to have characterised their Church in former times.' Mr. O'Connell had been specially invited to attend the meeting at Exeter Hall on the ground that he had thrown out a challenge to Protestants, and said it would be his delight to grapple with 'the No Popery hypocrites.' Roman Catholic priests were also expected to attend; and as the subject was political as well as religious, there was immense

excitement in London. Exeter Hall was crowded long before the appointed hour. Among the distinguished public men on the platform was Mr. Gladstone. No one then dreamt that he would be the statesman who would abolish the Establishment which that great meeting was intended to uphold. The first speaker was the Rev. R. J. McGhee, by whom the documents had been collected, and who, in 1840, had them deposited in the University Library, Cambridge, the Bodleian, Oxford, and the Library of Trinity College, Dublin, under the head ' A Report on the Books and Documents on the Papacy.' His subject was ' Dens' Theology.' Dr. Cooke followed on the ' Pope's Bull, *Unigenitus*.' Dr. Cooke gave the following account of the meeting in a letter to his son:—
' It would have given me great delight to have had you with me on Saturday. We had a splendid meeting, the great hall was crowded; we had but three speakers, McGhee, O'Sullivan, and my poor self. McGhee is the greatest speaker I ever heard. He electrified me; he bore me away. He overwhelmed everybody with admiration of the man and conviction of the truth. O'Sullivan was a cataract, tumbling from a mountain. McGhee, a thunder-bolt, flashing and laying prostrate. O'Sullivan, in winding up, almost made me start to my feet, by one awful picture of Rome, rising as a dead body with all the noisomeness of the grave and with all the activity of a demon.'[1]

Archbishop Murray wrote to Lord Melbourne, denying that ' Dens' Theology ' had been adopted as a text-book. But the volume of documents collected and published by Mr. McGhee in 1853, makes it a matter of question after all whether Cardinal Cullen or Archbishop McHale was the true witness when they gave their testimony in the Vatican Council as to the views of the Papacy held by the Irish Hierarchy. The Cardinal, in his great Latin speech, stated that the Irish Church had always held that the Pope was infallible. This Dr. McHale positively contradicted before the Council. It was certainly understood by the general public in Ireland that the Western Metropolitan, in his well-known antagonism to the Ultramontane Cardinal, represented the moderate constitutional liberal Catholicism of the old National Church. It was, therefore, considered that he was acting

[1] ' Life and Times,' &c. p. 286.

quite consistently, and might count on the general support of the priesthood when he resisted with great courage and with all the remaining strength of an octogenarian, the dogma of Papal Infallibility, agreeing with Dr. Newman that it was absurd and mischievous. But like Dr. Newman, he has succumbed, against his reason, to the Papal Absolutism which places all the canonical rights and liberties of the bishops and priests at the feet of a single man, to be trampled on whenever he pleases, or whenever he may be invoked by such a prelate as Cardinal Cullen, to excommunicate and ruin such an independent priest as Father O'Keefe. The object of the meeting in question was to prove, that while the Irish prelates gave evasive denials to the assertion that they were obliged to receive all Papal Bulls and Rescripts, and to bow to the authority of the Sovereign Pontiff in all things, they yet at the same time inculcated on their clergy, as an esoteric doctrine, the dogma of the personal infallibility of the Pope.

However that may be, the dogma is now the cardinal law of the Church of Rome. This being a fact, we must be prepared for all its consequences. If, as I have elsewhere observed, the Irish people had the same experience of the rule of the Papacy that the Spaniards and Italians had, we might count on their resisting and rebelling against its tyranny. But they have never felt its sword or its chains. They love the Pope in proportion as they hate England; and this fanatical devotion to a hereditary protector believed to be the Vicegerent of God has so perverted their judgments, that they have learned to glorify despotism and execrate freedom. During the agitation for Catholic emancipation, the toast of 'Civil and Religious Liberty all over the World' was given at every public dinner by the Irish Catholics. But since O'Connell's death it is never heard. The Pope had denounced religious liberty as damnable heresy. And while in the very act of crushing it in Italy with the aid of foreign troops, the most ardent friends of popular rights in Ireland actually went out as volunteers to help the Holy Father in this good work of oppression. When they returned, after being badly treated by the Roman authorities and defeated by the Italians in spite of their bravery, they were hailed with enthusiasm. The Irish people saw nothing inconsistent in a foreign crusade against the liberties of other nations, while they were threatening to rebel against England for not granting to themselves all the freedom they asked for.

Therefore—so far as any political union is concerned—the Irish Roman Catholics might as well be naturally the most intolerant of bigots, and the most treacherous of allies, instead of being, as most of them are, naturally lovers of freedom and fair play. For the moment the word goes forth from the Church, which is the Pope—they must succumb. They must betray and desert their Protestant colleagues, not only for prudence', but for conscience' sake. To resist the Church in *any* thing, which the Pope commands, is now to fight against God—to become a rebel and a renegade. Papal infallibility leaves no footing in the universe for private judgment.

'Nevertheless,' said His Holiness, 'I must speak the truth to France. There is a more formidable evil than the Revolution, more formidable than the Commune, let loose from hell, with its men who fling fire about Paris—and that is *Catholic Liberalism!*'

This is a hard saying. But whosoever believes in Papal Infallibility—now the cardinal dogma of the Church—must receive it implicitly were it a thousand times as hard. There is no alternative left to Liberal Catholics but the revolt of outraged reason against legitimate authority.

Certainly, if we grant the Catholic premises, it is not easy to resist this conclusion. In the preamble to the 'Apostolic Letter' convoking this Council', Pius said: 'The Lord chose Peter alone from among all the Apostles to be their Prince, His Vicar on earth, the chief *foundation* and *centre* of the Church, so that in *the sovereign fulness* of *authority, power,* and *jurisdiction,* he might, at that high degree of rank and honour, feed the lambs and the sheep, confirm his brethren, govern the Church Universal, be the door-keeper of heaven, the judge of all that should be bound or loosed, his judgments and definitions being destined *to subsist in heaven* as upon earth. . . . And this power, this jurisdiction, this supreme primacy given to Peter over the whole Church, *belong in all their vigour and all their fulness to the Roman Pontiffs, his successors.*' The Rev. Canon Pope, a Dublin priest, who has published a book on the Council, and ought to know the mind of the Irish Hierarchy, tells us plainly what the situation of the priests and laity is. 'It is futile to say the Church has its own legitimate limits, and the world its boundaries beyond which the Church must not intrude. The Church claims its right to enter the world's domain, and recognises no limits but the circumference of Christendom, to enforce her laws over her subjects, to control their reason and judgment, to guide their morals, their thoughts, words and actions, and to regard temporal sovereigns, though entitled to exercise power in temporal affairs, as auxiliaries and *subordinates* to the attainment of the end of her institution.'

The establishment of the Belgian Constitution in 1832 provoked the Encyclical of Gregory XVI., in which he execrated the freedom of the press and everything liberal in politics as well as in religion. That memorable encyclical was adopted by Pius IX., who, in a not less remarkable allocution, dated June 22, 1868, condemned the Austrian Constitution and anathematised its authors. The *Syllabus* brands as a damnable error the statement that the Pope should reconcile his policy to modern society and civilisation: *Romanus Pontifex potest ac debet cum progressu, cum Liberalismo et cum recenti civilisatione sese reconciliare et componere.* In irreconcilable antagonism to this progress, and this Liberalism, and this modern civilisation stands the stupendous system of SACERDOTAL ABSOLUTISM, trampling down all national independence, all freedom of individual judgment, all episcopal rights—pronouncing, without appeal, upon all questions of religion, morals, science, politics, and social life.[1]

[1] 'Frazer's Magazine,' Dec. 1871, p. 776.

CHAPTER XX.

PROGRESS OF PRESBYTERIANISM.

WHEN the late Dr. Cooke entered the ministry, says his biographer,[1] he found 'the Presbyterian Church infected and almost paralysed by a deadly heresy. He found Irish Protestants generally indifferent to the claims of vital religion; he found the public mind deeply imbued with sceptical and infidel opinions; he found the education of the masses in a state of lamentable neglect. Seeing and deploring these evils, he resolved to become a reformer. He spent ten years in unceasing and laborious preparation. Then, during a period of fully thirty years, his life was a continued series of battles for truth. In every battle he was victorious. He freed the Church of his fathers from Arianism. He gave a new impulse to religious life and work among the Protestants of Ireland. He largely contributed to mould the Government schemes of elementary and collegiate education, so as to adapt them to the wants of the people. And he founded and consolidated a constitutional party in Ulster, which preserved the peace of the country and gave a death-blow to repeal.'

The proverbial partiality of a biographer, the affection of a near relative, and the admiration of a political partizan, have given too much colouring to this picture. It is true that Dr. Cooke held strong opinions, both religious and political; that he propagated and defended them with extraordinary powers of wit, irony, argument and eloquence; and that he bore down opposition with whatever intellectual weapons came to hand at the moment, never losing a victory through excess of scrupulosity. He was to the Presbyterians of Ulster something like what Mr.

---

[1] 'Life and Times of Henry Cooke, D.D. LL.D.' By the Rev. Professor Porter, D.D. London, John Murray, 1871.

O'Connell was to the Roman Catholics of the nation. He won his popularity by a protracted war against Unitarianism, the professors of which were then the ablest, the most learned and eloquent men in the Synod of Ulster. Their leader was the Rev. Henry Montgomery, who was physically and intellectually one of the most magnificent men, and one of the most accomplished orators that any country ever produced. Dr. Porter does ample justice to his powers. He says Mr. Montgomery's presence was commanding, his manner graceful, his style chaste and classic, his voice singularly sweet. His speeches abounded with sparkling wit, touching pathos, and powerful declamation. Referring to one of his speeches in synod, Dr. Porter says:—' Never perhaps in the annals of debate, never in the whole history of controversial warfare, were charges grave and terrible constructed with more consummate ingenuity, and pressed home with such overwhelming power of oratory. His denunciations were absolutely appalling; they sent a thrill of horror through the assembly. Once and again he turned in the midst of his vehement philippic, and with voice and gesture and look expressive of bitterest scorn, pointed to his adversary (who sat before him calm and motionless as a statue), and exclaimed : " Who or what is our accuser? Has the Almighty given any peculiar dignity of intellect or person to Mr. Cooke that he should speak so of us?" Towards the close the orator, with matchless skill, again changed the theme and manner. The glance of scorn melted into a smile of benevolence ; the voice of triumph gave place to the mellow tone of touching pathos; the flashing eye became dimmed by the gathering tear-drop ; the lip, before curled with indignation, now quivered as if with suppressed emotion. In language of classic beauty he alluded to the impending rupture of the Synod; he contrasted the stormy scenes of earthly conflict with the peace of heaven. When he concluded, the Synod, the whole audience, seemed as if under the spell of a mighty magician. When the enchanting music of that marvellous oratory ceased there was for a time a stillness as of death. Then thunders of applause burst from the assembly; they ceased, but were again and again renewed. The Arians were triumphant. The orthodox thought their cause lost. Even the warmest friends and most enthusiastic admirers of Dr. Cooke hung their heads, or conversed in anxious whispers. Many supposed his character was ruined; all believed his influence was gone for ever.'

The speech lasted two hours and a half. After a short interval for refreshment the Synod re-assembled. The crowd was, if possible, denser than before; and Dr. Cooke rose to reply amid profound silence. Not a voice ventured to greet him with an encouraging cheer. He proceeded with his defence quietly, winding himself into his subject until he gradually won back the sympathy of his audience. 'No description,' says Dr. Porter, 'could convey an adequate idea of the speech that followed. Mr. Cooke had no notes, yet not a point was overlooked. He had no documents, yet his marvellous memory enabled him to supply the designed omissions, to expunge the damaging interpolations of his adversary. The convictions of Synod and audience were won by the searching, incisive logic and wonderful lucidity of the speaker; their sympathies and hearts were won by the resistless force of his eloquence. He swayed them as by the power of a mighty enchanter; they laughed, they wept, they cheered in turn; the house rang with peals of acclamation. When he resumed his seat the whole assembly rose, and by repeated rounds of applause celebrated his victory. Those who were present have affirmed that they never felt till then the full power of eloquence; and that they never could have imagined the human mind was capable of such an effort, or that human language would have produced such an effect.[1]

It was indeed a battle between giants, arising out of questions in which the whole population took the deepest interest. The synodical debates were long remembered with admiration and wonder by the Presbyterian laity. Dr. Cooke succeeded in compelling the retirement of the Unitarian members of the Synod, who formed a body of their own called ' *The Remonstrant Synod of Ulster.*' In order to secure the orthodoxy of those who remained, Dr. Cooke also succeeded in pledging the Synod to 'Absolute Subscription' of the Westminster *Confession of Faith* and the *Westminster Catechisms;* and they appointed a Theological Committee to watch over the faith of the young

[1] ' Life,' pp. 196–200.

men entering the ministry. Dr. Cooke was for years the great leader in Ulster of the opposition to the National System of Education, the rallying cry of its antagonists being 'the Bible, the whole Bible, and nothing but the Bible!' He also took part in the discussions against the Church of Rome previous to the passing of Catholic Emancipation, setting up 'a free and open Bible' against the creeds, canons, dogmas, rescripts, and anathemas of the Church of Rome, as mere human authority, which could not bind the conscience. Yet neither he nor his followers were able to see that in binding upon the consciences of the ministers of the Synod the enormous mass of metaphysical and theological propositions, dogmas, and interpretations compiled by the Westminster divines—mere fallible men—two hundred years before, in an age when religious liberty was so little understood, and when the science of biblical criticism had hardly been thought of, they were doing all in their power to accomplish the very thing which Lord J. Russell so truly and tersely ascribed to the Roman system—that is, to 'confine the intellect and enslave the soul.' How far their model Kirk of Scotland succeeded in doing so may be seen in the pages of Mr. Buckle.

Dr. Cooke, however, became extremely popular throughout Ireland, not only as the defender of orthodoxy, but as the champion of Toryism. He was unsparing in his philippics against the Liberal party. He supported the Conservative landlords in every electoral contest, enabling them, by means of the Presbyterian vote, to keep the representation of Ulster exclusively in their hands. He defended Religious Establishments with all his might, especially the Episcopal Establishment in Ireland, in spite of its Prelacy, and in charitable oblivion of the cruelties that Prelacy had inflicted upon his own Church in past ages.

In 1834 a great Protestant demonstration took place at Hillsborough, the result of a requisition, signed by the leading men of Down and Antrim, presented to Lord Hillsborough, then high sheriff of Down. It was intended to denounce the Whig Ministry charged with 'truckling to Popery, and seeking to conciliate the priests by the degradation of Protestantism.' It was a gathering of Conservatives from the whole province. The meeting was held on October 30 in a large field, and it was estimated that more than 40,000 of the gentry and yeomanry attended. Dr. Cooke was present on the earnest invitation of Lord Roden. Among the speakers were the Marquis of Downshire, the Marquis of Donegal, the Marquis of Londonderry, and several other peers. But the speech of the day was Dr. Cooke's. It made a great noise at the time, and was long remembered on account of his proposed marriage between the two divided Churches—the Anglican and the Presbyterian. The nature of the union was rather awkwardly expressed, which, perhaps, necessarily arose from the fact that both the parties to be united in holy matrimony were of the same sex. He said:—' I publish the banns of sacred marriage, of Christian forbearance where they differ, of Christian love where they agree, and of Christian cooperation in all matters where their common safety is concerned; who forbids the banns? None!' This speech gave great dissatisfaction, and called forth loud remonstrances from many of his own brethren. The Conservatives, however, were glad to have thus publicly committed to their cause ' the Moderator of the Synod of Ulster, the *head* of the Church, and the representative of the whole Presbyterians of Ireland.' They exulted in the meeting ' as a great success, as it contributed largely to the overthrow of a time-serving Ministry.' Of course, it added greatly to the popularity of the Presbyterian champion of Toryism; and his congregation rather ungenerously persuaded him to avail himself of the tide in order to sweep off the debt upon his church in May Street, Belfast, a large building erected especially for him, and in which he ministered with eminent success to the end of his career. He went to London on this unpleasant mission and accomplished his object. ' I think it too hard,' wrote his friend Mr. Cairns, now Lord Cairns, ' that you should have to expend your influence and lay yourself under an obligation, in accomplishing an object in which you have only a temporary interest.'

Dr. Cooke, as his biographer remarks, had become a recognised political leader; ' he had long been an ecclesiastical leader.' It was remarkable that those whose councils he guided in the Synod of Ulster, were most opposed to him in politics. Many of them wrote against him, and spoke against him, as a politician.

Yet this did not affect his ecclesiastical position. The services he had rendered and was still rendering to the Presbyterian Church, prevented his influence from waning. But, popular as he was with the lords of the soil in Ulster, and great as the services he had rendered them as their ablest and most ready champion, it is a remarkable fact, he was never able, if he ever desired, to get a single member of his own communion returned to represent the Presbyterians in the House of Commons. The majority of his brethren had long felt pained and humiliated by the fact that, though their people far outnumbered the Episcopalians in Ulster, and nearly equalled them in the whole of Ireland, they were absolutely excluded as a denomination from any voice in the House of Commons. Taking this fact into consideration, the Assembly in 1843 adopted the following very mild resolution, notwithstanding Dr. Cooke's most determined opposition:—
'That the difficulty that has been experienced in having the wishes and interests of Presbyterians efficiently represented in Parliament—a difficulty particularly manifested during the struggles of the Scottish Church—and the serious injury which, from the aspect of the times, we have reason to fear from a similar course, warrant this Assembly in recommending the adoption of measures for securing a more adequate representation of the principles and interests of Presbyterians in the legislature of the country.'

Dr. Cooke, who had brought all the influence of the Church to bear in favour of Toryism, as a recognised political leader, vehemently protested against this resolution, which he said would give the Church the appearance and place before the world of 'an electioneering club.' But, says his sympathetic biographer, 'party spirit triumphed.' He should rather have said, 'the independence of the Church triumphed.' Dr. Cooke, however, felt that the motion was virtually a condemnation of his own acts, and a reflection on his political friends. Assailed vigorously by young and rising men in the Assembly, the great leader was chafed and dispirited; so mortified, indeed, at this insurrection against his supremacy, that he retired from the Assembly, retaining his position as permanent Moderator of the Synod of Ulster for certain legal and official purposes. He never entered the

Assembly again for four years—the obnoxious political resolution having been rescinded for his personal gratification. When sending in his resignation, he protested against the policy which the resolution was meant to inaugurate—among other things, because it would tend to bring into conflict a peaceful and industrious tenantry with landlords who, with few exceptions, were considerate, kind, and indulgent; and to whom, with scarcely any exception, the Presbyterian congregations were deeply indebted for sites for their churches and liberal subscriptions for their erection. And, finally, this great agitator protested, because the Word of God warned him, that 'the beginning of strife is as one that letteth out water; therefore leave off contention before it be meddled with.' He had himself been all his life a man of contention. He had fought with the Unitarians until he drove them out of the Synod of Ulster. He was so fond of a good fight, that when the Rev. Dr. Richie of Edinburgh, in 1836, went to Belfast, to deliver lectures on Voluntaryism, Dr. Cooke, though suffering from illness, went forth to resist him and put him down, making himself the champion of all ecclesiastical Establishments—the Irish as well as the Scotch. And when O'Connell proposed to visit Belfast during the Repeal agitation, in 1840, in compliance with the request of a deputation, Dr. Cooke availed himself of the occasion to rouse the Orange spirit of the North by challenging the agitator to a public discussion on the Repeal question. O'Connell declined the challenge, saying, at a public meeting—'My worthy Cock of the North knows I could not comply with his letter, therefore he sends it to me. Now let him crow as much as he pleases, but I won't contend with him, nor am I such a blockhead as to take up a political question with him. I have no notion to give him that advantage, which would be this: he is at the head of the Presbyterians of Ulster, and if I was to argue politics with him, it would be admitting that I was an antagonist of theirs in politics. I am no antagonist in politics with them; on the contrary, I am most desirous to serve the Presbyterians in every way in my power; and if in my present struggle I succeed, it will be as much for their benefit as for the Roman Catholics. Oh no, Daddy Cooke! I will not gratify your trick.'

However, as O'Connell had foolishly reviled Belfast on a previous occasion, Dr. Cooke's challenge, and the insulting manner in which it was received, set the Ulster Orangemen in a blaze of uncontrollable excitement. The proposed triumphal procession of Repealers into Ulster was to be resisted to the death. The descendants of the men who stood the siege of Derry, and fought at the Boyne, were eager to fight now, and show the Repealers that they could neither be cajoled nor conquered. The Government, dreading a bloody collision, hastily drafted large bodies of troops and police, and stationed them in the towns along the line. Strong detachments were placed at Newry, Dromore, Banbridge, and other points, while Belfast presented the appearance of a besieged city. The public procession was therefore abandoned, and on the 16th January O'Connell and a few friends arrived at the Royal Hotel at that town about six o'clock, on a dark cold evening, having travelled from Dublin in a private carriage, disguised, and under assumed names. He remained on Sunday in his hotel. On Monday he received his friends; and in the evening they entertained him at a banquet at which eight hundred were present. Next day he was to hold a public meeting; but the Orangemen managed to pack the hall. Consequently O'Connell did not appear, but addressed a crowd from the window of his hotel. There the Protestants assembled in overwhelming force, jeering and groaning so loudly and incessantly, that scarcely a sentence he uttered could be heard; while a huge placard was held up before him, containing in large letters Dr. Cooke's challenge. 'He thought,' says Dr. Porter, 'he might ignore Dr. Cooke, and affect to despise his challenge; but he found, when too late, that Dr. Cooke's power in Belfast was *supreme*. In fact, O'Connell, from the moment of his arrival, had been virtually a prisoner. He dared not venture to leave his hotel, except by stealth or under escort. The hotel itself did not seem safe, after the abortive attempt to address the mob on Tuesday. A demand for protection was addressed to the authorities, and a cordon of troops was drawn round the house. Early on Wednesday morning a close carriage drew up at the door, encircled by mounted police with drawn swords; lines of infantry and patrols of cavalry kept back the crowds. O'Connell and his friends entered the carriage, which drove rapidly off to Donaghadee under military escort. While he was embarking, a waggish Highland piper, who chanced to be present, struck up the appropriate air ' We'll gang nae mair to yon toon.'

Immediately after O'Connell's flight a requisition was signed by 41 peers, 14 right honourables and honourables, 18 baronets, 32 members of Parliament, 11 high sheriffs, 6 lieutenants of counties, 98 deputy-lieutenants, 335 magistrates, and 330 clergy of various denominations, calling a meeting, which was held in an immense building called the Circus. No such array had ever been seen in Belfast. The chair was filled by the Marquis of Downshire. Many of the Conservative leaders were present, but the hero of the day and the chief speaker was Dr. Cooke. The excitement spread throughout the province, and he was everywhere hailed as 'the saviour of the country.' Steps were immediately taken to present him with a suitable testimonial. It was rumoured, probably without any foundation, that the life of the conquering hero was threatened; and accordingly the testimonial assumed the form of an assurance effected on his life, for which the sum of 2,000*l.* was soon raised and invested. Honours the most signal were conferred upon him by his own body. The General Assembly in 1841 raised him by acclamation to the Moderator's Chair; and a public meeting, held in his own church, presented a marble bust of him to his congregation. When the Rev. Dr. Henry, of Armagh, was made President of the Queen's College, Belfast, the sinecure office which he held as Distributor of Regium Donum was conferred by Sir Robert Peel upon Dr. Cooke, with a salary of 300*l.* a year, which made his income from Regium Donum 400*l.*; and when the General Assembly's College was established with a State endowment of 250*l.* a year for each professor, Dr. Cooke was elected President, and Professor of Sacred Rhetoric, as well as Dean of Residence.

And this was the leader who rebuked the General Assembly for presuming to meddle with politics so far as to desire some representation in the Imperial Parliament! We are astonished—even the most bigoted Episcopalians would be astonished—on reading that, when it was proposed by the Presbyterians in 1705 to institute a seminary for the education of their youth in Belfast, the Irish House of Commons passed this resolution:—' The erection of any seminary for the instruction and education of youth in principles contrary to the Established Church and Government tends to create and perpetuate misunderstandings among Protestants; and, further, any teaching or preaching in separate congregations *tends to defeat the succession in the Protestant line, and to encourage and advance the interests of the pretended Prince of Wales!'*

Yet what do we read in the Parliamentary proceedings of the year 1868, after all that Dr. Cooke and the Presbyterians of Ulster had done for the Irish Establishment and the Conservative landlords of Ulster? The General Assembly had just resolved, by a majority of thirty, that the preservation of the Irish Establishment, with the ascendency of the Episcopal Church, was to be preferred to religious equality obtained by universal disendowment. A member of the Assembly, a few days after, went on a deputation to the Prime Minister, and conveyed to him the impression that a majority of that body had stood up in defence of the Irish Establishment—a result that great efforts had been made to obtain. But at this very time—when the Establishment was in a dangerous crisis—on the eve of a general election which was to decide its fate, the representatives of Ulster whom the Presbyterian electors had returned to Parliament, and whom Dr. Cooke had supported on every occasion, as their best friends, voted that Presbyterian ministers should not have the right of holding funeral services in graveyards without the express permission in writing of the rector or other Church incumbent!

Except during the latter half of the eighteenth century, when the policy of the Aristocratic Church shut the Presbyterians out of the Constitution, subjecting them to much of the rigour of the penal code, for the purpose of discouraging the pretended Prince of Wales (a very silly pretext), that body has always been devotedly loyal to the Throne. Nevertheless it is to the spirit of democracy that we are to ascribe the energetic character and self-reliance of this people. In the Kirk Session, in the Presbytery, in the Synod, and the General Assembly, the practice of representative government, the right of voting, and the habit of free speech among the laity, have mainly contributed to form the character of the Ulster Presbyterians. But these privileges could not have been preserved in Ireland without the basis of tenant-right in the agricultural population. Without this custom, rack-rents and insecurity of tenure would have reduced them to serfdom, and placed them nearly on a level with the Roman Catholic peasantry. For their landlords, though of the same blood and language, were gradually alienated from them in religion and joined to the Church of the ascendency. Lord Castlereagh's father was a steady Presbyterian to the last. But the son resolved to maintain Prelacy in full power, though Ulster should be reduced to a solitude. Hence the Presbyterian spirit of democracy (regarded by the ruling oligarchy as presenting a most dangerous example to the Catholics) the Government determined to corrupt or crush, so that a body forming nearly half the Protestant population of the country should become politically a nonentity, and yet should be made strong as a buttress to the Episcopal Establishment. This was done by exciting religious animosity against the mass of the nation. The policy was inaugurated by converting the rebellion of '98 into a religious war. The organisation by which this policy has been perpetuated is the Orange Society, which has been always more or less patronised by the nobility, magistrates, and clergy of the ruling class, and fostered by anniversaries of civil wars. The wounds inflicted upon a vanquished Church and a subjugated nation were thus triumphantly, tauntingly, and defiantly torn open afresh two or three times every year!

The far-reaching effect of this policy was strikingly evinced even on the very eve of the Disestablishment, when Mr. Gladstone's preliminary resolutions were already before the public. The General Assembly then voted, by a majority, for perpetuating the ascendency over them of an Erastian and Prelatic Establishment, though the ministers were each and all bound by their ordination vows to do all in their power to *extirpate Prelacy*. We see the effect of the policy in the fact that 500,000 or 600,000 Presbyterians, constituting the most industrious and wealthy portion of the population of Ulster, were not able to return a single member of their own body to represent them in Parliament, being obliged to supplicate the Episcopalians, whom their

landlords required them to return, to obtain for them any boon
they needed as a Church. One would suppose that when they
appealed to those representatives for liberty to pray over the
remains of their departed friends, while committing their bodies
to the grave, without seeking permission from the minister of a
rival Church, their request would have at once been granted.
This should have been done, if not on the ground of humanity
and Christian charity, at least from prudence and policy, at a
time when the Established Church was in imminent danger, and
when the whole Presbyterian vote was given for its support.
Yet even then the invidious, unchristian distinction was maintained by the voices of the Ulster representatives—a curious
illustration of the marriage union proclaimed at Hillsborough by
the Presbyterian leader, who deserted the Assembly because it
meekly sought the only means of putting an end to such painful
degradation!

But the liberal party in the Assembly, which grew stronger
every year, was now largely composed of the elements to which
its real progress in spiritual things is to be mainly ascribed; and
to those earnest men this state of subjection to another Church
could no longer be endured, even for the sake of keeping the
Regium Donum. They protested against the resolutions, because
they held it to be the duty of the Assembly at this juncture
to look in the spirit of Christian patriotism beyond its own immediate interests, and to declare they preferred a system of
general disendowment to a system of indiscriminate endowment,
because, looking at the aspect of the question of ecclesiastical
endowments in Ireland, and remembering that no chance had
ever before been offered for removing the evils and injustice to
which Presbyterians had been subjected for upwards of two
hundred years, and for at the same time securing the disendowment of error, they believed that the opportunity now afforded of
accomplishing those great ends should not be allowed to pass.
The Assembly should declare that a measure of disestablishment
and disendowment, such as Mr. Gladstone proposed, if impartially
carried out, would be for the good of all the Protestant Churches,
as well as for the benefit of the entire population. The question
was very clearly stated by several of the most eminent men in

the body. Mr. McClure, M.P. for Belfast, now Vice-Lieutenant of Down, in the absence of the Earl of Dufferin, a gentleman in whose family there has been a Presbyterian minister for a hundred and fifty years, said that the question raised, and upon which they must give their decision, was—' Is it expedient, just and right, that the ascendency of the Anglican Church in Ireland should cease, and that the Assembly should give no uncertain sound?' Let the Presbyterian Church, if it chose, throw its position, its honour, and its emoluments in the forefront of the struggle, and say she would stand or fall in defence of the ascendency of the Anglican Church. Then she would have nothing to look to but the gratitude of the body for which she had perilled so much, and for which in that case she must lay aside her Presbyterian principles, and put a slight upon the memory of their forefathers. ' I will not,' he said, ' bow down to the idol of Ascendency! Are we the degenerate sons of a noble ancestry, that we dare not say that we are fit to stand on an equality with any Church?' The Rev. Professor Wallace had the greatest respect for the Established clergy; but the question did not depend on the character of the Episcopal community; he objected to its establishment; he objected to its exclusive ascendency in the land. He was surprised that his brethren should lend themselves to the maintenance in any way of the assumed superiority of any Church over their own. He was not prepared to bring his Church to sit at the feet of Anglicans, however worthy. And now, when in the wonderful providence of God there was a probability of that ascendency being removed without wrong to any man, why were they disputing there the question of the Headship of Christ, which no one denied, as if they could throw that shield over the Church of England to save her? They had been asked to look at the position in which they would leave their successors, bereft of Regium Donum, and dependent on the voluntary principle. ' I will,' said Professor Wallace, ' I will tell you what we will leave our successors; we will leave them what our fathers did not leave us—*Religious Equality.*'

The Rev. John McNaughton believed that the honour of their own Church was involved in that great question. As for him, he would give up all endowments rather than sacrifice principle. If they did so, they would secure the hearty sympathy and the holy co-operation of all the Churches in the land and elsewhere. He believed the removal of the endowments connected with the Established Church, even though the Regium Donum should sink in the whirlpool, would widen their circle and increase their sympathies, while at the same time they would be protesting against the indiscriminate endowment of truth and error, and save their consciences from a great wrong! All agreed that many landed proprietors and men of property among themselves would imitate the noble example of Lord Dufferin, who had offered to secure to all the Presbyterian ministers on his estates a rent-charge equal in amount to the Regium Donum, for which his lordship received the thanks of the Assembly, voted by acclamation.

The most sanguine expectations of the supporters of disendowment in the Presbyterian Church have been more than realised by the results of Mr. Gladstone's measure. It has given entire satisfaction, and has put the Presbyterian Church in a position for usefulness such as it never occupied before. In fact, it has relieved the Church from a false position which prevented the development of its true character, and held it in a state of miserable thraldom. The new spiritual life which so powerfully influenced all Evangelical denominations during the past half-century had been felt to a large extent amongst the Presbyterians of Ulster, and the reverend author of the 'Life and Times of Dr. Cooke' may well exult in the changes which have been wrought, and the attainments which have been made. Forty years ago the whole 'Church was satisfied with the cold observance of the routine of worship. There was no power in the pulpit; there was no spiritual life among the people; missionary work, whether at home or abroad, was never thought of. It has now in its communion 630 ministers, 560 congregations, and above 100,000 families. It has made noble efforts to provide for the spiritual training and wants of the rapidly increasing population of the large towns. In Belfast alone twenty-two new churches have been erected since 1830. It has missionaries labouring in Germany, Austria, Spain, Italy, Palestine, India, China, and in nearly all the colonies of the British Empire.'

Professor Porter asserts that, ' for this wonderful success the Presbyterian Church is, under God, *mainly* indebted to the talents and labours of Henry Cooke.' But this is scarcely fair to a host of other labourers in the same field and in the same communion. Dr. Cooke was a great controversialist, a great political leader, a champion ready to measure swords with all comers who had aught to say against ecclesiastical Establishments, orthodox Presbyterianism, or Protestant ascendency. He was a great orator, a powerful preacher, a most effective propagandist of the principles which he cherished, and he was true to those principles to the end. He probably made more noise in the world than all the other ministers of the body during his day and generation. But, while he paraded on the walls of the city, blowing his trumpet of defiance and flourishing his sword, many other men whose voices were not heard in the streets were quietly building up the Presbyterian Jerusalem, working hard at Sunday Schools, Bible classes, prayer-meetings, missionary meetings, as members of various committees, as earnest preachers, as diligent and faithful pastors, busy in organising and working charitable institutions, and collecting funds—in everything, in fact, that contributed to spiritual edification and to the internal renovation and strength of the Presbyterian Church. These men should not be passed over in silence in any history of that Church for the last half-century. The Morgans, the Johnstones, the McClures, the Wallaces, the McNaughtons, the Gibsons, the Killans, the Dills, the Rogerses, the Rentouls, the Kirkpatricks, the Edgars, and many others laboured to sow the seed, till the ground, and prepare for the production of that great harvest to which Dr. Porter points with so much satisfaction. He has a right to do so. But he is certainly wrong in ascribing so much of the merit to Dr. Cooke, and so little to other distinguished labourers in the field, whom he almost ignores.

How unsatisfying, after all, is popularity ! There is no sadder spectacle than the picture of a great man who had been all his life surrounded by troops of friends, and had been daily listening to the sound of his own praises in the public journals and on public platforms, complaining in his old age of being lonely and desolate

—the friends of his youth having all passed away—and feeling incapable of supplying their place by the friendship of later years. Many of our greatest men in every department of public life have lamented this melancholy isolation, even when reposing on well-earned laurels, won in glorious battles, after making no small part of history by their own achievements. Strange to say, Dr. Cooke, though loaded with honours and surrounded by troops of admirers, was one of these. After the death of a favourite daughter he wrote to the Rev. J. Burns, saying:—' After my God and her dear mother, she was all the world to me; and it is now to me, and will remain to me, a *blank*. After the salvation of the souls in my charge, there is nothing that interests me. My days and nights are spent in tears.'

But everything possible was done to console him. His Church had conferred upon him the highest offices and honours in her gift; and his political championship had not gone unrewarded, although the whole of his emoluments were nothing to what his talents would have won for him had he devoted them to the Bar; for he would have been quite as likely to have reached the highest place on the Bench as some of the friends whom he had helped to raise to that position, such as Lord Cairns, Sir Joseph Napier, and Chief Justice Whiteside. In 1865, however, a meeting was held in Belfast, attended by Protestants of all denominations, the Marquis of Downshire in the chair, when an address to Dr. Cooke was presented by the Mayor of Belfast, accompanied by a cheque for 1,600 guineas, and a magnificently illuminated volume containing the address and the names of the subscribers.

The Presbyterian leader deceived himself when he said the world would be henceforth to him a blank. He was persuaded to make his appearance at a great Conservative demonstration made at Hillsborough on the 30th October, 1867, the object being to protest against the disestablishment of the Irish Church, and to make a last united effort to defend what were called ' the Protestant institutions of the country.' Dr. Cooke, we are told, took a leading part in its organization, giving it all the weight of his name and influence. The meeting was held in the open air, on the same spot where he had delivered his famous harangue with the same object in 1834. He was now surrounded by many of the same old friends—Lords Roden, Downshire, Erne, Templeton,

Sir Thomas Bates, &c. Very touching is the record of this last political appearance on any stage given by his son-in-law. 'Dr. Cooke on rising was hailed with an outburst of applause from the vast assemblage, so enthusiastic and so prolonged that it fairly unmanned him. His whole frame trembled and his eyes filled with tears. I had for a time to give him the support of my arm. It was with the greatest difficulty he could speak at all. Nothing but a strong sense of duty, and an invincible determination to advocate to the very last the great principles for which he had so nobly struggled through a long life, would have induced him to be present or attempt to raise his voice on that day. It was a grand, and yet a sad, sight. The great orator, the great political leader, the great Protestant chieftain, inspired by the same truths, animated by the same noble aspirations, with all the old vigour of intellect, yet with feeble voice and trembling lips, trying to address a few parting words to the tens of thousands who eagerly bent forward and with a silence as of death hung upon his lips. All felt and mourned the change which fourscore years had wrought in that prince of men, and none more keenly than himself.' [1]

It was cruel of the leaders of the Conservative party to impose this task upon their veteran champion. It is painful to witness the public exhibition of a mere shadowy remnant of former power. But, not content with this, when the general election came on, which was to decide the fate of the Irish Establishment, the support or repudiation of Mr. Gladstone's Irish policy being the testing question on every hustings, the venerable white-haired octogenarian was induced again to interfere in the political conflict which then so violently agitated the United Kingdom. On the 24th October, 1868, when on his death-bed, he addressed a letter to the Protestant electors of Ireland, in which he invoked them, as they valued their faith, as they loved their country, to vote for no man, however respected or honoured, who cloaked his views on the great question of the day; to be watchful against the insidious advances of Popish error and despotism, and to be united in defence of liberty and truth, because the Established Church and all the Protestant institutions in the land were then in danger.

[1] Life, &c., p. 488.

CHAPTER XXI.

THE DISESTABLISHED CHURCH—RELIGIOUS EQUALITY.

A ROYAL COMMISSION on the Revenues and Condition of the Established Church was issued on the 30th October, 1867, and the report was presented to Parliament in 1868-9. The Commissioners found the Irish Church Establishment to consist of 2 archbishoprics, 10 bishoprics, 30 corporations of deans and chapters, 12 minor corporations or quasi-corporate bodies connected with cathedrals, 32 deaneries, 33 archdeaconries, and 1,509 incumbencies, also 500 stipendiary curacies. The Commissioners recommended that, with the exception of eight, all the existing corporations of deans and chapters should be dissolved, and the deaneries and other dignities connected with them suppressed; that all the minor corporations should be dissolved, and that the twelve existing dioceses should be reduced to eight. A majority were of opinion that one archbishop, that of Armagh, was sufficient; that of Dublin to be reduced to a bishopric; that there should be provided for the primatial see of Armagh an income of 6,000*l*. a year; for the Dublin bishopric, 4,500*l*. a year; and for every other bishopric an income of 3,000*l*. a year; with an additional allowance of 500*l*. for such of the bishops as in each year attended Parliament. There were in Ireland 1,075 benefices, the net income of which was returned as under 300*l*. a year. About 355 of these were above 200*l*. a year, about 420 of the remainder above 100*l*. a year, and about 300 under 100*l*. a year. The annual revenues of the Church, and aggregate net value of houses of residence and of lands in the occupation of the bishops, dignitaries, and beneficed clergy, after deducting poor-rates, expenses of collection, and quit-rents, were found to be—from lands let to tenants, 204,933*l*.; from tithe-rentcharge, 364,225*l*.; from other sources, 12,674*l*.; value of houses and lands in occupation,

32,152*l.*; total, 613,984*l*. The annual amount of rents reserved in perpetuity grants, of rents and fines from leaseholds not converted into perpetuities, and the net income of capitular bodies available for maintaining cathedral and choral services, amounted in all to 158,590*l.*

The recommendations of the Commissioners were not adopted. The general election showed that public opinion demanded, not the curtailment of the Irish Establishment, or retrenchment of its expenditure with a view to 'concurrent endowment,' but complete severance from the State, and the establishment of religious equality. This was the object of Mr. Gladstone's Irish Church Act (1869), which was entitled 'An Act to put an end to the Establishment of the Church of Ireland.' In the Act were named three Commissioners to carry it out—namely, Viscount Monck, G. C. M. G., Judge Lawson, and Mr. Geo. A. Hamilton, late Secretary to the Treasury, who died in 1871. It was agreed on all sides that no better men could have been selected for the work, and they have done it in such a manner as to give general satisfaction. The Commissioners are a body corporate, with a common seal, and a capacity to acquire and hold land for the purposes of the Act. They are styled 'The Commissioners of Church Temporalities in Ireland.'

The 19th clause of the Act effected instantaneously one of the greatest miracles ever accomplished by human legislation. It gave freedom, and with freedom *life*, to the Church. It should, therefore, be commemorated by a day of general thanksgiving for all time to come. It enacted that—' From and after the passing of this Act there shall be repealed and determined any Act of Parliament, law, or custom whereby the archbishops, bishops, clergy, or laity of the said Church are prohibited from holding assemblies, synods, or conventions, or electing representatives thereto, for the purpose of making rules for the well-being and ordering of the said Church; and nothing in any Act, law, or custom shall prevent the bishops, the clergy, and laity of the said Church, by such representatives, lay and clerical, and to be elected, as they, the said bishops, clergy, and laity shall appoint, from meeting in general synod or convention, and in such synod or convention framing constitutions and regulations for the general management and good government of the said Church, and property and affairs thereof, and the future representation of the members thereof in diocesan synods, general convention, or otherwise.' The 21st clause abolished all ecclesiastical courts and ecclesiastical law, leaving the Church free to make laws of her own, to be binding, like those of any other religious community, on her own members only, with an exemption in favour of those ministers who might dissent from them, so that they might not be deprived of any annuity or compensation to which, by the Act, they might be entitled. The Act constituted a 'Representative Body of the Church of Ireland' to deal with the Commissioners, and take charge of the property and temporalities of the community. This body consists of sixty members, all elected, except the two archbishops and the ten bishops who are *ex officio* members. Of the others, there are two laymen for one clergyman. The Parliamentary experience of the bishops and of many of the lay members of the Representative Body was very useful to them in carrying out this great and difficult work, and preventing the Church from making a rash use of her new-born liberty. The Act indeed was wisely framed so as to guard against this danger; and they were helped materially by Dr. Ball, M.P., as assessor. The preponderance of laymen might have led to ultra-Protestant decisions, but this was prevented by the plan of voting 'by orders,' and giving a veto to the 'house of bishops.' In the Constitution they have shown themselves to be a law-loving people. They call their decrees 'statutes'; and these occupy no less than 172 sections. The title is 'The Constitution of the Church of Ireland; being Statutes passed at the General Convention, 1870.' As this transition from a State institution to a voluntary Church is one of the most interesting events in ecclesiastical history, as well as one of the most important in the history of Ireland, the preamble of the new Constitution deserves special attention. It is as follows:—

In the Name of the Father, and of the Son, and of the Holy Ghost. Amen: Whereas it hath been determined by the Legislature that on and after the First day of January, 1871, the Church of Ireland shall cease to be established by law; and that the Ecclesiastical Law of Ireland shall cease to exist as law save as provided in the 'Irish Church Act, 1869,' and it hath thus become necessary that the Church of Ireland should provide for its own regulation :

We, the Archbishops and Bishops of this the Ancient Catholic and Apostolic Church of Ireland, together with the Representatives of the Clergy and the Laity of the same, in General Convention assembled in Dublin in the year of our Lord God one thousand eight hundred and seventy, before entering on this work, do solemnly declare as follows :—

I.—1. 'The Church of Ireland doth, as heretofore, accept and unfeignedly believe all the Canonical Scriptures of the Old and New Testaments, as given by inspiration of God, and containing all things necessary to salvation; and doth continue to profess the faith of Christ as professed by the Primitive Church.

2. 'The Church of Ireland will continue to minister the Doctrine, and Sacraments, and the Discipline of Christ, as the Lord hath commanded; and will maintain inviolate the Three Orders of Bishops, Priests, or Presbyters, and Deacons in the Sacred Ministry.

3. 'The Church of Ireland, as a Reformed and Protestant Church, doth hereby re-affirm its constant witness against all those innovations in doctrine and worship, whereby the Primitive Faith hath been from time to time defaced or overlaid, and which at the Reformation this Church did disown and reject.'

II. 'The Church of Ireland doth receive and approve *The Book of the Articles of Religion* commonly called the Thirty-nine Articles, received and approved by the Archbishops and Bishops and the rest of the Clergy of Ireland in the Synod holden in Dublin A.D. 1634; also, *The Book of Common Prayer and Administration of the Sacraments, and other Rites and Ceremonies of the Church, according to the use of the Church of Ireland; and the Form and Manner of Making, Ordaining and Consecrating of Bishops, Priests, and Deacons,* as approved and adopted by the Synod holden in Dublin A.D. 1662, and hitherto in use in this Church. And this Church will continue to use the same, subject to such alterations only as may be made therein from time to time by the lawful authority of the Church.'

III. 'The Church of Ireland will maintain communion with

the sister Church of England, and with all other Christian Churches agreeing in the principles of this Declaration; and will set forward, so far as in it lieth, quietness, peace, and love, among all Christian people.'

IV. 'The Church of Ireland, deriving its authority from Christ, Who is the head over all things to the Church, doth declare that a General Synod of the Church of Ireland, consisting of the Archbishops and Bishops, and of Representatives of the Clergy and Laity, shall have chief legislative power therein, and such administrative power as may be necessary for the Church and consistent with its Episcopal Constitution.'[1]

The supreme authority in the free Church of Ireland is 'the General Synod.' It consists of 208 ministers and 416 laymen. The only test required in those elected is this:—'I, A. B., do hereby solemnly declare that I am a member of the Church of Ireland, and a communicant of the said Church.' The General Synod meets annually; and while I write it is in its third session, discussing the great and exciting question of the revision of the Book of Common Prayer. The formula of legislation sufficiently asserts the autonomy of the Church. After the preamble come the words—'Be it therefore enacted by the Archbishops and Bishops, and the Representatives of the Clergy and Laity of the Church of Ireland assembled in General Synod, &c.'

There are Diocesan Synods elected in the same manner by the communicants, and these include *women* who have property and pay rates in the parish. The position thus given to the laity, no matter how guarded, is in itself a complete revolution. Hitherto in the Irish Church the laity had no rights. If they interfered at all in Church matters, they were generally repulsed both by bishops and clergy; and the fact of their humbly petitioning to have a curate—who had done the duty of the parish for a generation, and had grown grey on a miserable salary, with a family to support—appointed as the rector of a parish, on the death of a non-resident or unpopular incumbent, was almost invariably rejected, on the ground that it was an unwarrantable meddling with matters too high for them. Now, the laity have a potential voice in the patronage of the Church, and it

[1] Charles's 'Irish Church Directory,' 1873.

is calculated that in the course of ten or fifteen years all the sees and parishes will be occupied by Evangelical men, who can be relied upon to carry on the war against the Church of Rome, instead of labouring insidiously to bring the Protestants of Ireland under the sacerdotal yoke which most of them detest.

The organisation is most elaborate. There are no less than ten standing committees to attend to the various departments of business. In every office, from the archbishop down to the vestryman—*merit* and fitness, proved by labour and character, determine the choice. The best men are sure to be called to the front. The old 'prizes,' dependent on favour, not on merit, have ceased to exist; but the prizes which most powerfully stimulate to exertion have taken their place. The best preachers and most efficient pastors will be chosen to fill the most important city churches, and from them the deans and bishops will be chosen. Then, no minister need starve while waiting for the prize. The smallest income is 200*l*. a year. The effect of these new principles is already manifest, and those who were most bitterly opposed to disestablishment are now free to confess that it was the best thing that ever happened for the Church. And as years roll on it may be confidently predicted that the conviction will become more general, that the Irish Church never had so great a benefactor as Mr. Gladstone.

By the operation of the Church Temporalities Act a very large amount of property became vested in the late Ecclesiastical Commissioners. The net annual revenue received by them was estimated at 113,662*l*. a year. The Commissioners also held as trustees some property appropriated for particular purposes, viz.: Primate Boulter's and Primate Robinson's funds, the former amounting to upwards of 89,000*l*. Government stock, and the latter to 985*l*. consols; a fund called Bishop Gore's Fund, and some private endowments for churches, amounting to about 4,240*l*. Government stock. Immediately on the passing of the Irish Church Act, 1869, in accordance with the provision made in its 11th and 12th clauses, the Irish Church Temporalities Commissioners took over all the property which the late Ecclesiastical Commissioners had under their control, and issued forms of claims, to be filled up before February 1, 1870, by every

clergyman or other person entitled to receive a continuance of
clerical income or compensation under the enactment as to vested
and life interests. About three millions have either been paid,
or agreed to be paid, to the Representative Body by the Church
Temporalities Commissioners, as commutation money, the portion
remaining unpaid bearing interest at 3½ per cent. The annuities
extinguished by composition and advances amount to about
145,000*l.* During the year 1871 fifty-seven annuitant clergymen
died, several of whom had not applied to commute. Up to December 31, 1871, the commutation money of eleven deceased
clergymen had been paid to the Representative Body, and the
annuities extinguished thereby amounted to 4,315*l.* 8*s.* 8*d.* The
average rate of interest on the investments made by the Representative Body, up to 31st December, 1871, is stated to be about
4*l.* 7*s.* per cent. During the year 1871, 82,394*l.* 0*s.* 10*d.* was
received for donations and subscriptions to the General Sustentation Fund, and 132,432*l.* 1*s.* 11*d.* for donations and subscriptions
to be appropriated to various Trusts. By a resolution of the
General Synod (May 9, 1871), donors to the General Sustentation Fund were allowed to change the destination of their donations and subscriptions from the General Sustentation Fund to
any particular Fund, provided they signified their wish before
July 1, 1871. They have largely availed themselves of this
permission, and the amount to the credit of the General Sustentation Fund, after all these deductions, is 153,070*l.* 15*s.* 10*d.*, the
balance, 345,697*l.* 11*s.* 4*d.*, being allocated to various diocesan and
parochial trusts.

In addition to the amount of 758,000*l.* advanced on mortgage
up to December 31, 1871, contracts have been entered into for
similar loans to the amount of 770,514*l.* 0*s.* 7*d.*, of which 428,514*l.*
0*s.* 7*d.* will bear interest at 4½ per cent., and the balance,
342,000*l.*, at the rate of 4¼ per cent. The fabrics of the
churches and school-houses throughout the country have been
claimed from the Commissioners; and some progress has been
made in arranging the principles on which provision is hereafter
to be made for insurance and necessary repairs, as well as for
periodical inspection.

The Representative Body are of opinion that, notwithstanding all that may be accomplished by diocesan schemes, a Central Sustentation Fund will still be imperatively required. It is chiefly by its instrumentality that the General Synod will be enabled to provide a remedy for such defects or deficiencies as may be found to exist in the general plan of church organisation, especially in poorer districts; and the Representative Body trusts that, by the aid of liberal contributions from members of the Church, this urgent want may be supplied.

The greatest danger to the Church will arise from the popular demand for the revision of the Prayer Book in a decidedly Protestant or Evangelical sense. There are two societies established for the purpose of bringing about a complete expurgation—'the Clerical and Lay Union,' and 'the Church Defence Association.' On the other hand, there is 'the Irish Church Society,' which objects to any change whatever, for the following reasons:—

I. Because the Prayer Book, being in its Doctrines the authorised manifesto of the English Reformation, must be maintained unchanged by those who desire that the Irish Church should not depart from the principles then laid down.

II. Because it has hitherto formed, and may still form, a basis and bond of union among members of the Church of every shade of opinion. Revision would put an end to this state of things, narrow the present comprehensiveness of the Irish Church, and make it the Church of a party.

III. Because Revision, following closely on Disestablishment and Disendowment, would give occasion to the enemies of the Church to charge its clergy with having taken payment from the State for teaching doctrines which they did not believe, and which they repudiated as soon as the payment was withdrawn; and because its friends would find it difficult to answer the charge.

IV. Because, while the Revisionists are all agreed in demanding doctrinal changes of some kind, they are not agreed with respect to the particular changes which would satisfy them as a party. They have not settled how much they would expunge from the Prayer Book, or how much they would leave behind. Thus, while the Revision Committee proposes to make

Baptismal Regeneration an open question, and to limit the doctrine of the Holy Communion by a new rubric—the Clerical and Lay Union, which professes to seek 'a wise and judicious revision,' demands the removal from the same Prayer Book of 'every pretext for preaching such erroneous doctrines as the Real Presence of the body and blood of Christ in or under the forms of the sacramental bread and wine; or the power of priestly absolution in the sense of an authority to convey the forgiveness of sins;' and another society, the Protestant Defence Association, proposes as its 'object' to 'prevent' the Church from being 'overlaid, marred, or defaced by Romish or other errors and practices contrary to its Protestant spirit;' and adds to the programme of the Clerical and Lay Union the exclusion from the Prayer Book of 'all passages that can be used for the teaching of the unscriptural doctrine of Baptismal Regeneration.' It is obvious that no change in the Prayer Book short of a doctrinal change would satisfy any of the Revisionists; but, at the same time, the smallest change would help them, and stimulate agitation.

V. Because Doctrinal change would necessarily cause a schism in the Irish Church, many of its members of all schools being resolved not to accept or use an altered Prayer Book. The schismatics would be those who made, not those who refused the change. On the other hand, to resist all change would not necessarily or probably occasion any secession on the part of those who seek it, and who, having so long submitted to the Prayer Book on grounds of convenience, would, doubtless, continue to do so for the same reason.

VI. Because Doctrinal Revision would separate the Irish Church from the Church of England and the several branches of the Anglican communion. It would also destroy the consentient witness to the truth now borne by the entire Anglican body, so important in the present condition of Christendom; it would injuriously affect the position and prospects of the Irish clergy everywhere except in their own country; it would deprive the Irish Church of all sympathy and help from the Church of England (as the threat of it has, to a great extent, already done); and it would place the missions of the Irish Church in the position of those of an inconsiderable, if not an heretical, sect.

As to the Church of England, alienation from it will not be regarded as an evil by Irish Protestants so long as Ritualism is in the ascendant. On this subject some remarkable utterances have recently indicated that the conflicting doctrinal forms in the English Church may soon burst the State bonds which hold them together, and that then all that is truly Protestant in it will seek the most intimate union with the Irish Church, which is committed to the mortal struggle with Romanism under such conditions as exist nowhere else in Europe. In no other nation is Ultramontanism so strong, and so arrogant. In no other country is Protestantism so pure and energetic. Young David has put off the armour of Saul; and it will go hard with him if he does not hit the Goliath of Ultramontanism in the forehead.

The removal of the Church Establishment, Mr. Gladstone was the first British statesman who had even the courage to attempt, or the power to effect. He undertook the gigantic task and succeeded nobly. Others had tried the Land question, but all had ignominiously failed. None of the pretenders could bend the bow of Ulysses. Mr. Gladstone did it, as he had done everything, with ease. To establish Religious Equality instead of the ascendency of a small sect over a nation—of thousands over millions, maintained in virtue of invasion, slaughter, burning, desolation, and confiscation, and wrought by ages of usage and conflict into the framework of the Constitution—was a glorious achievement. To rescue 60 or 70 millions sterling of property belonging of right to the tenants from the grasp of the landlords, who held it iniquitously by laws of their own making, and made it the instrument of their political and social denomination, was a work fully as difficult, scarely less glorious, and certainly not less beneficial to the country. Both together, these measures constituted a great revolution, putting an end to a system of injustice entailed by confiscation and persecution, and, though much mitigated by previous legislation, still grievously embittering the relations of social and political life.

But the third limb of the upas, the Educational grievance, though originally the worst part of the penal code, was greatly exaggerated in Mr. Gladstone's imagination. It had been from time to time almost entirely cut away, and the remnant of the poisonous trunk might have been quietly removed, by carrying out a little further principles already in operation.

This was done by the late Lord Derby in the establishment of the 'National System,' which has now flourished for forty years, though opposed and anathematised by each of the churches in turn. It is founded on the principle of 'United Secular Education,' combined with separate religious instruction. This principle was fully sanctioned by the hierarchy of that time. Archbishop Murray was one of the commissioners, and worked most harmoniously with Archbishop Whately and the other Protestants on the Board till his death. Bishop Denvir of Down and Connor was also a commissioner, until the Pope or Dr. Cullen compelled him to retire. The late Primate Crolly was a warm supporter of the principle of united education. So also was the late Bishop Doyle. Indeed, the National System fully realised all that the hierarchy had demanded, until Cardinal Cullen came with his ultramontane pretensions and restless aggressions. As it is, the Catholics enjoy about four-fifths of the grant, which amounts to 474,055*l*. Total since 1831, 7,342,356*l*. There is nothing of the upas here. If there is it bears an abundance of very welcome fruit.

There are a number of endowed intermediate schools, royal and diocesan, on which there was a commission about twelve years ago, and which, after long inquiry, recommended that they should be thrown open to Roman Catholics, as they were originally intended for the whole people. This could have been easily done, utilising the funds, and supplementing them with a grant, so as to have a complete system of high schools for all denominations, on the united principle, and it should have accompanied or preceded the Queen's Colleges. But it was strangely and culpably neglected, not only by Sir Robert Peel's Government, but by every Liberal Government that followed. The Queen's Colleges are founded on the same united principle as the primary schools, with every possible safeguard for the consciences of Roman Catholics and others, and a careful provision for their religious instruction and direction by 'Deans of Residence,' selected by the authorities of their respective Churches. Roman Catholic students felt no scruple, and incurred no danger, until the Synod of Thurles, in obedience to orders from Rome, denounced the colleges as 'Godless,' and 'dangerous to faith and morals.' There never was a charge more unjust; and consequently a fair proportion of Catholic students have continued to attend the Queen's Colleges, which—all adverse circumstances considered—have been remarkably successful.

The College of Maynooth was established in 1795, from no love to Catholicism, but from State policy. Those were revolutionary times; and the priests, who had been obliged to seek education abroad, returned with no great fondness for the paternal government of George III. Up to 1835 the College received an annual grant of nearly 9,000*l*. The grant was always entered in the 'Irish Estimates,' and for many years the late Mr. Spooner, and after him Mr. Whalley, made a motion to have the sum struck out, which led to an irritating debate on the doctrines and moral principles for the propagation of which the Protestant tax-payers were obliged to pay. The late Sir Robert Peel, to avoid this evil, brought in a bill, which was passed (8 and 9 Vict., c. 25), making the endowment permanent, and placing it beyond the reach of debate on the Consolidated Fund. It was arranged that the college should accommodate 520 students, who should have 'commons,' *i.e.*, board, as well as education, at the expense of the State. The grant was thenceforth 26,360*l*. per annum, and there was a lump sum of 30,000*l*. for buildings in addition. When the Irish Church Act was passed, the College of Maynooth got 372,331*l*. as compensation for the withdrawal of the grant. This the hierarchy has got absolutely, without being subject to visitation, or any sort of responsibility. Considering the nature of the teaching of Maynooth, and of the text-books touching heretical, or 'atheistical Governments'—to adopt the Pope's phrase—it cannot be said that the British Parliament has acted very illiberally towards the Irish Catholics in the matter of education, especially if we allow for the almost uniform hostility of the young priests to the Government at contested elections. This is surely not a religious grievance.

Let us see how the different denominations now stand, under the system of religious equality in the matter of clerical education. The Church of Rome, as I have just said, has got under the late

Act, 372,331*l*., with all the buildings erected at the cost of the State. The General Assembly of the Presbyterian Church, which comprises nearly half the Protestant population, has got 43,976*l*. as compensation for 1,750*l*., which was paid for six professors, all theological, in a college quite distinct from the Queen's College, Belfast. The Dublin University, which has an average of 1,200 students, enjoys an income from land amounting to 36,000*l*. a year, and earns 27,000*l*. in fees. She has sizarships and scholarships, which may be won by hard study; but she does not, nor does the Presbyterian Church, give gratuitous education to the ministry, as the State enables Maynooth to do. In this most important point, therefore, Rome is a specially favoured Church. This Protestant State manufactures priests, but it does not manufacture Protestant ministers.

So much for the clergy, now for the laity. The Queen's Colleges belong to Roman Catholics quite as much as to Protestants. Sir Robert Kane, a Catholic, was one of the first Presidents appointed; and the first President of Galway College was actually a priest. Catholics may, and do, graduate in the Queen's Colleges and in the Dublin University; the most eminent men among them at the bar have done so; or they may, and do, graduate in the London University, which sends Examiners to their own halls, to enable them to qualify on the spot. Altogether, Catholics have as many young men, or very nearly as many, receiving a University education as their social condition can well afford. Of course, the disestablishment of the Church requires a change in the Dublin University to adapt it to the regime of religious equality, and make it neutral ground—separating Trinity College and keeping it apart for theological and ministerial training. This the governing body are ready and quite anxious to do, throwing open to Roman Catholics the professorships and fellowships, the ruling power, and all its privileges, so that this new element might be absorbed in the Academic system and grow into it, as it were, while maintaining its identity and its splendid historic prestige. Of all the institutions planted by the English in Ireland the University is the most successful. It is the only one of which all parties are proud. It owes this pre-eminence, this unique glory, to its independence—to its recognising, honouring, and rewarding merit alone. It has always been free from the manipulation and contagion of the Government and from the control of political parties. It is a grand old tree, which has 'stood the battle and the breeze' for three centuries, striking its roots deep in the soil of every county in Ireland, enabling many a poor scholar to wear the ermine and the mitre—to sit with princes. It is well, therefore, that it has been spared. Mr. Fawcett's Bill will enable it to accomplish fully its mission, and will remove everything that can be fairly regarded as a disability. If there is a disability it is what the Ultramontane party have to encounter in the most Catholic countries of the Continent. That party cannot be satisfied unless, as Earl Russell says, the sovereignty of Ireland be transferred from our Queen to the Pope. We can resist its aggressions with a good conscience when we take our stand on the ground of political equality, and the neutrality of the State in matters of religion.

LONDON: PRINTED BY
SPOTTISWOODE AND CO., NEW-STREET SQUARE
AND PARLIAMENT STREET

www.ingramcontent.com/pod-product-compliance
Lightning Source LLC
Chambersburg PA
CBHW022024240426

43667CB00042B/1082